Is the Vicar in, Pet?

From Pit to Pulpit –
My Childhood in a Geordie Vicarage

BARBARA FOX

sphere

SPHERE

First published in Great Britain in 2014 by Sphere
Reprinted 2014

A CIP catalogue record for this book
is available from the British Library.

ISBN 978-0-7515-5301-7

Typeset in Bembo by M Rules
Printed and bound in Great Britain by
Clays Ltd, St Ives plc

Papers used by Sphere are from well-managed forests
and other responsible sources.

MIX
Paper from
responsible sources
FSC
www.fsc.org FSC® C104740

Sphere
An imprint of
Little, Brown Book Group
100 Victoria Embankment
London EC4Y 0DY

An Hachette UK Company
www.hachette.co.uk

www.littlebrown.co.uk

To everyone who was there

Druridge Bay

I can't remember being at Druridge Bay –
It was going that was important.
We might not get there, anyhow:
It might rain, or Father change his mind.

But going! The car's leather smell,
The bright blue drive, mile after mile
Down shimmering tarmac lanes.

At last, the sea –

Can you see it yet? – *the magic line*
Rising over coarse dune grass.
I could stand on the seat to gaze through the open roof
Or ride on the running-board
For the last few thrilling miles.

The silent engine's petrol smell in sunshine.
Father's first picnic cigarette.
Heaven about to happen.

R V Bailey

To a Pit Pony

O blackbrowed beetling pony standing there,
In darkness standing, gulping in the air;
You are not more cold in heart than we,
For the green earth in shadowy dreams you see.

Those eyes, inured to night, have seen
Sparkling rivers, clouds, fields were green.
So in the dark you snuffle, kick the dust,
And stretch your weary head to take my crust –
Crunch steadily, while tremors rippling run,
Induc'd by visions of a half-remembered sun.

Sid Chaplin

Chapter One

My mother is supposed to have told my father when they were newly married, and as he began his training for the priesthood, that she would go anywhere on earth with him except Ashington. She had never been to Ashington, just heard about it — everyone had. It had the dubious claim to fame of being the biggest mining village in the world.

'Why is the North-East always famous for the grim things, like coal?' her own mother would grumble. 'Coal and ships and guns. People think we're savages up here.'

Ashington simply seemed to belong to a different North-East from the one Mum and her parents belonged to. She was proud enough of its claim, it just didn't have much to do with her and her city-centred life in Newcastle where she had grown up, gone to school and trained as a nurse. Her father worked in a bank. Her mother's father had been a gifted violinist named

Walter Stratford. Grandma was so proud of her maiden name and its associations with Shakespeare, you would think she was descended from the Bard himself.

Somewhere along the way Mum must have changed her mind, for, one afternoon, she left us all at home with Grandma and accompanied my father to meet the church council of the parish of Seaton Hirst, which covered a large part of Ashington. It was a parish on the Catholic wing of the Church of England, and its vicar – who had been in the job for over twenty years – was a single man, as had been the one before. If there had ever been a married vicar in the parish, no one could remember him, and there had certainly never been one in the current vicarage, a generously proportioned five-bedroom house designed by its first occupant in the 1930s for himself and his housekeeper. Yet despite some reservations over his marital status – and probably even more over his having four children – the council had decided that Dad was the man they wanted to be their new vicar.

Mum and Dad must have wondered just what they were letting themselves in for as they stood on the doorstep that afternoon.

'Alder, how lovely to see you!' boomed Canon Morton, the present incumbent, as he opened the door to them. My father's first name was William but he had always been known as Alder, his middle name and an old family name that had been handed down to various Goftons for several generations. 'Come in, come in! Let me take your coat.'

My mother, who was wearing an outfit borrowed from her elegant friend, Murial, in order to make a good impression, smiled and held out her hand too, but the old priest had already turned away, his hand on Dad's back, ushering him inside. Mum stayed where she was for a second, wondering if he had even seen her, if he might be coming back to give her an equally effusive welcome. When she realized that this was not going to happen, she stepped inside the porch, closed the front door behind her and followed the men into the hallway. She stood there awkwardly as they chatted, smiling in readiness to be included in the conversation as Canon Morton said for the third time how much everyone was looking forward to meeting his successor – but he didn't once look her way. Just when she thought that there might be something wrong with his eyesight and that he didn't actually know she was there, he glanced at her briefly and pointed to the cloakroom at the foot of the staircase. 'You can put your jacket in there,' he said.

The cloakroom was dark and she couldn't find the light switch. She draped her jacket over what appeared to be a heavy black cassock, glanced at herself in the tiny mirror and gave a forced smile at her ghostly reflection. 'Chin up,' she said to herself. 'He can't be any worse than some of those dragons you worked with at the hospital.' Perhaps Canon Morton wasn't comfortable with women. As he had never seen any need for a wife himself, he probably wondered why this young priest, whom he otherwise appeared to think quite highly of, had thought to acquire one. Or perhaps he just hadn't been expecting her, and that was the reason for the decidedly cool reception. But Alder had been quite clear, she remembered, that she was to come to meet the council too. Well, someone had their wires crossed. She sighed, took a deep breath and went out into the hallway, now empty and almost as dark as the cloakroom. The doors that led off it had all been closed. She had no idea which room the men had gone into and had to listen at each door to find out.

My father was being introduced to a group of people. No one took any notice of Mum as she slipped inside and quietly closed the door. An elderly lady, squeezed into a navy nylon dress, was sitting in a corner away from the others, her large legs slightly apart, fanning herself with her hand.

'Eeh,' she said when my mother wandered over, 'I've been on me feet all day and they're killing us.' She nodded towards the chair beside her. 'Have a seat, pet.'

Mum sat down and introduced herself, slightly apologetically. She would have words with my father about this on the way home. Trust him to get the wrong end of the stick! But the lady, who said she was called Margaret Dobie and that she had done some baking for the occasion, didn't seem surprised to see her and chatted away about her varicose veins and how Ashington wasn't the place it used to be, and asked Mum what the church they were leaving behind was like and how big their Sunday congregation was. After about twenty minutes, people began to leave. Canon Morton came over to where Mum was sitting, said, 'Thank you, Margaret,' to Miss Dobie, and helped her to her feet. She gave Mum a little nod, said a few words to Dad and departed along with the others. Only one person had stayed behind: a smart, nicely spoken lady who asked Mum if she would care to come to the table. Mum now saw that a dining table at the other end of the room had been laid for three people. She, my father and Canon Morton sat down to a huge spread of sandwiches and cakes, while the lady, who introduced herself to Mum as Phemie Templey, wife of one of the church-wardens, waited on them. Mum said she had only expected a cup of tea and a biscuit and wasn't very hungry, but she ate what she could to be polite. And Miss Dobie's orange cake was one of the nicest she had ever tasted – rich and moist with a creamy butter icing and pieces of candied fruit on the top. Canon Morton was very attentive to Mum now, including her in the conversation and even asking after the children. There was no reason or apology given for his reception earlier. She put it down to his being a confirmed bachelor, with no real idea of how to behave towards women, and laughed about it all the way home.

Chapter Two

Not long after that, when Canon Morton had left Ashington to see out the rest of his working life in a quiet country parish – and in another house that was far too big for one man – Mum and Dad took me and my sister Sarah to see our new home. Our younger siblings, Ruth and Mark, were being looked after by Grandma and Papa, Mum's parents, but Sarah and I were allowed to accompany Mum and Dad as they went to take measurements for carpets and curtains, so that we could choose our own bedrooms. We could hardly believe that we would each have a room of our own.

'Poo!' said Mum, as we got out of the car into the smoky air. She looked across to the row of houses on the other side of the road. 'I think there must be a chimney on fire.'

The thought of a fire was exciting, but to my disappointment I could see no evidence of one, just a long line of chimneys chuffing out smoke. Dad didn't seem to have heard what she said. He rubbed his hands together and grinned at me and Sarah. 'Well, what do you think, kids? Is it up to scratch?'

We had parked at the bottom of a driveway in front of a garage that was attached to a large red-brick house. The house had towering chimneys at each end and lots of windows. A path ran along the front of the house and kept on going, disappearing through some bushes into the churchyard next door. Dad pointed to a large rectangular plot alongside the drive that he said we would grow vegetables on. On the other side of that, separated from it by a beech hedge, a narrow path ran from a small wooden gate straight down to the front door. Beyond that was a lawn, about the size of the whole garden at our current home in a suburb of Newcastle, but Dad said if we thought that was big, we should see what was round the back.

He led the way along the front of the house, past the front door and through a gap in the hedge. If there had been a gate, I thought with a thrill, it would have been like entering a secret garden, just like the one in the book I was reading. We found ourselves in the corner of what might have been a tennis court if the ground hadn't been covered in gravel, and beside it, directly behind the house, was another lawn, bigger than the front one and dotted with shaggy rosebeds.

'I can get my game back up to scratch,' said Dad, giving a swing of an imaginary tennis racket. 'My backhand was terrible when I last played with Colin.'

Mum came up behind us. 'Aren't you lucky,' she said. 'All this space! It's like having your own park.'

'Can we go and play?' Sarah and I pleaded, looking longingly at the lawn. The grass was long and wet, and the trees and bushes that bordered it on two sides gave it a look of territory waiting to be explored.

But Mum and Dad said no, there was too much to do and we had years ahead of us for playing, and so we reluctantly followed them back through the gap in the hedge and into the house.

It was February, and the house was cold and bare apart from some dead flies on the windowsills and woodlice scuttling into the corners. Mum said to be careful, there might be the odd nail lying around. Sarah and I stood in the hallway, silent for a few seconds, breathing in the smell of emptiness and chilled air. We both felt slightly shy at our good fortune. Then we took off, tearing from room to room, excited by the size of the place and the clattery sound our feet made on the floorboards.

'Casey Jones, mounted to the cabin!' I sang out. The television programme about the adventures of the railroad engineer Casey Jones was one of our favourites. The empty rooms threw my words back at me.

'Casey Jones, with his orders in his hand!' Sarah continued in her shrill singing voice.

We thought echoes belonged in caves and hills, so it seemed magical to hear our voices bouncing back to us inside a house. And to think that this was *our* house! We had never felt so lucky before.

In the centre of each room a large brass disc, curved like a mushroom, sat on the floor. It didn't take us long to discover that if we stood on these, a bell rang in the kitchen. A box on the kitchen wall indicated the room in which it had been rung.

Mum said that the first incumbent had been looked after by a housekeeper, and that he would have rung a bell when he wanted something. Sarah and I looked at each other, scarcely able to believe it. Ringing bells for servants belonged to a different world from the one we knew.

'We can have different meanings for different rings,' I told Sarah. 'One ring will mean, "Are you ready now?" and two will mean "Yes", and three will mean "No".'

Sarah nodded. 'And we can ring when it's dinnertime, like ringing the gong when we're on holiday.'

But Mum was already shaking her head and saying certainly not, they would drive her mad, and anyway, we would have carpets covering them up. We tried to reason with her but she had made up her mind.

'I can't believe he's taken all the curtain rails and light fittings,' she said to Dad, and we realized that there was no more to be said on the matter.

When we had run round each of the downstairs rooms and jumped out on Mum and Dad from the walk-in pantry, we shot upstairs to do the same on the next floor. We stopped when we found a single piece of furniture left behind in one of the bedrooms. It was made of wood and had a tiny step and a shelf for holding a book, like the pulpit in church but far smaller.

I stood on the step, half closed my eyes and screwed up my face. 'Let me tell you a story from when I was in Borneo.'

Sarah giggled, knowing that I was imitating Father Hetherington, an eccentric old priest who often turned up at mealtimes. Mum, who had followed us upstairs, laughed from the doorway then told us to shush. She had explained to us that

men without wives developed strange habits, not having the
benefit of a woman to moderate their behaviour. A vicar without a wife, it seemed, was even more of a hopeless case than
other unmarried men. 'Think what your father would have been
like if I hadn't married him,' she would say, as she gave his hair
its weekly wash at the kitchen sink. It was true that Dad needed
Mum to look after him, and that in our house the more practical jobs fell to her. 'Or John Grainger, with that train set of his.
He wouldn't move from that room if Elspeth wasn't there to
give him a good kick in the pants when he needed it. What is
it with vicars and trains?'

I didn't know if Father Hetherington was a train nut too, but
he often began a sentence with: 'When I was in Borneo ...' refer-
ring back to his days as a missionary there. Apart from closing
his eyes when he spoke to you, he made strange gulping sounds
when he ate and his black cassock had hardened food stains down
the front. Sarah said they made her feel sick. Mum usually offered
to stick it in the wash for him when he came round, but had only
been successful the time he had bounced Mark on his lap and
Mark's nappy had leaked. Dad said she had arranged it deliber-
ately.

'Why's there a pulpit, Mum?' I asked as she disappeared into
another room with her tape measure.

She called back, 'It's not a pulpit, it's a prayer desk, to put your
Bible on. You're supposed to kneel on it.' She popped her head
back round the door. 'It's hideous. You can keep it in one of your
rooms, if you like.'

'I'll have it,' Sarah said, 'for when I'm playing schools. I can
use it for taking the register.'

Sarah was going to be a teacher when she grew up, and this

was one of her favourite games. I decided not to argue about it. I hadn't decided if I even liked it.

After we had explored all the bedrooms – three large, two slightly smaller – we saw there was another staircase.

'Bags I the attic – I'm the oldest,' I said, pushing past Sarah in my rush to get to the top. But I stopped short when I saw the darkness that lingered on the final stair.

Sarah barged up behind me. 'Go on, then,' she said, giving me a shove.

I walked a little way inside. The attic had a smaller window than the other rooms, too high up to look out of, and a cold, musty smell. A ripped mattress was propped up against the wall at the far end.

'There's your bed,' Sarah said.

'Very funny. Anyway, I was only joking when I said I was having this room.'

'Why? Are you scared?'

'Of course not. But it's not for sleeping in, it's for storing things.' I had a vague idea this might be true. Mum was always complaining about having no room for the trunks she had brought back from her travels in America, along with a passion for the latest labour-saving device, earning her the nickname Gadget Gwenda.

I walked a little further in and jumped up at the window. All I could see were the tops of trees, and part of the graveyard beyond the back garden. Apart from a box on the wall like the one in the kitchen showing where the bells were rung, there was nothing to see. While Sarah was pulling down the mattress – 'We could turn it into a trampoline' – I edged closer to the door then cried out to her, 'Who's that little old lady sitting in the corner?' She stopped what she was doing, looked to where I was pointing, then at me, and we both screamed and ran back down the stairs.

'I made you look, I made you stare, I made you cut the barber's hair!' I cried triumphantly as we ran.

'I knew there wasn't one,' she said, but we both kept on running all the way down to the kitchen.

Sarah wanted one of the big bedrooms. It had its own washbasin – the only one that did – and overlooked the back garden. Mum said that was fine, as long as she understood that it would also be the guest room and that when we had visitors she would have to move in with me. I chose the corner room that had two different views: one over the back garden and another, through a small side window, over the flat garage roof and on to the road. Sarah's room would have a double bed and mine would have twin beds, but when we had lots of guests, like when our aunt and uncle and cousins came to stay, we would both have to vacate our rooms and be banished to the attic in our sleeping bags.

'I'm not sleeping up there, there's a ghost,' said Sarah, flashing me a look, and Mum asked if I'd been telling my sister stories again.

I ran through the house one more time to count all the rooms. A kitchen and dining room all in one with a massive fireplace and cooking range in the centre; a study for Dad – he had chosen a light, sunny room with a view of the garden, rather than the room off the porch that the previous vicars had used; a sitting room with the same garden view; a proper cloakroom – there was even an old jacket left behind, hanging on a hook – with a separate toilet and washbasin. And there was still one room left over downstairs: the old study. Mum said that could be our playroom. A *playroom*! The very sound of it seemed to belong to the world of the books I read, where the children had their tea made by faithful old nannies, went to boarding school and spent a lot of their free time solving mysteries, seldom bothered by parents. I couldn't help thinking that we might have adventures too, if we lived in a house like this.

Chapter Three

We lived in Gosforth, a nice suburb of Newcastle, on a road where cars backed out of drives at eight o'clock each morning, returned at five-thirty, and were washed lovingly every weekend. Where neighbours took us for polite walks and the air smelt of petrol and freshly trimmed hedges.

'Ashington?' I overheard my friend's mother say to Mum outside school one afternoon. She laughed. 'Isn't that called one of the sacrifices of being married to a vicar?'

Mum replied with something about Dad testing his calling, and that she was doing the same. I didn't know what either of them were talking about. All I could think of was the big new house and garden and having my own bedroom at last. Sarah and I had been excited for weeks, and were most put out when Mum told us we had to go to school as usual on moving-in day, and that Grandma and Papa would pick us up and take us to our new home. I was so excited, I hadn't given much thought to the fact that it was the last day I would see some of my school-friends, and that I would be starting a new school after half-term, just over a week later.

We drove up Gosforth High Street with its banks and building societies, past the smart hairdresser's with the pictures in the window I liked to gaze at. I felt sure that if I had my hair cut there, rather than at the hairdresser's on our local shopping parade, I would come out looking like a film star. Mum said I would come out bankrupt, more likely. I reached for the end of my plaits and gave them both a tug, satisfied to see how far my hair was reaching down my back.

The Great North Road passed the Gosforth Park Hotel, almost hidden behind its high wall. 'Four stars,' Mum always said proudly, as if not quite able to believe that we deserved such a fine place in the North-East, yet what I could see of the building looked surprisingly ordinary. We carried on, and as we travelled north we left the smart houses and shops of the city behind and entered a new, grimy world – one of working-men's clubs and scruffy corner shops and the buildings that came with coal mines. After passing through some villages where remnants from disused collieries languished, we came to an estate of low, grey factories where men with haversacks stood smoking at bus stops. Ahead of us at the top of a steep bank stood a large, hand-some house. Grandma said it had been built for a wealthy mine owner and was now a home for injured miners. As we approached it, the road grew dark with overhanging trees, then plunged like a rabbit hole down the bank, wound its way over a stream and up the other side, passing behind the building that was now hidden from view in the thick woodland.

'Wheee!' Grandma said as we shot along the road. 'Who needs to go on the roller coaster, with Papa driving?'

Sarah and I grinned at each other in the back seat. We could hardly believe the day was finally here. I had sometimes wondered if the world would come to an end first. I was excited, but there was another feeling too that I didn't quite understand. Though I wanted to be there so badly, something in me also wanted this journey to go on for ever, so that nothing could spoil my dreams. To be always on the way to Ashington that first time.

A bit further along the road, Grandma caught my eye in the rear-view mirror. 'You two are unusually quiet,' she said. 'Nearly there now, you'll be pleased to hear.'

We came to a place where a gang of untidy boys kicked a football on a patch of grass next to a bus shelter. Papa slowed down then had to brake hard as the ball bounced into the road. Grandma tutted and shook her head at the boys, who didn't look as if they cared.

And then Papa said, 'Hold on to your hats, girls' – though only Grandma was wearing one – and took off down another bank, over a bridge that crossed a wide grey river, its banks glistening with slag heaps, and up a hill to where a sign announced that we were now in Ashington.

'Well,' said Grandma. She turned round to look at us. 'Well,' she said again, 'the cat's well and truly got *your* tongues today. Aren't you excited?'

'They're bound to be with that blummin' big house to live in,' chuckled Papa. 'I wouldn't mind it meself.'

Grandma said, to no one in particular, 'I suppose there's got to be *some* consolation to living in this place.'

We bumped over a railway line and carried on along a road lined with endless terraces of red-brick houses. Apart from different-coloured front doors, each house looked identical to its neighbour. Half a mile further on we came to a junction where a large building, topped with an assortment of chimneys and pinnacles, stood proudly on the corner. With its huge bay windows, wedding-cake turret and layers of contrasting stone and brick, the North Seaton Hotel looked far grander than the Gosforth Park Hotel we had left behind in Newcastle.

'Do you think that's four stars as well?' I asked Grandma.

Papa snorted, and Grandma said, '*Tsk*, that'll be the day.'

On our right, opposite the hotel – which we would soon discover was known to everyone as the White Elephant – was St John's Church, and next door to that, almost hidden from view behind untidy trees and bushes, was the vicarage, our new home.

Papa had to park on the road as the drive was full of cars, but there was no sign of the removal van.

'Perhaps we should have had tea and turned up a little later,' said Grandma, looking at him anxiously as we stood at the top of the path.

He tutted. 'We're here now.'

Papa opened the wooden gate and Sarah and I charged down the path. We stopped suddenly on the step, even though the front door was open. Loud hammer blows and the sound of unfamiliar voices coming from inside made us feel shy all of a sudden, and doubtful that this was really our house after all.

'Sounds like chaos,' said Grandma, coming up behind us. 'But get a move on, I need to put these bags down. Go carefully, now.'

When we opened the door into the hallway, the first person

we saw was Mark being pulled along the floor in a cardboard box by a man with a friendly, deeply lined face and wearing a flat cap. Mark beamed at us all for just a couple of seconds, then turned his attention back to his makeshift car, his hands round an imaginary steering wheel. He made a rumbling sound with his lips.

The man looked at me and Sarah, winked and said something I didn't understand.

Grandma poked us both in the back and said, 'They're very well, thank you. I think they must have lost their manners on the way here. Introduce yourselves, girls.'

We told him our names, while Mark pleaded with him, 'Faster! Pull me faster!'

'Please would be nice,' said Grandma.

Papa chuckled. 'You'll be doing that all night if you're not careful,' he said.

'I think she's conked oot, let's have a look at her and see what's wrong,' said the man with another wink, as we squeezed our way past boxes to the end of the hall and down the little corridor that led to the kitchen.

'Yoo-hoo!' Grandma said. 'No rest for the wicked,' and Mum looked up from the crate she was unpacking.

The kitchen, which was full of women washing and drying crockery or unpacking boxes, had changed since our last visit. The large fireplace and old-fashioned range, which had been the focus of the room before, had vanished and the room split into two with a dividing wall, complete with serving hatch, forming a narrow dining room down one side. I was pleased to see that the walk-in pantry was still there.

'Ah, here are the girls,' Mum said to everyone, 'and my parents, Gwen and Arthur Brady.'

The ladies briefly stopped what they were doing to smile and say hello, and I could tell that some of them were looking at me and Sarah closely, no doubt trying to decide which parent we looked like, one of the annoying habits that grown-ups had. The lady with her hands in the sink waved an arm in greeting and said, 'Your daughter's a hard taskmaster, Mrs Brady,' and all the adults laughed.

'I've been dying to see you two,' said a solid-looking lady half in and half out of the pantry, looking and sounding so purposeful I thought she was about to bound across the room and grab us both. Luckily, her way was blocked by boxes and she stayed put. 'I thought to meself, I bet you're both gorgeous, just like your little brother and sister, and I can see youse are. Ooh, wait till I get me hands on you both!'

Grandma, who believed modesty to be the utmost virtue, said something about us spending enough time already in front of the mirror without hearing comments like that. Meanwhile, Mum was trying to introduce her helpers. 'This is Mrs Bennett, Mrs Kirkup, Mrs Oxberry, Mrs Turner . . .'

'I'm your Aunty June,' said the lady in the larder, 'so you can forget your Mrs Oxberry nonsense. Hee, hee, hee.' She had a funny, rasping sort of laugh. Sarah and I looked at each other and laughed too.

'Have you seen your rooms yet, girls?' asked another of the ladies. 'They're smashing. June . . . your Aunty June's given them a good hoover and made your beds. I'm thinking of moving in myself.'

'But I've not touched your things,' said Aunty June, holding

up both her hands in a gesture of innocence. 'I'm not getting
meself into trouble. I know what our Carol would say if I started
rearranging her knick-knacks. "Mam," she would tell us, "do *not*
meddle with my stuff." And I always do as I'm told.'

We would discover later that this wasn't strictly true. Mum
gave Sarah and me a look that we recognized. 'Thank you,' we
chorused.

'Go up and have a look,' said Mum. 'You'll have plenty to do
later when my lovely helpers have gone. Oh, ladies! What would
I have done without you? You must all be worn out by now.
Come on, let's call it a day and put the kettle back on.'

'But you've got loads to do still,' one of the women protested,
and as we slipped away we heard Mum saying something about
having all the time in the world, and how lucky she was to have
two hard-working daughters, which we suspected was intended
for our ears too.

Unfamiliar male voices were coming from one of the downstairs
rooms. Mark's cardboard car was now half in and half out of the
playroom, but he had disappeared. I experienced a fleeting
moment of disappointment to see that the house wasn't quite as
big as I'd remembered it.

Our bedrooms were a sanctuary from the mayhem below,
with the beds made and our belongings, like Aunty June had
said, waiting to be unpacked. One box, however, had been
opened, and a few books were arranged in neat piles on my
bookcase. I knelt on my bed and looked into the back
garden. The lawn had been cut, and large pink and yellow
roses were bouncing showily in one of the beds. Sarah's teddy
was sitting on top of my bedspread. I picked him up to take

him to Sarah but stopped when I heard someone coming up the stairs. I peeped out from behind my door. A tall slim man with a ruddy face was carrying a tea chest. When he got to the landing he paused for a second, jiggled the chest a bit higher in his arms, then carried on up the next flight of stairs to the attic. Dad, coming up behind him with a far smaller box, was laughing apologetically. 'Oh to have your strength, Wilf!'

When I heard their footsteps on the attic floor, I made my escape.

Sarah was sitting on the edge of her double bed, swinging her legs. I saw with pleasure how high the bed was, with lots of room for hiding underneath.

I handed over the teddy. 'Do you like your room?' I asked her, looking admiringly at the size of it. 'My room's blue, like I wanted.'

'Well, I wanted white. And look, I've got Mum's old dressing table.'

It was positioned in front of the window, a proper dressing table with a stool in the centre and three mirrors so that you could see yourself from all angles. I would have loved one too, but there was no room for extra furniture in my room, and the top of the chest of drawers would have to do for my treasured collection of Avon cosmetics and my jewellery. But I did have something nobody else had. 'I've got a secret cupboard in my room. Do you want to come and see it?'

'In a minute.' She kicked her legs importantly. 'I bet you can't do this on your bed.'

'Are you going to start unpacking now? Let's do one box each, then go outside before tea.'

Sarah came into my room a few minutes later. 'Let's see what's so special, then.'

I showed her how the cupboard was built into the wall, and that there was a smaller cupboard underneath the main one. We lay on our stomachs to see inside. 'We could keep our treasure in there and not tell anyone else.'

'Like what?'

I thought for a few seconds. 'Well, that penny with the old king on it – it must be worth lots of money. And the heart necklace with the Lord's Prayer written on the back. You can keep yours there as well, if you want.'

We both jumped when someone came up behind us. 'Aren't youse two just the luckiest girls! Ooh, I'd love to live in your house. Wait till I tell yer Uncle Andy about youse all. He's on foreshift this week. Our Carol and I can't stand it. We have to tiptoe around so we don't wake him. You've never known such a light sleeper as your Uncle Andy! Now, who can tell her Aunty June where your mam's nets are? We can make a start on getting them up.'

Neither of us spoke.

'What?' I said at last. 'I mean, pardon?'

'Her nets. You want to get them up now before it's dark.'

'Um, I don't know where they are.' I looked at Sarah, who shrugged and pulled a how-should-I-know face at me.

Aunty June padded round the room in her slippers, prodding at boxes and opening drawers. She pointed to the jewellery box I had just unpacked. 'Mind, that's a proper bobby-dazzler you've got there,' she said.

'It plays a tune,' I said, jumping up. 'I'll show you.'

I wound it up and the three of us watched the ballerina turn on her little stand to the music. Aunty June clutched her hands together with delight.

'I love that show. I love a good musical, me. Yer Uncle Andy laughs at us, you know, when I pretend to be Doris Day.' She gave a little wiggle to make us laugh, then went out of the room, saying over her shoulder, 'I'll ask yer mam about her nets when she's got a second. I don't suppose there's any chance of yer dad knowing, not after what she said about him.' She chuckled to herself as she went back downstairs.

Sarah and I looked at each other and giggled.

'What kind of nets can she mean?' asked Sarah.

I wanted to have the answer to this, but couldn't think of one.

One of the women downstairs was shouting to everyone else now in a pretendy-posh voice that tea and biscuits were being served, and people started making their way to the kitchen from the other downstairs rooms. I was thirsty too, but didn't want to be fussed over and asked lots of questions about school or what we thought of our new house.

The main way into the garden was out through the back door by the kitchen, but that would mean braving the crowds. Instead, we peered over the banister and, when the coast was clear, ran downstairs and out the front door, slipping through the gap in the hedge.

'Race you to the top of the tennis court,' I said to Sarah, giving her a small head start. We peered over the fence at the far end. 'The graveyard is huge,' I said. 'I wonder if we're allowed to ride our bikes on the paths.'

'We could have races on it! We could start at different ends and meet in the middle.'

'Shall we time ourselves now, running the length of the tennis court? I've got a second hand on my watch.'

'You always have to make it a competition.'

'OK, we'll do it just for fun.'

Sarah pretended to be looking at something, then ran ahead gleefully when I wasn't ready. 'Come on then, slowcoach!'

'We might be tennis champions one day,' I said, as we leant against the wall of the house getting our breath back after running several lengths. 'I'm going to play every single day in the summer.'

'I'm going to play *every* day, even in winter.'

'Well, it was my idea. Maybe we can both be champions.'

We walked along the path that ran between the house and the lawn. Although it was May, the day had been dull and overcast and someone had switched the lights on inside. People had taken their tea to different rooms. They could have seen us if they had looked, but everyone was too busy or talking too much to know they were being watched. We could see our sister, Ruth, on someone's knee in the sitting room, being read a story. Aunty June and another of the kitchen ladies were looking down at her fondly. In Dad's study, the next room along, the man who had been playing with Mark on our arrival was talking to a man in paint-spattered overalls, while Wilf, the man who had carried the tea chest to the attic, was doing something with a hammer to one of Dad's many bookcases. Further along in the dining room sat Grandma, still wearing her coat and hat, nodding politely at the conversation of two of the other helpers from the kitchen. I knew she had brought pans of mince and potatoes for tea, and wondered when everyone was going to leave so that we could sit down and eat.

When one of the ladies seemed to look straight at us, we ducked, then crept on to the lawn. The trees and bushes at the back of the lawn were thick and jungle-like and hid the churchyard from view. As we hunkered down in the wet grass, I hoped there was nothing hiding in them.

'We can spy on everyone from here,' I said.

'The light's on in my bedroom,' said Sarah. 'There'd better not be anyone in it.'

'That's Mum and Dad's room, not yours.'

'Oh.'

'It's like looking into a doll's house,' I said, suddenly enthralled by this image. Each room was a story with its own characters, playing out its own scenes. Grandpa Gofton, a builder, had made a doll's house for me and Sarah three or four Christmases ago, and I could still spend hours moving the little figures around, rearranging their furniture and making up stories about their lives.

'Everyone talks funny,' said Sarah.

'I know. Did you hear that man when we came in? It sounded like this . . . ' I made a thick guttural sound in my throat and put the word 'pet' on the end.

'No, it was like this.' Sarah's version sounded almost exactly the same.

'Mum says some of my friends can come and stay in the summer holidays. Will you invite yours too?'

'I don't know.' Sarah pulled at a clump of moss. 'Maybe. If I don't have any new ones.'

A new school. A new teacher. New friends. I had put these thoughts to the back of my mind, and the thought of them now was both exciting and terrifying. What if I didn't make any new friends? I hadn't been a new girl before. Would I know what to do? I was glad it was the holidays first, and that I could forget about such things for a week. A week was a long time. Something might happen, and I might never need to go to school.

'Girls!' a voice called from somewhere.

'Mum's shouting for us,' said Sarah. 'Quick, let's hide.'

But before we had the chance, she appeared round the corner from the tennis court and saw us. 'I've been looking for you two. Come on, people are leaving. Time for tea.'

Chapter Four

As I lay in bed, I could hear Dad singing downstairs. Dad had a good voice, and often said he wished he had had proper vocal training. In church he was always the loudest one singing the hymns. I thought that all vicars must be the same – that it was a requirement for the job – so was surprised when I discovered that some couldn't sing that well at all, or that they sang hesitantly, like other people did. His only failing was that when he sang at home, without the benefit of a hymn book, he didn't always remember the words, so we got used to hearing his favourite lines repeated over and over again, often followed by improvised lines of his own or by whistling. For he was a whistler, too, of jaunty tunes from his past, of show tunes, of popular North-Eastern songs.

'If I were a rich man,' he was singing tonight. He sounded happy. 'A teedle-deedle-deedle-deedle-deedle-deedle-dum.' He whistled it next, then sang it again, making a whole verse out of the teedle-deedles. He and Mum were unpacking boxes. I didn't feel tired at all. I wanted to help. 'We're just doing one more,' they said, as Sarah and I were sent to bed. But I learnt the next day that they had stayed up until three in the morning.

My room smelt of fresh paint, but there was another smell that permeated the house, the rubbery smell of carpet underlay. Our old house and school felt like a long way away and a long time ago. Had I really woken up this morning in the bedroom Sarah and I shared in Gosforth? It hardly seemed possible.

Mum interrupted Dad's singing, and I could hear the faint sounds of snatched conversation and things being moved around. The melancholy drone of a foghorn reminded me how close we were to the sea. The house creaked and groaned, protesting at this rowdy intrusion after months of solitude. I thought I heard Sarah walking along the landing to my room and I quickly sat up in bed.

'What do you want?' I called out. She didn't answer. 'I know you're there.'

I decided she must have gone to the toilet, which was next to my bedroom, and waited for her to come out. When she didn't, and it was obvious that no one was there, I lay back down and pulled my blanket over my head, trying to block out all the unfamiliar sounds.

'La, la, la, la,' I sang to myself. 'There's nothing there. La, la, la, la. If you keep talking you won't hear anything.' I wished I felt sleepier. I was impatient for the new day to begin. There was nothing I wouldn't do in this house. Sarah and I would solve mysteries. We might discover another world, like Narnia in *The Lion, the Witch and the Wardrobe*. We would hunt for fairies in the garden. I also hoped that I might make a new best friend to share everything with. It was nice to have a sister just a year younger, but a best friend was a special thing too.

I was helping Mum put things away in the kitchen the next morning when I heard the doorbell. I ran off importantly to answer it.

'Is the vicar in, pet?' asked the sharp-faced lady, who was already stepping into the porch when I got there. 'I'm Mrs Russell — from the big house up the road. You know, the one with the Venetian blinds.'

She moved past me into the hallway. 'I was Canon Morton's right-hand woman,' she went on. 'This place is like my second home.'

Mum came out of the kitchen and Mrs Russell repeated what she had told me.

'Oh, that's a lovely house you've got,' Mum agreed. 'Canon Morton told us all about you. How lovely to meet you.' Then she added, somewhat unnecessarily, 'Do come in.'

Mrs Russell looked surprised. 'He did? Oh, well, yes.' Her small head twitched like a bird as she took in the boxes in our hallway and glimpses of untidy rooms.

'My husband is . . . I'm not sure where he is, actually,' Mum said, after popping her head round the study door. 'Come to the kitchen and have a cup of coffee.'

Mrs Russell followed her down the passage, her head still turning this way and that as if desperate not to miss the slightest speck on the wall. 'Of course, I will miss Canon Morton,' she was saying. 'I won't pretend otherwise. Ernie and I both will. I dare say he'll miss — eeh, that's a big kitchen you've got there!'

She stopped, slightly flustered, before carrying on. 'Of course, I've been in it before. Canon Morton relied on me, he did. But, as I was saying, it's nice to have a family here. Ernie and I always said the house was made for kiddies.'

She jumped as Mark came tearing down the hall on his wooden sit-on lorry, made a ninety-degree turn into the kitchen and performed a wheelie round her ankles.

'Oops, you nearly lost the skin of your legs there,' said Mum. 'You'll regret your last remark, Mrs Russell! Come and sit over here in safety. Mark, out of the kitchen, now!' She narrowed her eyes at me, indicating that my brother was now my responsibility.

Dad appeared as she was sitting down. 'Alder Gofton! Lovely to meet you!' he exclaimed, holding out his hand.

As I chased Mark down the hall to the playroom, I could hear Mrs Russell telling Dad, 'The house with the Venetian blinds. Stops my furniture getting faded. Ernie likes the best quality, and so do I. I'm sure you're the same, Father . . . Yes, the big house on the end . . . I was his right-hand woman.'

When she left twenty minutes later, Mum gave a big sigh.

'Well, I hope they're not all like her, that's all I can say.' She saw me listening. 'You never heard that.'

She brightened up when George Templey dropped in. George was one of St John's two churchwardens and the husband of Phemie, the lady who had waited on Mum and Dad at that fateful meeting all those months ago.

'I've come to see how you're getting on, and Phemie sends a cake and some home-made jam.'

'How lovely, thank you.' Mum took the gifts, then said in a theatrical whisper, 'We've just met Mrs Russell.'

'Ah,' said George.

'Apparently she spent most of her time here, despite having such a lovely house of her own. If I had Venetian blinds, I'm sure I'd want to tell the world about them too.'

George laughed. 'That sounds like her. She and Ernie made a bob or two when they sold their business, and she thinks she's better than everyone else. Mind, I don't think she ever made it past the front door. Not many of us did.'

When Mum and Dad looked surprised, he explained how, as there was a door leading from the porch straight into the room Canon Morton used as his study, few people had been admitted to the main part of the house.

'Honestly!' said Mum. 'You'd think he'd want to share it, especially being on his own.'

'Takes all sorts,' said Dad.

'Typical bachelor,' said Mum. 'Coffee, while you're here?'

The men disappeared into Dad's study.

The telephone rang as Mum was putting the kettle on again. There was a phone in Dad's study and another in the cloakroom. 'Go and get it quickly before your dad picks it up, there's a good girl,' Mum said. 'You can take a message if it's for him.'

'Hello, bonny lass,' came a cheery voice. 'This is John Grenfell, your local undertaker. Now, I know your daddy hasn't started work yet, but I've just had a funeral in and they're asking for him in particular. Is he busy, pet?'

'Um, I'm not sure. I'll just go and see.'

And so began our new life.

Chapter Five

The weather was miserable that half-term. We looked out of the windows, desperate to find the sun, and it just kept on raining. I soon got sick of unpacking boxes. Mum said it was a choice between that or keeping Ruth and Mark amused, and sometimes it was hard to know which to pick. Luckily there were lots of interruptions, with people popping in to say hello and introduce themselves.

We had guests one day. David Parker, one of Dad's friends from his training days, came for lunch with his wife, Aunty Cathie and their sons, Michael and Jeremy. Things always got boisterous when Sarah and I were with the Parker boys, and the second the rain stopped, the four of us were sent to play outside.

We wandered into the churchyard, and when we saw how perfect the large gravestones were for hiding behind, decided to play sardines instead of hide and seek. Michael, Jeremy and I faced the road and counted to one hundred while Sarah went to hide.

'Don't go too far,' I said, 'or we'll never find you.'

'No peeking – and that means you too, Jeremy,' Sarah called over her shoulder as she skipped away.

'Yeah, no cheating, Jer!' cried Michael, who took our games as seriously as we did.

Jeremy sniggered and turned his head back. When the three of us had finished counting and turned round, the churchyard was a sea of long swaying grass, and the stones that were visible – for some were completely swallowed up in the vegetation – were the ships that sailed on it. We split up, Michael taking the path to the left that went behind our back garden and the gardens of the neighbouring houses. I carried straight on to the far end, looking to both sides as I walked. We should have narrowed down the hiding area, I thought – the graveyard was so big, it was going to take ages to find her. I read some of the gravestones as I went. Charlton, Armstrong, Dodds, Milburn – the same names kept popping up. I wondered if I might come across a Gofton. Dad said it was a good old North-Eastern name, but I had never met a Gofton who wasn't a close relation.

Apart from a couple of people tidying up a grave, there was no one around. The only noise was the traffic on the main road a few hundred yards behind us. When I had reached the far end, I began to walk back in a haphazard pattern across the grass. I saw Jeremy in the distance, disappearing behind the church, and wondered if Sarah had been sneaky and hidden close to where we had been counting. I realized I couldn't see Michael any more and I started to run in the direction where I'd last seen him, guessing he had found her. I had to be careful not to trip over the grave kerbs, many of them covered over with grass and weeds.

I discovered Sarah and Michael, flat on their stomachs in a large grave. This grave was neater and newer-looking than some of the others and the bottom of it was covered in shiny green stones, like jewels. I lay down beside them, running the stones through my fingers. Michael asked if we'd heard of a game called Totopoly, and said we'd have to play it when we came to his house. We talked about what we were going to do when we met up on our summer holidays and what the best part of last year's holiday had been.

'See if you can see Jeremy,' Sarah said after some time. 'We might be here all afternoon.'

I propped myself up on my arms and saw him in the distance. 'I think we should give him a shout. He's miles away.'

We all sat up, counted three and called his name together, then ducked back down. We were startled when a woman called to us from the path as she walked past: 'Show some respect, won't you? There's a funeral going on. This isn't a playground, you know.'

When she was out of earshot, Michael said, 'Bloomin' cheek. This is your churchyard. Why don't you tell her?' But he said it half-heartedly.

We looked to see what she was talking about and saw a group of people, who must have come from the church, gathered round a newly dug grave.

Just then Jeremy, who had heard our cry and was getting closer, yelled at the top of his voice: 'If you're keeping on moving it's not fair, and I'm telling on you!'

Michael jumped to his feet. 'Shurrup, Jer, and get over here. Can't you see it's a funeral?'

Jeremy ran up, happy to have found us, and threw himself down. 'Eh? What's the matter?'

No one needed to answer, as at that moment a small brass band began to play a sad tune. The four of us were silent for the first time that day. Two men held a large banner with pictures on it high in the air, their faces grimly determined as the wind snapped at it. The white vestments of the priest – not Dad, for he hadn't started work yet – fluttered round him so that he looked like a giant bird about to take flight.

'Must be a miner's funeral,' said Michael, when we decided it was safe to speak, though he spoke quietly.

'How do you know?' I asked.

'Well, that's their hymn. And this is a mining town.' He added scornfully, 'You do know where you live, don't you?'

'Of course I do.'

'And mining is a dangerous job. Not soft, like what our dads do.'

Although I had heard the words 'pit village' being used to describe our new home, they were still just words to me and had little meaning. I decided to ask Dad later whether mining really was dangerous. I knew it had been in the olden days, but I couldn't believe that it was today.

'Some of the pits are under the sea,' Michael went on, and though I nodded, I thought that sounded very unlikely.

The odd word floated over to us on the breeze. The band started playing again and people began to drift off.

'Your turn to hide now, Michael,' I said, but we seemed to have lost our enthusiasm.

'I'm freezing,' said Sarah.

We followed the path back to the house, but when we saw that Alan Routledge, the gravedigger, was filling in the new grave, we made a detour to talk to him.

'Alan!' we called out, and he stopped what he was doing. He was a small, slight man, but his body moved like a machine as he shovelled. He had a cheerful, boyish face that was nearly always smiling, and pale reddish hair.

Alan had joined us twice for lunch that week after Dad had found him taking shelter under one of the trees to eat his sandwiches. The previous vicar sometimes used to let him have his 'bait' in the garage, he explained, but he had never been invited inside before. He had a bowl of Mum's soup, all his sandwiches and two of Mum's biscuits before Ruth and Mark dragged him into the playroom, where he happily pushed cars around the floor and joined in games about Ruth's farm animals – each one of whom had a name and a distinct personality – for another half-hour before going back to work.

'What youse up to?'

'We've been playing hide and seek. Well, sardines.' I stopped when I caught a glimpse of the coffin.

'It's just a young 'un,' said Alan, looking from the grave to our four faces. 'Terrible. Terrible.' He shook his head. 'Ye divvent want to be doing this job for a young 'un, that's when it gets to you.' He looked serious for a few seconds, then he beamed at us again. 'Whey, I'd better get on or your dad'll be after us. Enjoy your games.'

Back in the garden, we decided to play at being miners. We made a tunnel by draping a rug over the bars of the swing, but it was time for Michael and Jeremy to go home before we got very far.

Chapter Six

The next morning Mum dragged us all out to see a lady up the road who, she had found out, was a friend of a friend of Grandma's and would appreciate a visit.

'We're only going to say hello, we won't stay long,' she said as we grumbled along behind her. The wind blew down Newbiggin Road straight into our faces. We must have looked like the children's-home outing: Mum holding Mark on his reins, Ruth holding Sarah's hand behind them, me tagging along last, desperate to get back to the mountain ash tree Sarah and I had just discovered was perfect for climbing, before it started raining again.

Mum couldn't see a bell, so knocked on the door. It didn't seem to make much noise so she did it again, a bit harder, then stood back, giving us all a nervous smile. 'We won't be a minute,' she said quietly. 'It'll make her day to see you all.' She cleared her throat and looked expectantly at the door.

'I think I can hear a telly,' said Sarah.

'Television,' said Mum. Still no one came, and she knocked a

third time. This time, sounds of life seemed to start up and grow
within the house. Footsteps got closer, a muffled voice spoke to
itself. Someone was behind the door now and we heard cum-
bersome items being moved, something sliding over a hard
surface, the strain of human effort. After what seemed like ages,
a voice called out: 'Who on earth is it? Can't you come round
the back like everyone else?'

Mum seemed to freeze for a split second, then she cried out,
'I'm so sorry, Mrs Elliott. It's Gwenda Gofton. From the vicarage. And I've brought the children to see you. We'll be round
in a jiffy.'

'Oh, Gwenda!' There was the sound of more shuffling. 'No,
no, I'm almost there. Hang on, pet. If I can just shift these . . .
Eeh, that'll teach us.'

After a few more seconds, the bolts were undone. A key was
inserted into a lock and wiggled until it turned and the door
burst open, to the sound of splintering wood.

'I'm so sorry, Mrs Elliott, we seem to have caused a lot of
bother. I didn't . . . ' Mum trailed off, sounding embarrassed.

Mrs Elliott propped herself up on the doorframe and patted
her chest. 'Eeh, pet, I keep my junk there, out of the way. We
don't use our front doors here except for funerals, or when it's
hot and we want to let a breeze through. If you keep on doing
that you'll have people thinking the bailiffs are round! Now, how
is your mam keeping?'

She ruffled Mark's hair and regarded us all warmly. I scowled
and looked at my feet. I hoped no one had seen us. We were in
a new world, and there were new rules to be learnt. Newcastle
seemed a long way away.

*

All that week, people came and went. Word had got round that this vicar was different from the ones before and that callers were being allowed over the doorstep. I got used to having my games interrupted by a head popping round the door belonging to someone who wanted to see 'the bairns' before leaving. Miss Dobie, the lady Mum had met on her first visit, came struggling down the path one morning with one of her cakes and a tin full of home-made shortbread. She'd been expecting company at the weekend, she said, and it hadn't arrived, so would we like the cakes instead?

George Templey came again, and was soon 'Uncle George' to all four of us. His fellow churchwarden, Jack Watson, likewise became Uncle Jack. They looked like a double act, Uncle George very tall and Uncle Jack small, both full of smiles. Ruth and Mark would rush to greet them whenever they arrived, throwing themselves into their arms. (Ruth once did this with such enthusiasm she split her head on the skirting board and had to be carted off to hospital to have stitches.) Uncle Jim, who belonged to St Andrew's, the other church in the parish, was in and out a lot too, usually with a book or two under his arm, and it wasn't long before he developed his own way of announcing his arrival – three quick rings of the doorbell, then straight inside.

One morning, not long after we had finished breakfast, the porch seemed to shudder and heavy footsteps sounded down the hallway.

'Hello, my darlin's!' bellowed Aunty June as she came into the kitchen, where Sarah and I were emptying the dishwasher – Mum's leaving gift from the last parish – and Ruth and Mark were playing on the floor. .

'Oh, hello, June.' Mum sounded only slightly surprised.

'I've come to give you a hand putting your nets up,' she said, after scooping up Mark and giving him such a fierce squeeze he immediately started wriggling to be put down.

'Oh, June, I'm not sure I'm going to bother. We're far enough back from the road not to be overlooked.'

We had learnt by now that 'nets' were net curtains, and that all of our neighbours had them at their windows.

'No nets? Why, everyone has nets, flower.'

'Look, I've decided to go for these half-curtains – I think they're called café curtains – here in the kitchen.' Mum pointed at the wide kitchen windows. 'But I really think that's all the privacy I need. We're not exactly running around naked all the time. Only some of the time. Now, have a coffee while you're here.'

Aunty June looked at me and Sarah and shook her head. 'You tell your mam,' she said.

'They're such grubby things,' Mum continued.

'Only if you don't wash them!' Aunty June said.

Mum laughed and admitted she had a point. 'But life's too short to spend washing net curtains,' she pleaded.

'That's why you've got me!' said Aunty June. It had already been decided that she was going to help Mum with the house two mornings a week and babysit on Dad's night off. She flexed her arms like a weightlifter. 'Feel these, girls. I'm as strong as your Uncle Andy.'

I looked at her admiringly. Aunty June wasn't fat, but she certainly wasn't thin either. She was simply as sturdy as a barge, and it was hard to imagine that she would ever be anything but as solid and cheerful as she was at that moment.

She and Mum were both laughing now. 'I'm going to let the side down, aren't I,' said Mum. 'I can just see the headline in the local paper: "New vicar's wife hounded out of town over net curtains".'

'You're dead right. And where are your fires? What sort of woman in Ashington keeps a house without a coal fire?' She looked to me and Sarah to explain our mysterious mother to her. I shrugged. 'Eeh, I don't know. I see I'm going to have my work cut out with you.' She picked up Ruth this time, planted a huge kiss on her cheek and said, 'At least you'll let your Aunty June get her own way, won't you, my darlin'?'

Dad was often out when visitors called, something we would grow used to over the years, so the kitchen turned into a sort of holding area, full of people drinking tea or coffee and talking to Mum as they waited to see him. We were getting to know some of the regulars quite well. When Grandma and Papa came for a visit, Grandma was taking off her hat in the hallway mirror when Uncle Jim, who had announced himself with his three rings, walked jauntily past her. He gave her a cheery, 'Hello, pet,' as he made his way to the kitchen where he knew he'd find Mum.

Grandma shot into the sitting room. 'Who is that man?' she hissed at me. 'Honestly, I think any Tom, Dick or Harry could walk straight into this house and you lot wouldn't bat an eyelid. Mind you' – her eyes took in our plain second-hand furniture, tiny black-and-white television that took ages to warm up and floor studded with children's toys – 'there's not much to tempt a burglar here.' Papa gave a small chuckle as he sat himself down with his pipe in his favourite seat.

'Oh, that was just Uncle Jim,' said Sarah breezily. 'He comes every day when Dad's out.'

I overheard Grandma telling Mum what Sarah had said later, and wondered why they were both hooting with laughter.

Chapter Seven

Half-term was over, and Sarah and I started at Hirst South Junior school. It was a slightly severe-looking, two-storey red-brick building with tall, narrow windows that afforded views of sky from the inside, and a concrete yard wrapped around it. Boys were downstairs and girls upstairs, so that in fact they were two separate schools. Litter drifted around the playground, which had high railings dividing the boys' area from the girls'. My teacher, Miss Stewart, introduced me to the class. Everyone stared and some of the girls whispered, though most of them looked friendly. I was told the names of the girls on my table – Susan, Sandra, another Susan, Karen. There was one girl whose name I couldn't catch and she hissed it into my ear, but I still couldn't understand her thick accent.

I was told about merits (pink cards) and demerits (blue ones), about pencil monitors and bell monitors and about having to

bring a note in if I'd been bad. I was horrified. Why did my
teacher need to know if I'd been naughty at home?

We did maths first, and for part of the lesson we went into the
playground to take measurements by pushing a wooden wheel
on a stick which clicked with every metre.

When the bell went for playtime, some of the girls took skipping ropes and rubber balls from their bags. Though I would
have liked to skip, Sandra took my hand and whisked me off like
a prize trophy to play with her big sister and some other older
girls. There were about twenty of them standing holding hands
in a circle, singing a song about a princess long ago who was
locked up in a tower. The girl chosen to be the princess stood
in the centre of the circle, and with our arms we made the thick
walls of the tower and the trees of the forest growing round it.
Then a handsome prince came riding by, and one of the girls
skipped round the outside of the circle and finally broke through
all the obstacles to rescue her. I was overcome with embarrassment when, after two girls had taken the part of the princess,
Sandra's sister pointed to me and said I should have a turn. The
older girls all nodded in agreement, Sandra prodded me and I
unwillingly took my place in the middle. I looked shyly at all the
faces I didn't know dancing around me. Was this really happening? I knew they were being kind to me, the new girl, but I
couldn't get the feeling out of my head that they were taunting
me. I longed to be back in my old playground at school in
Gosforth, playing anonymously alongside my friends.

'You've got to do the actions,' Sandra mouthed at me, making
a pillow out of her hands as the princess was put to sleep after
a witch pricked her finger. I made a lame effort to play my part
with more enthusiasm, and wished it would all end soon.

After another lesson, a bell rang and Miss Stewart sent four girls to put on their coats. These were the girls who went home for their dinners, what my mother would have called 'fussy eaters'. One of them was a girl called Kathryn Egdell, who I had met at church the day before.

The school hall, on to which all the classrooms opened, had been transformed into the dining room, with three rows of tables down the length of it and a serving area at one end. Mrs Neal, the chief dinner lady, took Sarah and me to one side to explain how the system worked.

'A girl in my class didn't come to school today because she was naughty,' Sarah whispered to me as Mrs Neal left us for a minute to march someone whose hands had failed her inspection back down to the toilets to wash them again.

By now I had worked out my earlier misunderstanding. 'You mean she was bad? It doesn't mean naughty,' I gloated. 'It means ill!'

Sarah looked disappointed. 'How do you know?'

'Everyone does.'

When Mrs Neal came back, she told us that we all sat on tables of six, each with an older pupil at the head. We collected our main course from the serving area as we filed into the hall, but our puddings were served at the table by a group of privileged fourth-years. Everyone had to walk in a clockwise direction, even if it meant walking almost all of the way round the hall to reach our seat. At the end of each course, third-years called 'scrapers' gathered up the empty plates and scraped the slops into a large plastic dustbin. She pointed out two of them, looking very superior in their pretty aprons.

'You might be a scraper, too, come September, if you play

your cards right,' she said, nodding at me. I couldn't help feeling pleased. 'You've got to be a two-scooper, mind.' My heart
dropped a little until she explained that all this meant was that
a scraper had to have two scoops of mashed potato with her
dinner and not just one, a sign of the maturity required to take
on such a responsibility. And it went without saying that scrapers and servers had to eat everything on their plates.

'I've got eyes in the back of my head, and all,' she added
ominously, though her front pair were twinkling a bit when she
said it.

She put me and Sarah together for dinner that day. The potato,
which was very white, had small shiny lumps in it, though the
spam fritters were delicious. I was determined to eat everything,
whatever happened. And when I saw some of the older girls
parading round the hall, holding their stacks of dirty dishes in
front of them like offerings for Baby Jesus, I knew I had found
my calling. Sarah, however, picked at her food in tiny mouthfuls.

'You won't ever be a scraper,' I warned her.

'I wouldn't want to be. Did you see inside that bin? It looked
like sick.'

But I was already dreaming about the lacy apron I would ask
Grandma to make me, identical to the one the girl with the long
blonde ponytail was wearing.

The headmistress sat at the head of a table with some of the
older girls, and had her own special server. I guessed it must be
a real honour to have that job, and saw how Mrs Neal fussed
around her table for longer. When the scraper on our table said
to me, 'Are you finished, pet?' I thought nothing in the world
could beat being as grown up as she was.

Pudding wasn't so nice – something white and gloopy with

a dollop of raspberry jam in the middle – but I managed to force it down. At home we were used to having to eat everything on our plates, though neither of us had encountered anything like this before. Mrs Neal sighed when she saw Sarah's dish still half full. 'We'll let this go today because you're new, but you'll have to bring a note if you're going to leave anything in future, mind.'

As the tables filed out, I noticed a few girls sitting on their own, gazing miserably at their leftovers. One girl was crying. Mrs Neal went over to her.

'One more mouthful. Howway, just a tiddly bit.'

She whipped the plate away and winked at me and Sarah as we passed her. 'Don't look so scared. Me bark's worse than me bite.'

In the afternoon, we wrote stories about what we had done in the half-term holiday. That was perfect for me. I loved writing, and my holiday had been more interesting than usual. I covered five pages of my jotter, though I noticed that some girls sat gazing into the air or wrote painfully slowly.

'Why are you not writing, Julie Huddleston?' asked Miss Stewart. She was marking our maths books from that morning. There were so many Julies in the class, as well as Susans and Sandras, that the teacher had to use their surnames whenever she addressed them.

''Cos I didn't do nowt,' said Julie.

'You must have done something. Think harder.'

Later, we had to share some of our stories. One girl had helped her grandad on his allotment; another had made a skirt, which Miss Stewart asked her to bring in to show us all. My friend Sandra had played skippy with her sister in the back lane.

Joanna had gone 'up the street' with her nana – a funny thing to mention, I thought. I learnt later that this was the way everyone described going to Ashington's main shopping area. Kathryn, the girl I had met at church, had been to a museum in Newcastle with her dad. Kathryn wore glasses and had a face that often looked serious, but when she laughed she put her head back and exploded. Mum had invited her to come and play after the service, and we had discovered a shared love of reading. Kathryn promised to lend me the Enid Blyton books I didn't have. It sounded as if she had hundreds.

It was afternoon playtime before I knew it, and I found myself surrounded by lots of girls, but it wasn't a game this time.

'You're the vicar's daughter,' said one of them. She was right, of course, but it was the first time in my life I had heard myself described like this and it gave me a weird feeling, not exactly like being punched, but physical all the same and not very pleasant. In my old school nobody had ever mentioned my father, and I didn't remember his job once coming up in conversation. But here, even girls from other classes seemed to know who I was.

'Me mam goes to your dad's church.'

'We live dead close to you.'

'Your dad's doing our Susan's wedding next year.'

'Are you not scared, living next door to the cemetery?'

I didn't know what a cemetery was and shook my head, thinking that was the safest answer.

'I saw your dad yesterday!'

I was sick of hearing about my dad. Why did everyone care about him so much?

'So what do your dads do?' I asked in the end, realising that fathers were an important topic round here.

They all gawped at me. One or two looked at each other and sniggered. 'Whey, he's a miner,' said one, as if I should have known this already.

'Aye, a miner,' said another.

'Miner.'

'Miner.'

'Mine's a deputy,' said one proudly, and I thought that at last I had found someone with whom I might have something in common.

'He's still a miner,' corrected her friend.

A girl from my class called Kirsty said that her dad was a policeman.

'And she lives in one of the police houses,' said her friend, admiringly.

Kirsty nodded. 'But he used to work down the pit,' she said, and she and her friend skipped away, holding hands.

'Don't you talk posh!' said someone else.

That was news to me. When I tried to protest, they just started laughing and imitating my reply. 'But you do! It's dead funny, man! Say that again!'

Sandra smiled and linked my arm. 'We can teach you Geordie. It's dead easy.'

'Aye,' said Elaine, a friendly, skinny girl, handing me the end of a long skipping rope. 'If us lot can speak it, anyone can! Howway, let's play skippy before the bell goes.'

There weren't any other cars outside school, but our lumpy old Morris Traveller was waiting by the gates. Some of my new friends stood and stared as I got into it. I waved self-consciously from the back seat and watched enviously as they linked arms and began to walk home. Some of them were already in the sweet shop a few doors away when we drove past.

'We could have walked,' I said.

Mum ignored this. 'How was it, then?' she asked. 'Made some nice friends?'

'Yes, lots. They're going to teach me Geordie.'

'Don't be silly,' she said. 'You talk very nicely.'

'No I don't. People think I'm posh.'

'They think I'm posh, and all,' Sarah wailed, and I sneaked her an admiring glance. She'd already picked up some of the dialect!

When Mum didn't respond, she continued, 'It's really stupid because posh is how some of your friends talk, and we don't talk nothing like them.'

'*Anything* like them.' Mum corrected her this time. She made a tutting noise. 'They're just jealous. All the ladies at church yesterday said how nicely you spoke.'

Being admired by old ladies was little compensation.

Mum changed the subject. 'Aunty June found your hairbrush, Barbara. You'll never guess where it was. She can always put her hand straight on whatever you need. She's babysitting tomorrow night.'

We cheered up at that news. Aunty June had promised us sweets on babysitting night, as well as watching a good *fillim* on the telly.

'Will you go out every Tuesday night?' I asked.

'Please!' said Sarah.

The car was at the bottom of Milburn Road now, beside the

White Elephant, facing the church. Mum laughed. 'As many as we can.' After a few seconds she added, 'It's not easy for your dad, either, you know, being new. And it's such a big parish. Probably the busiest in the whole of our diocese. He's going to have a lot on his plate. Canon Morton simply laid down the law and everyone did as they were told and didn't have to think for themselves, which isn't your dad's way of working. He didn't have a family, either, so he could dedicate every waking moment to his parishioners.' She met my eyes in the rear-view mirror. 'Your father has you lot to think about as well.'

I wasn't really listening. Michael had been right about our dads having soft jobs. Miners came home with dirt on their faces. One girl said her dad never washed his back, as that would make him weak. And it was even true that some of them went to work in tunnels under the sea. My new friends had all seemed so proud of their fathers in a way I'd never encountered before. I'd never thought much about what my dad did until now, apart from popping in and out of the house a lot and taking a service on Sundays. I'd certainly never thought it worthy of a conversation.

Mum pulled into the drive. A man who was digging the vegetable plot looked up briefly and then carried on with what he was doing.

'That's Dougie,' said Mum. 'He's giving us a hand with the garden. Just think, we'll have all sorts growing here next year – runner beans, corn on the cob, carrots . . . '

'From out the ground? Ugh!' said Sarah. 'What's wrong with ones from the shop?'

'They taste far nicer, that's what,' Mum said. 'And where do you think the ones in the shop come from?'

'Well I'm not eating them.'

'Mum, can we serve our mashed potato with an ice-cream scoop like they do at school?' I asked.

'I don't see why not. Come on, hop out.'

'Oh, and Mum, I'm going to be a scraper when I'm a third-year. I bet you don't know what that is. I can't wait!'

Chapter Eight

Sarah and I found Alan jumping up and down in a grave.

'It's been stottin' doon for so long,' he explained, 'sometimes the holes fill up with watter and the coffin starts floating. We've just buried this poor chap and he's come bobbing back up.'

We found this inexplicably funny, both the way Alan told us and watching what he was doing. The graveyard in the other parish in Ashington had a different problem – it was on fire deep underground. Dad said that it was the only place where you got buried and cremated at the same time.

'Can we have a go?' I asked him when we had got over the giggles.

'No, I don't think your dad would like that. And you'll do me out of a job. You wouldn't do that to poor Alan, would you?'

We shook our heads.

I pictured the whole graveyard underwater, the coffins bobbing up and down all over the place and Sarah and I jumping from one to the other as if they were stepping stones.

'Let's go and look in the window of that funny shop,' I suggested as Alan picked up his spade again.

Next door to the church was a small terrace of three shops, and on the other side of that, a sad-looking building that had once been grand – the Hippodrome – now used as a warehouse. But it was the two end shops that interested us. Charlton's the sweet shop was at the far end, nearest the Hipp, as it was known, where the kind-faced Mrs Charlton stood in front of row upon row of jars – a bafflingly large assortment that included sherbet lemons, Kola cubes, butterscotch toffees, Black Jacks and lurid gobstoppers. Closest to the church stood a dusty old store that had surely closed down years ago. A peeling sign announced that it had been called Spedding's, a post office and newsagent. Such a shame, said Mum and Dad when we first saw it – a newsagent right on our doorstep would have been so handy!

We pushed our faces up against the murky glass and saw treasures in the window frilled with spiders' webs and gently coated with dust: there were faded birthday cards, felt pens, a washing line and pegs, a packet of weed killer and countless sunlight-scorched boxes of unidentifiable but intriguing objects. A pharaoh's tomb could not have looked more promising.

Today a dim yellow light seemed to be coming from inside. I pressed my nose against the glass of the door and pulled back quickly when it opened and a woman walked briskly out.

'Ta-ta, Jack,' she called over her shoulder. 'See you th' morra.'

She held the door for me with a questioning expression. I

took it, just to be polite, and looked at Sarah, wondering what we should do.

'I don't bite, you know,' boomed a loud voice from inside the shop, 'at least, not on a Saturday,' and though we felt like running, we shuffled inside.

A man stood behind a counter. He was very tall and had a long bristly chin, like a giant in a fairy tale. His shirt was unbuttoned at the top and he wore a shabby brown cardigan over it. But his smile was surprisingly gentle.

'Can I help you young ladies?'

'Er, can we just look, please?' I said.

'Look away! There's lots to look at here.'

There were so many surfaces in the shop, each one filled with so many items, that we didn't know where to start.

'You're not the new inhabitants of the vicarage, are you?' asked the man as we stood there dithering.

We nodded.

'I was wondering when I was going to meet you.' He held out a long arm across the counter, then seemed to think the occasion demanded more and vaulted over it in one leap. We looked up at him towering over us as he shook our hands. 'Jack Spedding's the name. And what are yours?'

We told him, and Sarah added, 'We thought you were closed down.'

'Did you? Why's that?'

'It's because the shop is all ...' I nudged Sarah and she stopped, gave me a bewildered look, then carried on. 'All old-looking,' she said, and glared at me.

'Ah, that's because I'm old,' he said. 'Me and my shop are one and the same.'

I looked at him. I wasn't sure if he was old or not. There were different kinds of old, and I couldn't tell which kind he was. Older than my parents, perhaps, but not as old as my grandparents. Though I couldn't be sure about that as I had never seen my grandparents looking as rumpled as this man was. If he didn't speak so nicely he might have been the sort of man you would keep out of the way of in the street.

He grinned at us both. 'Well, you have a good look round, then you can go home and tell your parents that I'm open and that if they want a morning paper, this is the place to get it. I'm open seven days a week. And for all sorts of other paraphernalia, too.'

I had never heard that word before, but it made sense immediately.

The shop was almost as dark and dusty inside as it appeared outside, but it was true that there was lots to see. There was a wide counter covered in comics and magazines and a separate cubbyhole for the post office. Behind the main counter were shelves crammed with paper and boxes. Near the door was a stand full of greetings cards, and beside that an old chest of drawers that I would have liked to open if I'd dared. There were other things too, all mixed up together – tins of paint, packets of seeds and other items for the garden, pots of glue, small toys, batteries.

I wished I had some money to buy a comic. Mum always told us not to waste our money on them but to read books instead. I loved books, but having a comic was a treat. I always spent as long as I could turning the pages of the copy of *Woman's Own* that Grandma Gofton brought every Saturday afternoon. I particularly loved the pictures of film stars lounging in their

Beverly Hills homes, and the smooth-skinned, shiny-haired
models advertising night creams and shampoos. And I was
always intrigued by the problem page, even though I couldn't
always understand what the problems actually were. I had made
up my mind to write to Mary Grant if I had a problem with
boyfriends when I was older, as she looked kind and always had
an answer.

'*June and Schoolfriend*,' said Sarah, holding her favourite comic
up at me with a smile.

'I know, and *Princess Tina*,' I said, 'but sshhhh, put it down, we
haven't any money.' I stole a glance at Mr Spedding, wondering
if we would be told off for picking things up we weren't going
to buy, but he was engrossed in whatever he was doing at the
post-office counter.

We could have spent all afternoon in the shop, flicking
through the comics and discovering unexpected items on the
shelves or piled up on the floor. A few customers came in while
we were there. All of them addressed the owner as Jack, and
most stayed to chat with him.

'My two newest customers, Barbara and Sarah, from the vicarage,' he said to some of them. He said it as if we were adults,
too, and of just as much interest as anyone else, something I
wasn't used to grown-ups doing.

Then, as we slipped towards the door, he called out, 'Don't
forget to take these with you.'

He was holding the comics we had been looking at earlier.

'Oh, but . . . ' I said, confused.

'They're a present,' he said. 'I can tell we're going to be
friends, and friends are allowed to give presents, aren't they?'

'Yes, I think so,' I said shyly.

We took the comics, trying not to seem too eager. 'Thank you,' we chorused. We ran home, each of us wanting to be the first to share our news.

'I wondered where you two were,' said Mum as we dashed down the side path and almost bumped into her coming to look for us. 'I was getting quite worried about you.'

'We've met Mr Spedding,' Sarah cried.

'Who?'

'The man in the shop you thought was closed.'

'And he's really nice. And funny.'

'And look what he gave us. Free!'

Mum looked at our comics. 'You mean that filthy old place is actually open? Well, heavens above.'

Mum and Mr Spedding hit it off straight away. If we were ever in the newsagent's with Mum, the two of them would spend ages chatting about all sorts of things, and it wasn't long before they were trading good-natured insults. Mum joked about the mess in the shop, the huge quantity of things for sale and how he must surely stock everything but the kitchen sink. He said no, she was wrong there, and came out of the back room, where he kept a whole host of other goods that he had no room to display, holding just that. I don't think it really was for sale, but it made us all laugh. But the nicest thing about Mr Spedding was that he didn't forget us children either, because our parents were there, or speak to us in the patronising way some adults did, or – even worse – in that matey way that made you wish they had just kept their mouths shut. He spoke to us as if we were his friends, too, like Mum, but different.

Now that we knew the shop was open, we were in and out

all the time. It was always worth trying Mr Spedding first if we needed something, and he often had it. Not long after we moved, Mum sent me to buy an air letter. Two women were gossiping by the post-office counter, and I tried hard not to stare. Was that lady wearing slippers? I stole another look, and saw that not only was I correct, but that she was also wearing her pinny, as if she was still in her own kitchen. Her companion was quite smartly dressed in a dark coat with high heels, but did she realize that she had come out of the house with her curlers in? The scarf tied over the top only accentuated them. As they were standing where I wanted to be, I went to look through the magazines. 'Though don't go accepting one,' Mum had said. 'Mr Spedding will be going bankrupt if he keeps on doing that.'

I couldn't see Mr Spedding, but Mary Sobey (soon to be Aunty Mary), a member of our congregation who worked for him, was behind the counter. She was a smart lady – such a contrast to Jack, exclaimed Mum and Dad – with a pretty face and a welcoming smile. I wondered if she had noticed the ladies' attire, but if she thought it unusual she showed no sign of it.

'Hello, pet,' she said. 'Just looking? That's fine, flower. I'll be out the back, making Jack a cup of tea.'

I wished Sarah was with me so that we could laugh about the ladies together. She might not believe me when I told her. I heard them discuss someone's chesty cough and someone else's *arthuritis*. I flicked through *Bunty* and was wondering if I had the chance to read a whole 'Four Marys' story when something in their conversation made me listen more closely.

'She's been here two weeks and she hasn't even got her nets up,' the slipper lady was saying.

'June says she'll not have them,' said Curlers. At the mention of June my ears pricked up even more. Aunty June knew everyone, so there was a good chance she was the one being mentioned. 'Says they make a place look dirty! Did you ever! June says she told her that you just take them doon and wash them – she's got a machine, like, and a one that dries. Doesn't use a washing line, ye knaa.'

'No!'

'Aye, June says to her, "How do you get the air through your sheets and the bairns' clothes?" but she says she sticks them in the dryer like everything else. Says she got fed up of getting black spots on them when she lived in Newcastle. Mind, the city's a dirty place.'

'Filthy!'

'But no nets!'

I realized with growing embarrassment that it was my own mother they were talking about. Waves of hot and cold were washing over me.

Then one of the women said in a more sympathetic way, 'Mind, with all them bairns – four? five? – they must keep her canny busy.'

They carried on, sympathizing while they condemned.

I hardly dared move. I felt strangely guilty, as if it was my fault that I was overhearing this. I wondered if I could slip out of the shop without being noticed.

'Barbara!' Mr Spedding called suddenly from some dark recess. 'What can I do for you?'

'Um, I've come for an air letter, please, but ... ' I shrugged apologetically and put down the comic I was reading.

'Ah, your mother's writing to America again, no doubt! I told her the last time she was in, she needs to write a book about all her adventures. It's bound to be a bestseller! Tell your father to type his own sermons and iron his own vestments and then she might find the time. Don't you agree, Mrs Hudson?'

The women stopped talking all of a sudden. Curlers nudged Slippers and said something under her breath. They stood, almost motionless apart from their heads, which looked from Mr Spedding to me and back to Mr Spedding again.

Mr Spedding was enjoying himself. 'Ladies, may I introduce you to the vicar's eldest? Barbara, meet Mrs Hudson and Mrs Patterson, two fine upstanding ladies of this parish.'

'Eeh, Jack, listen to you,' said Curlers, looking coy all of a sudden.

'Hello, pet,' said Slippers. 'Are you settlin' in, darlin'?'

'Yes, thank you.'

'What do you think of Ashington, then?' There was definite pride in the way she said the name.

Jack called out, 'Don't answer that, Barbara, if you want to get out of here alive.'

The women chuckled, and Curlers said with mock indignation, 'I bet she loves it here, don't you, pet?'

I nodded.

'It's a big house you live in,' said Slippers. 'I hope you bairns are good for your poor mam, now, she's got a lot on her plate.'

'Eeh, you can say that again. We were just saying, Jack, what a wonder the vicar's wife was, weren't we, Ruby?'

Ruby – or Slippers – nodded. 'Your Aunty June's told us what a grand job your mam's doing. Mind, so's your dad. Everyone says how friendly he is and how he makes everyone feel so welcome.' She turned to Jack. 'You know, I didn't think I'd get used to a married vicar, it didn't seem right, somehow, but now I can't imagine having anyone else. And I've only met him to say hello to.'

I smiled awkwardly and picked a bobble off the sleeve of my cardigan. Mr Spedding pulled an understanding face at me.

'He's certainly quite a fellow,' he said. 'And as for Gwenda,' he carried on, in a final sort of way, 'she's second to none.' And he banged the words out on the counter with his fist. The women and I jumped and they both laughed nervously. 'It's good for all of us to have someone like her here, shaking things up a bit. You need a bit of a shake, don't you, Mrs Hudson?'

'I dare say I do,' she laughed, slightly uncertainly.

'Now, let's see about that air letter. Or did you ladies need anything before you carry on putting the world to rights?'

I skipped home a few minutes later with my purchase. Thanks to Jack Spedding, the incident had changed from horrible to funny, and I couldn't wait to tell Mum. I waved to Dad and Alan, who were taking measurements beside a freshly dug grave. Alan grinned and waved back at me. Dad said he'd never met anyone who enjoyed his job as much as Alan did.

As I had expected, Mum threw her head back and laughed when I told her.

'Good old Jack! What a hoot!'

'Can't we have some net curtains, though?' I pleaded. When it was dark outside and I saw the yellow light glowing behind them, I always longed to be in those rooms too.

'Not you as well!'

I was annoyed with her all of a sudden. 'When I've got my own house I'm going to have them at every window. And I'll wash them once a week.'

'No, you won't,' said Mum. 'You've got too much sense.'

I knew she was right. She really was the most irritating person at times.

Chapter Nine

We lived in the biggest house in the street, though it might as well have been the world, for Ashington was the centre of the universe to its inhabitants. It had everything you could possibly need – why would you venture anywhere else? We had shops of every kind – the big ones in a part of town known to one and all as 'up the street'; we had cinemas (two), swimming baths and parks (though our family rarely visited the parks, as we were blessed with the garden and churchyard, plus an abandoned mining village that lay behind them both and was as fascinating as any playground). We even had our own seaside – Newbiggin-by-the-Sea, at the end of the road, with its promenade and ancient church that stuck out on the point, or Druridge Bay, a little further up the coast, with its huge sandy beach for when we had whole afternoons to spare. Families like ours might visit Newcastle for the really big shops and department stores, while Aunty June saw nearby Blyth as the local metropolis. But plenty of others saw no need to go anywhere else as the town fulfilled all of their needs.

There was plenty of work, too, for the men. Boys followed their fathers down the pit. No doubt many had hoped for an easier, safer job for their sons, but work was work and here it was, right on the doorstep in one of four big collieries – Ashington, Woodhorn, Lynemouth and Ellington (a fifth one, Linton, had closed before our arrival).

In 1849, when the first serious colliery undertaking was established there, Ashington was little more than a random collection of farms and hamlets. Another hamlet was Hirst, from the Old English 'hyrste' meaning copse or wood, which grew to be more than twice the size of Ashington when two new collieries were sunk in the 1890s. Now, our part of town was still known as the Hirst – or Horst, as it was pronounced by the locals – and the parish of Seaton Hirst was three times bigger than the parish of Ashington, but Ashington had become the name of the town and that was the name on the map.

Despite claiming to be the world's biggest mining village, with its thirty thousand inhabitants, you couldn't really call Ashington a village by the time we got there. It was too big, too sprawling and too, well, town-like. It was made up of rows of terraced houses, so straight and so methodical that in an aerial photograph taken in the year of our arrival the town looks like a giant railway yard. Mum joked that it was like Manhattan – one of the places she had visited on her American travels – long and thin and with parallel numbered avenues, but that even New York City couldn't have produced more smoke than

Ashington's chimneys! Mining families received free coal, so every house – except ours, for Mum had had all the fireplaces boarded up – had a fire blazing in the hearth whatever the weather. Sometimes we would go to Aunty June's to find her peeling potatoes at the sink wearing just a slip, and I rarely saw Uncle Andy in anything other than vest and trousers when he was relaxing at home.

Newer houses in estates that sprang up on the edge of town had patches of garden and indoor bathrooms, but few of the colliery houses had such luxuries when we first arrived and the toilets were in the backyard, next to the coal shed. To sit in Aunty June's outdoor netty, with the clean, sharp smell of disinfectant up your nose, the pile of *Sun* newspapers on the floor and the sunlight dancing through the slats, provided a sense of tranquillity you never felt in any other loo. Of course I'd never had to go out there at night, or in the winter, or in the pouring rain, at least not on a regular basis.

And then there were the back lanes, full of children playing, people walking and talking, the coal van delivering. They were the canals to Ashington's Venice! Because we had our garden, and our mother liked to be able to see where we were playing, Sarah and I didn't spend much time in them, and so they maintained an allure that the dog mess and the dirty puddles probably didn't merit.

As the warmer weather arrived, front doors that had been jammed shut for almost a year were being opened – I still felt my cheeks flush remembering that episode with Mum at Mrs Elliott's during our first week! – and ribbon curtains hung in the doorways, fluttering in the breeze. I would come to think of this annual phenomenon like seeing summer personified, as significant as the first day you wore your summer dress to school or had tea in the garden.

We were only seventeen miles north of Newcastle, but we lived and behaved and spoke differently here. If only I'd known during those first weeks that the Geordie spoken in Ashington was almost as different from the Geordie spoken in the rest of the North-East as it was from Cockney! It was a language of its own that had developed from the pitmen, from shared experiences in an underground world I would never know. Ignorant of this, and keen to fit in, Sarah and I did our best to emulate our friends' way of speaking.

This was our new home, and we quickly grew to love it. We children, at least, would come to believe what everyone who had been born and brought up in the town believed – that Ashington, with its smoking chimneys and ponging pitheaps, was paradise.

When Dad came home on his first Saturday after being installed as vicar of Seaton Hirst, we heard his slightly manic laughter coming from the kitchen. 'Would you credit it?' he said to Mum. 'I don't know what Canon Morton was playing at!'

It turned out he had had four weddings booked back to back with only half an hour between each. By the time the first ceremony was ending, the second lot of guests had arrived and were waiting at the doors. They had to be asked politely to stand aside while the newly married couple had photographs taken as they were leaving the church. Then the newlyweds and their guests had to be gently steered to the side of the building to have further photos taken so that the second service could begin. As things were now running late, the third wedding party had already turned up and the bridal party was driving round the block to kill time. To cap it all, there had been some 'argy-bargy', as Dad put it, between some of the guests.

'A good photographer is worth his weight in gold,' Dad said, as Mum nodded her agreement. 'You need someone with authority, like Dennis, to organize everyone, or it can turn into chaos.' (Dennis Swinton, owner of a successful photography business, was a family friend and had been Dad's churchwarden in Gosforth.) He looked at his watch. 'And now I've just got time for a quick cup of tea before I do those sick visits. We'll have to do my sermon when I'm back.'

Sarah and I had had a lovely time watching all of this from the tennis court. We had enjoyed seeing the pretty brides in their frilly white dresses, the grooms and ushers who shuffled their feet and smoked cigarettes at the church door before going cautiously inside, and counting all the bridesmaids. One bride had eight! We had laughed as one little bridesmaid, who couldn't have been more than two, stamped her feet and refused to do as she was told until someone popped a sweet in her mouth. And it had been even more exciting when the best man from one party had suddenly squared up to the photographer from another, threatening to smash his 'bloody camera' if he wasn't careful, before being dragged away by his friends.

'We almost saw a fight,' said Sarah to Mum, disappointed that it hadn't come to anything. 'And he swore.'

Dad resolved that today's chaos wouldn't happen again. 'Everyone deserves not to be rushed on their special day,' he said. Saturdays would always be busy – while we were in Ashington he officiated at up to eighty weddings a year – but nobody had to feel they were on a conveyor belt. And while Canon Morton had done his wedding interviews all in one group, Dad liked to talk to each couple separately, even though that meant spending Wednesday nights at back-to-back meetings. Sarah and I would answer the door to the earlier ones before we went to bed. The couples were always very young, though how young I didn't really know. It was Mum who sometimes made comments later, like, 'I thought they'd come to ask if you were going out to play'. The boys – for many of them were too young to think of as men – had fashionably long hair and sideboards. The girls had 'shags' or feather cuts, or very long hair. They usually looked nervous, probably not helped by being stared at by me and Sarah as we were sent to ask if they'd like anything to drink while they were waiting, giggling at any who we thought looked or sounded funny.

Chapter Ten

Sunday morning meant church, and Sarah and I had adopted regular places in one of the two choir stalls at the back. Mum brought Ruth and Mark in later, after the sermon, when any disruption Mark might cause was less noticeable. St John's was an attractive building of golden stone, built in the 1890s, with a single bell tower. Inside, it was serene and simple, with white-washed walls and rows of slightly wobbly wooden seats. Each seat had a slot in the back of it for the person sitting behind to store their hymn and service books, and a hook for their kneeler. Though there were choir stalls, we didn't have a proper choir at St John's. Our sister church, St Andrew's, where we would sometimes go on feast days, had a flourishing choir whose members paraded importantly out of the vestry during the first hymn wearing white surplices over blue cassocks. Our choir consisted of two people, Uncle George the churchwarden and his sister, Sadie – known to us children as Miss Templey, or Brown Owl, depending on where we happened to see her. Sadie Templey was a smart, large-built woman with a kindly face and eyes that twinkled behind her glasses. She stood tall and proud, her head high. She seemed to have been made for wearing a uniform, for marching and singing.

It was a service full of ritual, of bells tolling at particular moments, of kneeling here and standing there – up and down we went countless times throughout the service. And we would soon discover that there was nothing the congregation liked more than a waft of incense and a procession on saints' days and other special occasions.

From our places at the back we could see everything that was going on. Aunty June beckoning to Aunty Mary to tell her that she'd saved a seat for her, her husband Albert and their children, Anne and Barry. My friend Kathryn, the fussed-over only child, sitting between her parents about halfway down on the left. The family of churchwarden Uncle Jack on the other side – a blonde mum and three pretty blonde daughters, all older than me and so grown-up-looking I would have paid anything to be as old and glamorous as they were. The old lady who smelt, sitting on her own near the back, her head bobbing up and down. Uncle George ringing the bell by pulling on a rope outside the door of the vestry. The organist, Eric Perkins, ruddy-faced and smiling. He had been sacked from another church, where his habit of popping out for a drink during the sermon had been tolerated until the day he had forgotten to come back. Dad said he was a good organist and that everyone deserved a second chance.

Today there was a lady with two dark-haired girls sitting at the back of the church. I looked admiringly at the shiny black ponytail of the older girl. Her sister's hair was cut short in a little cap round her head. When the service was over, Mum rushed to the girls' mother as they were leaving and they exchanged a few words.

Our house was always full of bustle after the service. Mum had the churchwardens in for coffee and a glass of sherry. There might be guests for Sunday dinner – visiting preachers, Franciscan friars from the friary at Alnmouth who Mum and Dad were friendly with, people we didn't know but who seemed to have had an important role in our parents' lives such as old teachers, nursing colleagues, older bachelor members of the clergy. Of this latter group, some were fun and jolly, with hands that turned into tickling machines; others so unused to children they behaved as if we weren't there. Some talked too much about church and God and what the archdeacon had said, though my ears would prick up when the adults' voices got lower and they spoke more confidentially. Sarah and I would catch each other's eyes across the table and try hard not to laugh at the persistent throat-clearers or the ones with strange habits, or if Father Hetherington started talking about Borneo again. All of them, however, were grateful for Mum's cooking, which on a Sunday was always a roast with four or five vegetables followed by a home-made pudding and with cider or shandy or even wine to drink if the guest had brought any. Sarah and I were allowed a small glass too. But we were always itching to leave the table and get outside again into our garden kingdom.

While we loved the house, the garden was our real playground, and after school we usually had friends to play. We could run races and shout and skip and jump and not disturb anyone. Our next-door neighbour, Mrs Robson, whose detached house was one of five large properties that stood alongside the vicarage, was a reclusive widow who lived happily with her Toby jugs and never complained about us making a noise. (I used to visit her sometimes, but she remained a mystery to most locals.)

Today we had planned a circuit on the lawn: start at the climbing frame, run once round the garden, crawl under the swing, up and down the slide, round the central flowerbed then back to the climbing frame, touching the top. We let Ruth and Mark have a go too, then to get them out of the way told them we would time them riding their bikes round the tennis court.

I stopped my circuit for a second when I saw Mum come into the garden followed by the lady and two girls I had noticed at church that morning, then carried on, hoping they would be impressed at my speed and agility.

Mum called us over. 'This is Krishna and Nicola De and their mum, Beryl – that's Aunty Beryl to you. Now, why don't you all get to know each other while Beryl and I have a chat?'

After we'd all said hello, and Aunty Beryl had admired the garden, the adults went back inside.

Nicola looked incredulously at the lawn and all our toys on it, and tugged her sister's arm. Krishna nodded and shook her off. We all looked at each other shyly.

'You can play on whatever you want,' said Sarah, and we both ran to the climbing frame to show them how we could turn somersaults on the bars.

Nicola asked her sister to push her on the swing, but Sarah offered to push her instead. Nicola's giggles as she went higher were infectious. Krishna and I grinned at each other.

They lived in Ashington too, Krishna said, not very far up the road in one of the newer houses. But they went to a different school from us.

'Is your dad a miner?' I asked, waiting for the usual answer.

Krishna shook her head and said quietly but matter-of-factly, 'A doctor. But he died.'

I looked at her, waiting for her to laugh and tell me she was joking. I didn't think people's fathers died in real life. In the books I read it was quite common to have dead parents, and I sometimes envied the orphan children their freedom. But they were stories. I didn't think parents died in ordinary everyday life, at least not when their children were young. Krishna was my age, and Nicola a few years younger.

When she said nothing more, and stood high on one of the bars on the climbing frame, waving at Ruth and Mark who were still riding their bikes, I said, not wanting to appear to have been taken in, 'He didn't really!' But she looked at me with her large eyes and said, 'He did. Honest.'

I did a somersault and hung upside down for a few seconds, wondering what to say next. When I came back up, Krishna said, 'I think our mums are going to be friends.' She gave a laugh. 'They probably want us to be, too. My mum's a nurse as well, you see.'

I knew what she meant. Nurses gravitated towards each other. Though Mum hadn't worked in a hospital since she got married, she still talked like a nurse and was often called on to dispense advice.

I felt secretly pleased, and did another somersault to hide my grin. I wished I was brave enough to go straight on to my hands and do a crab from there on to the lawn, but I always landed heavily on my back when I tried to do that. My friend Elaine at school had a body like a piece of elastic and could even walk like a crab.

Nicola and Sarah were doing handstands on the lawn now. Nicola did one, hovered in the air for a few seconds then collapsed in a heap of giggles.

'Can you do this?' I asked, and a minute later, all four of us were lying on the lawn bicycling in the air.

'We could be a circus act,' I said, and I couldn't have been more impressed when Krishna showed us how she could do the splits. She and Nicola did ballet and were as stretchy as Elaine.

Mum and Aunty Beryl came into the garden a bit later with their cups of coffee and a tray containing beakers of squash for us.

'Aunty Gwenda takes her coffee black as well,' Aunty Beryl said to her daughters, giving them a meaningful stare, and Krishna and Nicola sneaked glances at the tray. 'They thought I was the only person in the world who did.' She and Mum exchanged looks that seemed to contain years of understanding.

'Your mother's not so strange, there's plenty of us,' said Mum, holding out the drinks to our guests. 'With me it dates from my days in America. We couldn't carry fresh milk around with us when we were travelling, so we got used to drinking it without.'

Aunty Beryl said, 'Ooh! You hear that, girls? America!'

'What's America like?' asked Krishna, sitting on the bench beside Mum.

Sarah and I raised our eyes at each other. We heard about America a lot. So many of Mum's stories started with, 'When I was in America', and though we secretly liked some of them – tales of thirty-one flavours of ice-cream, of taking a dinghy

down the rapids, of surfing in Hawaii – we still acted uninter-
ested a lot of the time. In my *Children of the World* book, Helen
and Hank from the USA walked among skyscrapers, went to
outdoor movies and led lives perhaps even more exciting than
Enid Blyton's orphans with their boarding schools and midnight
feasts. But Mum could go on for ages, and we wanted our new
friends for ourselves. Sarah and I finished our drinks and tried
to coax Krishna and Nicola back to the lawn, but they weren't
ready to play again just yet.

'There were five of us, in a battered old car that we called
Flatus,' Mum began.

'Gwenda, you didn't call it that!' said Aunty Beryl, and the
two laughed the laughter of nurses in their shared knowledge.

'She saw someone killed by a bear,' I offered, thinking that we
might as well listen to the best stories.

The three guests gasped. Mum said, 'Well, no, I didn't actually *see* that happen, these stories get exaggerated in the telling.'
She looked at her audience and shook her head sadly. 'You had
to be so careful in Yellowstone and places where there were
bears around. There were plenty of signs telling you how to store
your food, but you know what people are like . . . Would you
believe that some of them used to feed the bears from their car
windows as if they were pet dogs.'

Aunty Beryl and Krishna shook their heads. Nicola moved to
sit on her mother's knee.

'And you haven't told us yet what you were doing there,
Gwenda,' said Aunty Beryl.

'We were nursing for a year in Cleveland. I went out from
Newcastle with my friend Pat after we saw an advert. They think
British nurses are the bee's knees out there. "Oh, we just lurve

your accents!"' Her audience giggled delightedly. 'Well, after our training with Sister Gunn at the General, we had to be good. Talk about battleaxes ... I bet some of your tutors were the same, Beryl. Of course the first thing we did was buy a car – we weren't going to sit around on our backsides with such a big country to see. Pat and I got quite a name for ourselves at the hospital, tearing all over the place in our off-duty.'

'You should have gone, Mum,' said Krishna, nudging her mother, and Aunty Beryl laughed and said she wouldn't have been brave enough.

'And don't they drive on the right?' said Aunty Beryl. 'How did you manage with that?'

'Oh, that was the least of our worries. Holes in the floor and doors that wouldn't close were more of a problem.'

'You still haven't told them the bear story,' I said, getting restless. 'That's the best bit.'

So Mum told them how a woman had stopped her car to take a picture of the little bear cub, all alone at the roadside, and how she had put her two-year-old son on the bear's back. But while she was taking the picture the mother bear appeared from the bushes and swiped the child away with a careless sweep of her huge paw, killing him instantly.

Aunty Beryl and Krishna looked shocked. Nicola looked as if she didn't know whether to laugh or cry.

'How terrible. And were you nursing at the hospital where the child was brought in?' Aunty Beryl sounded concerned for Mum as well as for the child.

'No, it was something that happened before we got there. But I did have a patient who'd been given a bear hug.'

Krishna caught my eye and we smiled at each other.

'That's what they call it. The claws leave the most beautiful imprint. And it turned out the man had been camping just downstream from our own camp. I didn't tell the others, of course; they'd have had a fit.'

'Oh, Gwenda!'

Mum finished her coffee. 'You see, you'll never be bored if you choose nursing as a career, girls,' she said. 'I'm sure you've got plenty of your own stories, Beryl.'

Aunty Beryl smiled. 'Oh, one or two.' But she looked sad all of a sudden, and perhaps Mum sensed that her stories were bound up with memories of her husband.

The sun went behind a black cloud and Mum stood up and gave an exaggerated shiver and suggested they go inside. Aunty Beryl shuffled Nicola off her lap and followed her in.

We were quiet for a few seconds. An ice-cream van played a jangly tune from one of the back lanes. Suddenly I had a great idea. 'Does anyone want to play a bear game? The person who's on is the mother bear and the rest of us are people at Yellowstone. You're safe when you're on the climbing frame, but if the bear catches you, then it's your turn to be on. But you can't stay on the climbing frame for ever. That's cheating. I'll be on first, if you like. I'll count to three.'

Later, I remembered hearing at school about Doctor De – it was pronounced *Day* but most of the girls said *Dee* – a popular Indian GP who had died very suddenly. 'I was bubbling when me mam told us,' said Elaine, looking as if she was going to start crying again. Everyone was shocked at his tragic demise at such an early age – not even forty – and at the fact that he had left a wife and two daughters.

Aunty Beryl was a very private person, but she told Mum that she got to know the man who would become her husband, known to everyone as Robin, when they were working at a North Wales hospital. She joked that their eyes met over the surgical masks when they were both in theatre. She had pretty brown eyes so I could quite believe this. They used to dress her little sisters up in saris for fun, and get together with the other Asian doctors to cook curries. They were happy days. An Indian husband can't have been what her Welsh coal miner father and Lancashire cotton mill mother had been expecting for their eldest daughter, but they accepted him into their family. He had been the love of her life. There would never be anyone else.

Chapter Eleven

You could spend ages in Spedding's, just looking, even if you didn't know what you were looking for. It was the sort of shop where you might come across something unexpected and suddenly realize that you needed it very badly. Mum would complain that she went in for a packet of paperclips and an air letter and came out twenty minutes later with half a dozen other things, probably having forgotten what she'd originally gone in for.

Down the right-hand side of the shop was a counter that was almost hidden behind the items piled up in front and on top of it – seed displays, rolls of wire netting, unsold newspapers, boxes containing rubber balls or high-bouncing balls (forbidden in the school playground now ever since one had broken a window) or plastic frogs on springs, and all sorts of hardware.

But there was another reason for being there – to absorb all the comings and goings, to listen to snippets of people's conversations, to get sucked into this strange new world in which we were living. In came the ladies in their pinnies and slippers – I was used to that sight now – and the men in their donkey jackets, some as chatty as their wives, others who communicated with just a nod and a wink.

'Eeh, hello, Jack. Hello, Mary. How's your Albert, Mary?'

'Oh, he's canny, pet. How's your Len?'

'Canny an' all. I've left him in front of the telly while I get his paper and pop over to George's for his fags.'

Today Mrs Hudson came in, one of the ladies I had overheard talking about Mum. She always had plenty to say and sometimes, when she wasn't looking, Mr Spedding would roll his eyes at his assistant to try to make her laugh. But Aunty Mary always kept her interested face on.

'Eeh, Mary, I feel aaful the day,' said the customer after Aunty Mary had enquired as to her health. She coughed noisily and patted her chest. 'I just canna clear it, it's been sitting there for days and I've tried everything.'

Aunty Mary tutted in sympathy and said she should see the doctor, but it turned out she had, more than once, and whatever he had given her had done 'naa good'.

'What about stopping those cigarettes?' came Mr Spedding's voice from the post-office counter.

'Eeh, Jack, it's not them! I've been smoking all me life!' Mrs Hudson looked to Aunty Mary for some sympathy over this foolish idea. When Aunty Mary just nodded and gave a small smile, she carried on. 'I've tried everything. It's getting us doon now. And on top of all that, there's me legs.' She paused for dramatic effect and clutched the counter. 'Aye, well, it's me knee,

really. It keeps seizing up. I'd better not stop much longer, else
I'll be stuck in here all day.'

'And we wouldn't want that,' chimed Jack.

'No,' said Mrs Hudson, missing the sarcasm in his tone.
'Specially not when I've been having a bit of trouble too,
with—' Her voice fell to a hush and she whispered something
to Aunty Mary.

'Oh dear,' said Aunty Mary. 'You are in the wars.'

Mr Spedding, who had come out from the post-office
booth to stand beside Aunty Mary, facing his customer, shook
his head slowly. 'You do sound bad, Ruby,' he began, 'but tell
you what, I've got an idea.' He leant across the counter confidentially. 'I've got a spade in the back and the churchyard's just
next door. Why don't I nip round there and dig you a nice big
hole and you can go and have a lie-down? Save you the walk
home.'

There was silence for a few seconds. Aunty Mary turned away
and started to busy herself tidying the shelves. Mrs Hudson
straightened up, gave a theatrical gasp and said, 'Jack Spedding,
that is not nice,' and marched out of the shop, quite niftily considering her condition.

When she had gone, Aunty Mary said something quietly to
Mr Spedding and they both laughed.

'She'll be back,' announced Mr Spedding. Then, as if he'd suddenly noticed me, he added, 'We hear her tales of woe every day;
we're not really being unkind.'

'I know,' I said, not sure what else to say.

'How's things in the vicarage? Got everything sorted yet?
Hey, did I ever tell you about the day your father's predecessor
came in here for a packet of drawing pins?'

I shook my head. Aunty Mary smiled and nodded, as if she knew the story and agreed that it was worth hearing.

'Well, in comes Canon Morton, looking very busy, can't stop, just wants the drawing pins. I sell him a packet, and an hour or so later he's back again for another. Then, lo and behold, not long after that he wants more. This time I asked him what he was doing that required so many drawing pins, and I couldn't believe it when he told me.'

Aunty Mary was chuckling to herself now and saying, 'Aye, who'd have thought it?' as she whisked a duster over the shelves.

'Turns out he was trying to repaper his living room using drawing pins instead of wallpaper paste.'

I told Mum this story when I got home. 'It doesn't surprise me in the least,' she said. 'Stingy beggar. He took all the curtain rails and light fittings when he left, and he's moved into a rectory twice the size of this place with huge windows, so he won't have been able to use them. Some people.' And she gave one of her can-you-believe-it tuts.

Stingy or not, Canon Morton was a hard act for Dad to follow. He had been in the parish for twenty-two years, and people had got used to him. More than one person insisted to Dad that his predecessor had visited every one of his parishioners every week, and asked why he hadn't been round to see them yet. It was no good Dad telling them that would have been impossible, that there were twenty-one thousand people in the parish of Seaton Hirst and that not even the saintly canon could have got round them all. Some of them believed it. And in truth, he *had* been a good visitor, bounding down the back lanes to greet his flock, sometimes just sticking his head in the yard to check that everyone was all right, other times staying long enough for his favourite tot of whisky. Some people spoke as if Canon Morton was still around, stopping Dad in the street to ask how the canon was keeping today, as if Dad was a temporary replacement.

But if there was one thing the parish felt aggrieved about – even if they were only starting to feel it now, for they hadn't known anything different until Dad arrived – it was that they had never been invited inside the vicarage. Canon Morton had conducted all meetings in his study, and it was doubtful anyone would have been brazen enough to ask to use the lavatory and thus sneak a look at some of the other rooms. Apart from Phemie Templey, who was allowed into the house to serve meals to visitors on special occasions, the house was his personal domain. Dad felt strongly that the vicarage, though it was our family home, belonged to the parish too, and to help rectify matters, he and Mum threw a party one Sunday night, a few weeks after our arrival, to which all the adult parishioners were invited.

Sarah and I helped to get the house ready as Ruth and Mark were being put to bed. Floors were cleared of toys, a duster flicked over tables and windowsills, spare chairs and stools fetched from the rest of the house and placed in the sitting room, dining room and hallway. Dad had a quick run round with the vacuum cleaner, one of the few domestic duties he occasionally performed. Under Mum's guidance we poured bottles of lemonade, pineapple juice, wine and brandy into her jam pan for her home-made punch and made up jugs of squash for anyone who didn't drink. We put crisps in bowls, plates and glasses on the trolley and retrieved ashtrays from under the sink.

Mum had told people to eat before they arrived, so Dad raised his eyes to the heavens when he saw the trays of sausage rolls and things on sticks, farmhouse flan, chocolate crunchie, apple slice, tiffin and fruit cake.

'You told them there was no food!' he cried.

'Well, there's not. The cake's left over from Christmas because you lot won't finish it, and everyone can manage a sausage roll,' said Mum, as if that explained all the other platefuls as well.

'Your mother has an answer for everything,' Dad grumbled to us. He liked Mum's cooking, and was probably worried that he was going to be living on leftover party food for the next week.

Sarah and I put on the maxi dresses we had got for Christmas, and Mum wore her gypsy top and skirt and gold charm bracelet, as it was a special occasion.

At ten to seven – forty minutes before the guests were due to start arriving – the doorbell rang and Mum shouted for us to get it, reminding us that no one was coming to play this evening. I rushed to the door and there stood the Bennett family from St Andrew's. Cecil, a small man with a face that creased into a wide smile, was churchwarden of our sister church; his wife, Vera, and teenage children Brian and Sandra, were in St Andrew's choir. They didn't say anything about being early as I showed them inside. No sooner had they been seated and Dad had gone to get them drinks than the doorbell rang again. This time it was Wilf and Jean Kirkup, and as they were coming into the house, a whole stream of new arrivals were snaking down the path behind them.

'Are you sure you said seven-thirty?' Mum mouthed at Dad as he poured the punch, and she quickly applied her lipstick in the mirror on the pantry door.

'You know what time it said – you typed the notice up.'

Only slightly flustered, Mum sent me and Sarah into the sitting room with the trolley and to make sure that everyone was helping themselves to the nuts and crisps. The room was filling quickly and cigarette smoke curled up into the air.

'They're asking for more ashtrays,' I told Mum when I went back to the kitchen.

She stuck her head under the sink and pulled out a pile of oyster shells. 'I knew these would come in handy one day.'

'Can I give you a hand, Mrs Gofton?' said Joyce Turner, coming into the kitchen as I was on my way out, and Mum set her to work cutting up one of her cakes.

As I was putting out the ashtrays, Aunty Mary's husband, Uncle Albert, touched my arm and asked if he could have a beer instead of the punch, and when I delivered it, two other men asked if they could have one too.

Back in the kitchen, Mrs Turner smiled at me and said, 'Your boyfriend was looking for you in the playground the other day.' I must have looked puzzled, because she added, 'Our Brian. He's at South Boys. He sees you sometimes.'

'Oh,' was all I could think of to say.

Mrs Turner nudged Mum, who was coming in from the garage with yet more cakes, and said, 'Did you know that our Brian's got his eye on your Barbara?'

Mum smiled at me, then her attention was diverted by someone asking for a cloth as there'd been a little accident. I offered to take it in with the beers, and quickly made my escape.

By twenty-five past seven we had ninety guests in the house; they filled the sitting room, dining room and hallway, and some of them sat on the stairs. Mum hissed at me and Sarah from the kitchen and asked us to cut the sausage rolls in half, just to be on the safe side.

Kathryn's parents, Bill and Rita Egdell, were among the last to arrive. Bill Egdell was a butcher, and such a popular man that his queues in the White Shop butcher's were always the longest. He was also a keen amateur photographer. Rita was a smart, anxious-looking woman who had worked at Ashington Hospital as an auxiliary before having Kathryn. When she spoke to you, she gave you her full attention and nodded vigorously at whatever you said, making you feel as if you were the most interesting person in the world.

I was introduced to Mr and Mrs Paton from St Andrew's. Their daughter Angela was in my class at school, and we'd become friends.

Sandra Bennett wanted to know how old I was, and began to tell me about the Girl Guide company she helped to run before Mum apologized for interrupting, but I needed to help her start bringing in the food.

'Where are me bairns?' asked Aunty June, barging into the kitchen behind me, and Mum thrust a tray of food into her hands as she told her that the little ones had been put to bed earlier.

'I can't believe you've never been inside before,' Mum said to Vera Bennett, who had come to the kitchen to fetch one of the older ladies a glass of water. Vera confided that on the occasion of the Mothers' Union tea party, which Canon Morton had generously allowed them to host in the vicarage garden, only one lady had been allowed into the kitchen at a time.

'He got into a right flap and threw me out when I came in to give Jean a hand,' she confided, and she and Mum clutched each other with laughter.

Alan the gravedigger had arrived with a large lady he introduced to me and Sarah as Joan. He sat her down in one of the
most comfortable seats, searched for a cushion that was just right
for her back – she rejected one as being too hard and another
as too soft – and went off to fetch her a glass of lemonade as she
didn't like the look of the punch.

'Who's that lady with Alan?' I whispered to Dad, and when
he told me she was his wife I was shocked. We didn't know Alan
had a wife. He belonged to our family – Ruth and Mark even
called him 'our Alan'. He was as much a part of the churchyard
as the gravestones, and when he wasn't visible himself, his
donkey jacket would be draped over a neighbouring grave while
spadefuls of earth flew up in the air. We didn't imagine him
having a home life, and certainly not sharing it with this lady,
who was twice the size of him. But Alan appeared to be devoted
to her, racing off to get whatever she needed and rarely leaving
her side.

'I've nivvor had punch before but I'll certainly be having it
again,' declared Wilf, smacking his lips. 'Mind, I'd better not get
meself tiddly in a vicarage.'

Mum said, 'Have another, it's more juice than alcohol,' and
topped his glass up before he could protest.

Mum got talking to a smart lady called Jean Wilkinson from
St Andrew's. Mrs Wilkinson had her hair pinned up in an elab-
orate bun. I thought that all ladies of Mum's age and older had
short, curly hairstyles – that it was a badge of being a grown
woman – so I looked at Mrs Wilkinson with admiration. She
was blowing cigarette smoke over her shoulder while Mum told
her how she had always wanted to start a church drama group.

'I haven't been in a play since I was a student nurse at the

General,' Mum was saying, 'but if we put a notice in the next magazine and have a meeting before the holidays, we could get going on a production in September.'

'Men are always the problem,' said Mrs Wilkinson, and Mum said they would just press-gang them as necessary. 'It's amazing what a bit of sweet-talking does as well,' she said, fluttering her eyelashes. Seeing me hovering nearby, she added, 'Barbara wants to be an actress.'

'The more the merrier,' said Mrs Wilkinson.

I pretended I hadn't heard.

A few minutes later, in the kitchen, Mum said, 'Well, there might be a part for a child, and you said you wanted to act.'

'But not that sort of acting, Mum! Proper acting.'

'Acting is acting, you silly billy, and everyone starts somewhere. Even your Laurence Oliviers and Sybil Thorndikes probably started off in their local drama group.'

'Who?'

She raised her eyes and was about to say something when someone called her name and she disappeared.

My idea of acting meant giving my admirers aloof stares, tossing my long hair behind me and galloping off on horseback. Though I also liked the idea of being Truly Scrumptious to Dick Van Dyke's Caractacus Potts in *Chitty Chitty Bang Bang*.

About an hour after everyone had arrived the phone rang, and I went to answer it in Dad's study where it was quieter. It was Grandma. 'What on earth's going on there?' she asked. 'It sounds like the last night on the *Titanic* at your end.'

I told her we were having a party. 'And Aunty June and Aunty Mary are here, and Uncle George and Uncle Jack, and guess what—'

'Hmph,' interrupted Grandma. 'You do know they're not your real aunties and uncles, don't you?'

'Of course I do.' I felt slightly hurt at this statement. 'But we've hardly got any real ones,' I added.

'Well, just don't go forgetting them, whatever you do.'

'If you'd had more children . . . ' I began.

'Cheeky young madam. If I'd had more like your mother I'd be in my grave now. Tell her I'll speak to her tomorrow, and see if she can settle an argument between me and Papa. We're trying to remember which school Winston Churchill went to. Papa says it's Charterhouse, I say Harrow. Enjoy the madhouse.' And she rang off.

It was true that we didn't have many aunts and uncles of our own. Mum and Dad had just one brother each, and Uncle Peter wasn't even married. Mum's brother, Uncle Doug, did have a wife and children but lived near London, so we didn't see him as often as we'd have liked. We'd never even been to visit him, though he and his family came to stay with us a couple of times a year. In some ways, America, which we heard so much about from Mum, seemed more familiar than the South-East of England, always referred to in our house as 'Down South'. Thanks to *Children of the World*, I probably knew more about Lapland and New Zealand and countries in Africa than any- where in England south of Yorkshire.

Ted Nichol had been one of the last to arrive. Ted was one of the brawny men who Dad admired so much – a practical man who could sort out every problem our house threw at him with a few nails, a bit of wood and the occasional swear word. He worked with Uncle Andy as a power loader at Woodhorn

Colliery, working the big cutting machines underground, but he was a skilled carpenter, plumber and jack of all trades the rest of the time, who brought his son with him whenever he could. Simon, dark-haired and gangly, was somewhere between me and Sarah in age. Something had happened to him when he was born, and he was different from other children. Though he smiled when he was happy and cried when he was sad, he did not speak properly and his movements were awkward and jerky. People patted his curls and called him a bonny lad, then recoiled in fear when he put his face close to theirs and they saw the blankness in his eyes.

Mum had got all the background from Aunty June. Ted's wife, Elsie, found it hard to cope; she would have put the lad in a home if she could, but Ted was devoted to him and wouldn't hear of it.

'But it's hard work for the poor lass and when Ted's not around, she struggles. Mind, she has it easy when he is at home, 'cos he does more than most dads do with their bairns. There's nowhere he'll not take that lad, and he doesn't care what anyone says.'

Mum said Ted was a wonder, and Elsie too, and that some schools did amazing things with children like Simon, if only you could find the right one.

If we were at home when Ted came round, we would be called on to entertain Simon, and his face lit up when he was with other children. We would take him by the hand into the garden, where he liked to trot around the lawn and would get excited by strange things – the sight of a distant aeroplane, a bird singing noisily in a tree, Mark jumping from the moving swing. If he got upset – not often, but it could happen quickly – we sang to him and did silly dances to make him smile again. Once he got into such a state that Ted had to take him home, but usually his humour could be improved by a song, though we might have to go through our whole repertoire until we found the right one for the occasion. 'Michael Row the Boat Ashore', which Mum sang to him, and 'Skippy the Bush Kangaroo', sung by us and accompanied by lots of hopping, usually did the trick.

Though younger children hadn't been invited, Mum had counted on Ted bringing Simon. As usual, Elsie wasn't with them.

'We'll not stop long,' said Ted. He was the only person to have said that and to have possibly meant it.

'How's this fine lad?' Dad ruffled Simon's hair and Simon tilted his face towards him and smiled his dreamy smile. He could talk a little, in a strange, grunting way, but only his parents and a few others could understand him. Mum was one of these people, though I never knew if she really understood him or if she just pretended to.

'I'll go and get Simon a lemonade,' I said, skipping off to the kitchen.

'No, no, that'll go straight through him,' said Mum. She took his hand. 'Orange squash or Ribena, Simon?' she asked him slowly.

Simon made one of his grunts. 'Yes, I thought you liked that best. I've got a piece of that cake you like, as well.' She looked at me. 'Well, go on then.'

'But what does he want?'

'Orange squash, didn't you hear? Put it in one of those special cups so that he can't spill it.'

Suddenly Simon ran to the well at the foot of the stairs and stood there stamping his feet and jerking his body around like someone doing a war dance. The people in the hallway looked at him, amused but slightly nervous. I wondered if he was throwing a tantrum, but he looked contented enough.

'What's he doing now?' said his father. 'Simon! Come here, lad.'

But Simon's face was full of a happiness that we couldn't share, and he grew agitated when his father tried to lead him away.

'He'll be getting a good clout if he's not careful,' said Ted.

'He's not doing any harm,' said Mum. 'Just leave him.'

'It's the vacuum!' said Sarah suddenly. 'He was here the other day when Aunty June was hoovering and he was dancing away to it. He knows it stays in the cupboard there. I'll get it out.'

Mum grabbed Sarah's arm. 'Not tonight, pet, it's a party. We'll not be able to hear ourselves think. But what a clever lad, remembering that!' She nodded at his father. 'He's got far more than we give him credit for, Ted, you know that, don't you?'

'Aye, he's in a world of his own, that's the truth of the matter,' said his father wistfully. 'There's many a time I'd love to be able to read that brain of his.'

'You do a good job,' said Mum, patting his hand. 'Now, shall I get you a tot of whisky?' and she put a finger to her lips to make it clear she wasn't offering one to anyone else.

If Mum had envisaged the party as a sort of drop-in, with people popping in during the course of the evening, having a drink and a nibble and then moving on, so that the house was never completely full, then she knew now not to expect it again. Everyone arrived early – that was the Ashington way – and stayed until the bitter end – that was also the Ashington way. The whole house throbbed for almost four hours with chatter and loud laughter. What Mum and Dad had also forgotten when they'd issued the invitation was that Canon Morton had put an end to church social events during his tenure, reasoning that too much time and effort went into their organization – time that could be better spent on spreading the gospel. The congregations of the two churches had been starved of them for so long, they pounced on this occasion, just in case they didn't get the chance of one again.

Sarah and I were in our element, topping up drinks, clearing away plates and being thanked and complimented on every little favour we bestowed.

Later that evening, Mum dashed into the kitchen where we were loading the dishwasher. 'Is Simon in here with you?'

We looked at her blankly.

'Ted's about to go and he's lost Simon. Wasn't he with you a few minutes ago?'

It was true that we had taken him into the playroom and put 'Purple People Eater' on the old record player for him, but it had been too noisy to hear it and we had returned him to his father after that.

'The men are looking out the front in case he's got on to the road. Have a run round the house, please. Quick!'

There was no sign of him upstairs. As we came back down, through the landing window we could see some of the men patrolling Newbiggin Road. We met Dad at the foot of the stairs.

'No luck?' He scratched his head anxiously. 'He can actually move quite fast when he puts his mind to it, that's what worries me.'

We had just passed the longest day and it was still light outside. Sarah and I went into the back garden that Simon loved so much. Some of Ruth and Mark's toys were strewn over the lawn. We heard Simon before we saw him, humming in that way he had. He was in the mountain ash tree that bordered our neighbour's garden, the one we both liked to climb. Mum always forbade us from climbing it when Ruth and Mark were around, so as not to give them ideas. Mark was a daring child already, a boisterous boy capable of giving the adults a heart attack with his daredevil feats. He had already given Grandma the fright of her life by shinning up a drainpipe and waving to her, upside down, from the ledge above the sitting-room window. I had the feeling we might be about to get the blame for this.

'Simon, you've got to come down now, your dad's going,' I said as we ran to the base of the tree.

'Howway down,' said Sarah, whose Geordie accent was coming on a treat.

Simon laughed and uttered a string of garbled words.

'What if he tries to jump?' I said.

'He'll not.'

We peered up into the tree. He appeared to be safely ensconced in its branches.

A couple of the men came up behind us.

'Eeh, what a lad,' said Ken Turner. 'Howway, Simon, before your dad sees you.'

Simon ignored us all and carried on humming to himself.

'He's in a world of his own,' said Cecil Bennett. 'Probably best to leave him to come down in his own time.'

They stood debating tactics while Sarah and I carried on talking to him. He clearly had no intention of moving.

'I'll go and fetch his dad,' said Mr Bennett.

Satisfied that Simon wasn't going to hurt himself, they went to find Ted.

Two of the ladies now came across the lawn to see what was going on.

'Eeh, what a lad,' said one of them. 'You never know what he'll do next.'

'You're right there. Mind you,' the other one lowered her voice and looked around before continuing, 'I've heard Elsie ate a lot of foreign food when she was expecting. You've got to wonder if that had anything to do with . . . what he's like.'

Her companion looked surprised by the news. 'What kind, like?'

'She had a craving for them spicy things what you put in curry.'

'You mean curry powder?'

'Mebbes. I don't know exactly. But you know what fiery tempers them foreigners have.'

Mum was the next to arrive. 'Thank goodness he's safe,' she said. 'I had visions of him under the wheels of a lorry.'

'I wonder when he learnt to climb, Mrs Gofton. Nora was saying he might have a bit of foreign blood in him.'

'No, no, I never said that,' protested Nora, as Mum gave them both a puzzled look. 'Just that it's a funny way of eating chicken, if you ask me.'

Mum didn't ask them to explain. 'He's just a normal kid,' she said. 'It's probably these two who gave him the idea. Girls, you'll have to sing him down.'

'What! Not now, in front of everyone,' I said.

'Yes! Now! Ted wants to go. It's late for him – and it's late for you, too. What would do the trick?'

Without waiting for a reply, she started singing 'La Cucaracha', a song she'd learnt as a Girl Guide.

'Mum, shut up, you know you can't sing.'

The two ladies hooted with laughter.

'Come on,' I said to Sarah. 'We're not listening to this. One, two, three,' and we began to sing 'Kookaburra', one of our favourite songs from Brownies. Suddenly, a far more melodious voice accompanied ours. It was Miss Templey, our Brown Owl.

Laugh, kookaburra, laugh, kookaburra
Gay your life must be.

Miss Templey was a good sport. She always joined in all the games at Brownies, even getting down on her hunkers with us as we bounced up and down crying, 'Too-whit too-whit too-whoo!' three times before exploding into the air on the final 'Whoo!'. We sang 'Kookaburra' again, more confidently now. Miss Templey laughed and said something about it being rather appropriate. At Brownies we sang it in rounds, each Six coming in at a different point. We all loved it, and Miss Templey always beamed at the end and asked who wanted to sing it again, which everyone did.

We could hear Simon growing excited and the branches rustling. Mum indicated that we should start walking towards the house so that he would want to follow us.

A few seconds later a leg appeared, and Mum dashed back to yank him down, in case he changed his mind. He gave a wild laugh and looked pleased with himself as he gambolled towards us, humming the song in his own rather tuneless way. Sarah and I took a hand each and returned him to his anxious father.

When Ted and Simon had left, Mum made me and Sarah say goodnight to everyone and go to bed. We made this last as long as possible until Mum came up behind us and said, 'It's school tomorrow. Up. Now.' When we started to protest, she just said, 'Scram!' and there was no point in arguing.

Chapter Twelve

If Dad thought we'd be living on party leftovers for the rest of the week, he needn't have worried. When I looked in the three-tier cake tin at teatime the next day there was a new 'Dobie cake' – the name we gave to Margaret Dobie's now weekly offerings – but none of the previous night's delicacies. Every Monday now Miss Dobie arrived bearing food, with the story that her 'company' hadn't turned up and she didn't want to waste whatever baking she had done. As well as her orange cake, she made particularly good shortbread. I wondered if Mum had frozen the party leftovers, but she confirmed that everything had been eaten. One lady, who had been heard by Uncle George saying very loudly that she wouldn't be touching anything as 'fancy' food didn't agree with her, had been spotted a few minutes later with a teetering plateful. Sandra Bennett had admitted in that open way of hers that she'd tried a piece of everything, and two of some things, and was thinking of moving in with us if we ate like that every day.

That morning as I arrived at school, I thought about what Mrs Turner had said about Brian, her son. This was the time of day when some of the boys gathered round the railings that divided our two playgrounds, a few of them swinging like monkeys on the bars. I wondered if Brian was one of the boys there today. I had an idea we had been introduced at Dad's licensing, and stole a look at the boys who were there now to see if any of them looked familiar, but none of them did, and no one was looking at me. I wondered who had decided that he was my boyfriend – Brian himself, or his mother. Mum hadn't mentioned it, but I knew she wasn't interested in that sort of talk. It didn't occur to me that it might have been a joke, or that Brian might have been as surprised by the news as I was. It had been said by an adult, so it must be true.

In English, Miss Stewart asked us to write about something we were looking forward to, so I wrote about the forthcoming visit of Mum's American friends, Bob and Mary Ann Jones from California. In the last lesson, she sat marking our work in the corner while our student teacher, who had been helping for the past few weeks, read us some poetry. The student teacher's gentle Scottish lilt, and the rhythmical way she spoke the recurring line at the end of each verse, sounded as soothing as a lullaby in the warm, light-filled classroom. Soon, one of the girls from the top class would run around the hall ringing the bell to announce home time, stopping briefly outside each classroom door and at the top of the stairs. Miss Stewart was in a good mood today, because she allowed us to play with the hair of the girl in front as we listened. My friend Alison was turning my ponytail into a series of plaits, while I combed through Sandra's long brown hair. I saw Miss Stewart smiling to herself every now and then as she read, though she became quite fierce all of a sudden when she sent Karen Critchley to stand against the wall for five minutes for whispering. At the end of one of the poems she stood up, apologized to the student teacher for interrupting and asked me if it was true about *the Americans*. She said the words as if they were the title of a book or a film. Her enthusiasm radiated through the classroom. Karen Critchley, who had only just been allowed to sit back down, started to put on her American accent, but this time Miss Stewart laughed with the rest of us.

No one had met an American before, though one girl did have an uncle who had emigrated to Canada and who they spoke to on her grandma's telephone every Christmas.

'Let's try to think of some famous Americans,' Miss Stewart suggested. 'Hands up, please. No shouting out.'

We came up with a list that included James Drury and Doug McClure from *The Virginian* (almost everyone's favourite programme), Liberace, Elvis Presley, President Nixon (though only a few people had heard of him), James Stewart, John Wayne, Casey Jones and Dick Van Dyke.

'Has anyone heard of John F. Kennedy?' asked Miss Stewart, and Kathryn stuck her hand in the air.

'He was shot by Lee Harvey Oswald in 1963,' she announced. 'Though there are various conspiracy theories about what actually happened. A bit like the death of Marilyn Monroe.'

Miss Stewart's face was pink with pride, though I'm not sure the rest of us had a clue what Kathryn was talking about. Kathryn's general knowledge knew no bounds. I had gone to play at her house one night and she had begged her mother to give us a quiz, which she had easily won. I knew my capital cities and various other world facts that Mum had drummed into me, but when Mrs Egdell had shown us pictures of famous people and asked us to name them, I was baffled by most of them. They both thought it very funny when I identified one man as Prince Philip. The question was passed to Kathryn, who declared, 'It's the Pope, man!' I didn't know who or what a pope was, so was none the wiser.

Miss Stewart asked me where my mother had met these Americans, and I told her about the morning in the Grand Teton National Park – there were a few sniggers over the name – when Mum and her four friends had risen early to take photos of the sunrise. Bob and Mary Ann were working in the park as fire rangers for the summer, and when they heard the girls' accents they got talking and invited them to their lookout hut for coffee. They had lent them their tent for the rest of the summer, asking them to return it when they reached California later in their trip.

Miss Stewart was open-mouthed over their generosity. She asked if Bob and Mary Ann had any children and I told her that they did, but that they wouldn't be joining their parents as they would probably be at summer camp, and that American children had already finished school for the summer.

There were cries of, 'That's not fair! Why don't we get such a long holiday?'

'Not long to go now,' said Miss Stewart.

'I wish we had summer camps,' said Elaine wistfully. 'I've never been in a tent before.'

Miss Stewart asked what else I knew about America.

'They have thirty-one flavours of ice-cream,' I said, remembering Mum's oft-quoted fact.

'Good heavens, what could they all be?' wondered our teacher.

One of the Susans put up her hand. 'I can never decide between vanilla or raspberry ripple,' she said, 'so I divvent knaa what I'd be like if I had thirty-one to choose from.' The class laughed.

I thought of something Mum had said when I showed her a picture of the Osmond brothers in a magazine – a dazzling line-up of sequined outfits, thick hair and sparkling smiles. Some of my friends had been talking about them, and I was happy to know who they were now and to be able to join in their conversations. I told her I wanted to have a smile as white as Donny's, but Mum had her own theory about why they looked so perfect.

To Miss Stewart's astonishment, I announced, 'And all Americans have false teeth.'

Mum allowed me and Sarah to walk home from school now with our friends. Perhaps she realized that we were different enough without being picked up at the end of every day in the Morris Traveller when everyone else walked. But she gave us strict instructions not to ruin our tea by stopping off at the sweet shop, where you could buy four chews for a halfpenny and where girls came out with mouths full of bubblegum and gob-stoppers.

Today was the day the Joneses were arriving. I walked with Kathryn and Sandra, the three of us linking arms, an unspoken understanding dictating which of us would be in the middle.

Sometimes it changed as we walked, and one of us would rush to the other side, desperate to link the friend on the other end. Sarah walked a few yards behind us with her friends Dawn and Linda.

'They'll be there when I get in,' I said. 'Mum was picking them up from the station at dinnertime.'

'I wonder if they'll look like film stars,' said Sandra. 'I saw a film on Saturday night where the man says to the woman' – here she put on her best American accent – '"I guess you are just the priddiest thing I ever did see." And he kissed her, like this.' She pressed her lips to the back of her hand and circled them round and round. 'We should practise on each other so that we know what to do when we get a lad. Then he scooped her up and carried her up the stairs.' She paused, as if replaying the scene in her mind. 'And you didn't see anything else.'

Sandra was allowed to stay up later than me and Kathryn and watch things I'm sure Mum would have told us were unsuitable for children.

'Well, I might have a boyfriend,' I said. It just slipped out. I hadn't meant to share this fact. They both stopped walking and turned to look at me, and Kathryn let go of my arm.

'You never have!' she said accusingly.

'Well, I don't know who he is, but he goes to South Boys and his mam says he likes me,' I said.

'Sounds like his mam's the one who wants to go out with you,' sniggered Kathryn. We carried on walking.

'We'll have to find out who he is, though,' said Sandra. 'Our Susan might know. I'll ask her.'

'No, don't. I don't think I want to know. He might be awful. He might . . . I don't know what, but don't say anything. Promise!'

'Oh, all right. If you promise to be my partner for the trip to Druridge Bay next week.'

'You were going to be mine,' said Kathryn, squeezing my arm more tightly and glaring at both me and Sandra. 'You can't go and change your mind. You were going to be Diane's, Sandra.'

'Well, we've fallen out. And she's going to be Sandra Elliott's. You can be Julie Huddleston's.'

'I don't want to be Julie Huddleston's!'

When we left each other a couple of minutes later, I had no idea if Kathryn was still my best friend, whose partner I was going to be and even if anyone wanted me as their partner now. Being a friend was hard sometimes.

I waited for Sarah at the gate as she said goodbye to Dawn and Linda.

'Yee-hah!' yelled Mark, running up to us as we walked into the hall.

'I bet you can't do this. Yee-hah!' echoed Ruth. They both wore the cowboy outfits they'd got for Christmas.

Bob and Mary Ann got up to say hello as we entered the sitting room.

'I'm afraid Bob's taught your sweet little brother and sister some of our crude American expressions,' said Mary Ann, smiling.

I had desperately wanted the Joneses to look the way I felt Americans should look. The picture I had in my head changed from day to day. Today it was Sonny and Cher, who I had seen in *Woman's Own*. I secretly hoped that Mary Ann had some Cherokee blood, like Cher. The couple in front of me now may not have been as glitzy as Sonny and Cher, but they had enough charisma between them to make up for it. Bob was one of the tallest men I'd ever seen, with a bushy beard, untidy hair and a lively face. Everything he said was uttered with great conviction, as if he was reading for a play in which he had the starring role, as well as all the funniest lines. Mary Ann was tall, too, with a friendly face and a chirpy accent that came straight off the television.

As they commented on how we both looked like our mother, Mum said she could hardly believe that their eldest daughter, Laura, who had been a baby when they had met, was now a teenager.

'Brenda, our youngest, would have loved to meet you two,' Mary Ann said to Sarah and me, laughing as Ruth and Mark dragged Bob into the garden, all three of them hollering, 'Yee-hah!' at the tops of their voices. 'See if you can persuade your mom to come see us in California next time.'

Mum gave a small gasp and said it was one of her dreams that we would all go one day, if we could ever afford it.

Mary Ann said, 'We've got people all over the place who could put you up. It wouldn't cost you much more than your airfares.'

Mum said she didn't know if she'd ever manage to persuade Dad, but that it was everyone's job to work on him while Bob and Mary Ann were here.

'We are so looking forward to this vacation,' said Mary Ann.

A vacation! It was so exciting being an American. We only went on holidays.

Later, they gave us some gifts. Brenda had made some pretty beaded jewellery for me and Sarah. 'It's inspired by the handicrafts of our Native American population,' explained Mary Ann, and I nodded as if I understood what she was talking about.

'And we like to support our local artisans,' she said, as we opened a bag containing a selection of small wooden toys.

There was a little pipe that Bob blew a tune on. He gave it to Ruth and Mark and laughed with delight at the noises they made.

Another was a stick with a small metal ball attached to one end with a piece of twine. The aim was to hold the stick and flick the ball into the air, trying to catch it in a notch cut on the top of the stick. At first it seemed impossible, but eventually I got the knack and started catching more than I dropped. Sarah and I were soon competing to see who could catch the most in ten attempts.

'We'll have a league table while Bob and Mary Ann are here and see who's the winner,' we informed everyone.

'What are they like?'

The girls crowded round me in the playground. Mum was dropping Ruth and Mark at Grandma's and taking our visitors to York for the day. Dad couldn't go as he was conducting three funerals. I'd never been to York, and wanted to go too. Mum had said we would go somewhere nice at the weekend before Bob and Mary Ann went up to Scotland to see Aunty Pat.

'They're big,' I said. 'Bob is like a giant, and he has a loud voice and he laughs a lot. He's always telling jokes. And he knows some good tongue-twisters. When you say thank you to Mary Ann, she always says, "You're welcome".'

'Like this?' asked Alison, practising an American drawl.

'No, like this, man,' said Karen Critchley, doing her Doris Day impression and fluttering her eyelashes at the same time.

Later in class I told Miss Stewart how they both liked to sing and had asked us to teach them some English songs that they could teach their friends at the choir they belonged to when they got home.

'So tell us what you taught them. Anything we sing at school?'

I thought for a second. 'Yes! They liked "What Shall We Do with the Drunken Sailor?" And Bob loved "The Worm Song" we sing at Brownies.'

Miss Stewart wanted to know what that was, and those of us in Brownies had to sing it for her.

She pulled a face in all the right places. 'Is it about a bird?' she asked.

'It's just a song about someone who likes eating worms, Miss,' said Kirsty.

I remembered another. 'Dad tried to teach them "Cushie Butterfield" but he had to give up in the end. He said it was like teaching them another language.'

Miss Stewart put her hands on her hips. 'Don't tell untruths about your father, Barbara,' she said.

Some girls started to chuckle, but Miss Stewart glared at them. She had her stern, red face on now, and when that happened you had to be very careful indeed. 'I can't see a man like your father – a vicar! – teaching his visitors a song like that,' she continued. 'I'm surprised at you.'

I felt humiliated. I wondered what I'd said wrong. 'Cushie Butterfield' was a North-Eastern song about a keelman in love with the big and bonny lass of the title. I wondered if it was ruder than I'd thought, or if it was just another case of people thinking my father was too saintly for such popular entertainment. Our headmistress, Miss Bailey, always had a faraway look in her eyes when she mentioned him and said his name in a hushed, reverential tone, so I guessed the reason was the latter. I'm not a liar, I wanted to say, and my father is really quite normal. I wanted to tell Miss Stewart that his father was a builder and his grand-father had been a miner, and that both his parents spoke with Geordie accents. But I knew I couldn't answer her back. Girls who did that sometimes had their bottoms smacked.

Kathryn snorted and held her hand over her mouth. Miss Stewart glared at her.

'He did!' I mouthed across the table.

'Anyone who even moves while I hand out your jotters will stay in at playtime,' said Miss Stewart.

Before our visitors' arrival, Mum had warned me and Sarah that if we carried on copying our friends' accents, Bob and Mary Ann wouldn't understand us. Somehow I doubted that the odd 'howway' and saying 'us' instead of 'me' would render us incom-prehensible to them. After all, Americans had an unusual accent of their own, and used words that we didn't use or that had dif-ferent meanings from ours. Words like 'swell' and 'neat', or 'pooped' to mean tired – we didn't think we'd be able to con-tain ourselves if they actually said that in front of us.

They did look a bit baffled, though, when Uncle Jim came by to return a book Dad had lent him.

'Youse stoppin' long?' he began.

Sarah translated this for them in her nicest voice, now bear-ing a sing-song Geordie lilt. 'He's asking how long you're staying here.'

'They say it'll be a canny day the morra, but you often get a bit of a fret if you're gannin' to the coo-ast.'

'He says it's gannin', I mean, going to be a nice day, but you sometimes get a sea fret – that's a mist – at the coast.' She spoke the last word so poshly – the way the Queen might have said it – that she surprised herself as well as me and we had a fit of the giggles.

A bit later, Aunty June popped round in a state of great excitement to let us know that sometime next week they would be on the telephone at last.

'How neat!' exclaimed Mary Ann.

'I told them that our Carol's off to join the Army,' Aunty June said as they sat there, concentrating hard, 'and they've agreed to put us at the top of the list. Aye, I'll miss her, but at least I've got me bairns here, haven't I, me darlin's?' And she looked to see who was the closest to give one of her rib-crushing squeezes to.

But Aunty June was easy to understand compared to Dougie Lewins. Dougie was the miner who helped with the garden, mainly the vegetable plot, and often brought with him his son, Paul, who was the same age as Ruth. He'd started cultivating the plot before our arrival, so we were already eating the potatoes he had planted. Today he'd been digging these up before a sudden downpour brought him indoors. Not being able to find Mum, he stuck his head round the sitting-room door and declared to our baffled guests, 'Can yer tell Mrs Gofton, it's absolutely stottin' doon oot there so I'm gannin' hyem with the bairn and tekkin' a few tatties.'

Luckily Mum appeared just then, so they had no need to ask him to repeat it, which would probably not have made it any easier to decipher.

*

When Saturday came, Mum borrowed Papa's Austin and we drove in two cars up the coast, crossing the causeway to Holy Island for a quick walk round before having to leave because of the tides. We had our picnic lunch on Bamburgh beach. The sun shone and the sea sparkled and Dad said that Northumberland could beat the Caribbean on days like this. Though we children wore our swimsuits and Mum and Dad were both bare-armed, Bob and Mary Ann didn't remove their light jackets.

The adults were talking about the night before, when Aunty June had babysat while Mum and Dad took our guests to a medieval banquet in Delaval Hall in nearby Seaton Delaval. Girls at school told stories of the Grey Lady who haunted the hall, but disappointingly, she hadn't made an appearance the previous night. Mary Ann had worn one of Mum's long dresses and Bob looked like a different man in a borrowed jacket and tie. They had been the last to arrive, on which Bob and Mary Ann were whisked into a side room, leaving Mum and Dad wondering what was going on. When they reappeared, the organizers announced that their friends had been invited to be Lord and Lady of the Manor and showed all four of them to places at the head of the table, where they were the only guests to sit on proper chairs rather than benches, and where Bob had to read a few lines to all the minions gathered there.

'I thought they were going to show me some naughty postcards – close your ears, kids,' joked Bob.

Mary Ann gave him a light slap. 'They thought he looked just the part,' she told me and Sarah. 'You can see why, can't you? I'm so glad he kept the beard for this trip. Wait till we tell everyone back home. You loved it, didn't you, honey?'

'Silence, serf,' said Bob, holding up a hand, 'I only answer if my title is used.'

'He's going to be impossible now,' said his wife, shaking her head. She leant back on the rug and looked up at Bamburgh Castle, piled high on a rock like something out of a picture book. 'How lucky you are, to have all this history around you. So many castles! I think we've already seen four today.'

Dad, who had studied history at university, became serious and talked about lawless tribes and battles in this most northerly part of England. Sarah and I got up and raced each other into the sea.

'He's put his sermon voice on,' said Sarah.

When we drove home, we passed collieries – Ellington, Lynemouth and Woodhorn – whose towers and wheels made me think of some sinister fairground ride.

'You've got the Golden Gate Bridge,' said Dad as a towering slag heap came into view, 'and we've got the Ashington Alps.'

But to his surprise, Bob asked Dad to stop the car so that he could take photographs. 'I might never see a sight like this again. It's very special.'

Dad spoke more proudly this time. 'Ashington used to be known as the biggest mining village in the world. This part of the country was the real powerhouse for the Industrial Revolution. So much started in the North-East, you know – railways, street lighting . . . If you were here for longer, there's a lot more we could show you.'

Bob clicked away with his camera as Dad warmed to his theme. 'You watch the news and the weather and, blow me, you'd sometimes think that we didn't exist up here. But we're quite happy to keep it to ourselves most of the time, aren't we, girls?' He looked at me and Sarah for agreement. The rest of our party were ahead of us in Papa's car, and as Mum was a faster driver than Dad, probably home by now. 'No crowded beaches or traffic jams for us on a scorcher like today.'

Bob, still in his jacket, mimed a shiver, and laughed heartily.

Later, Uncle Andy managed to get Bob a proper miner's lamp as a souvenir of his visit. Bob was thrilled with it, but as he and Mary Ann were going to be travelling for several more weeks, he asked us to look after it for him. 'You can bring it to America when you come to stay with us,' he said. That meant we had to go one day.

Chapter Thirteen

Carol, Aunty June's daughter and only child, sometimes came to babysit with her mother. Today would be one of her last visits for a while as she was seventeen years old and leaving home to join the Army.

'I cannot wait,' she said, as she made herself comfortable on Sarah's double bed where she was about to read us a story. 'There's got to be more to life than this place.'

'You can't wait to leave Ashington?' I asked, feeling hurt on behalf of our new home.

I thought Carol had a perfect life with Aunty June and Uncle Andy. At 27 Monkseaton Terrace the television was always on, there were no brothers or sisters to bother her when she wanted to be on her own, no one to have to share toys, sweets – everything! – with and a plentiful supply of bottles of pop to drink. Aunty June was always talking about 'Our Carol', but as she was a few years older than me – practically a grown-up – we never felt any rivalry or the need to compete for Aunty June's affections. We listened, fascinated, to tales of what Carol had or hadn't done, what music she liked (Stevie Wonder, Wings – now that the Beatles were no more – and Cream) and didn't like (the Rolling Stones, jazz), the bad stories as well as the good, for Aunty June seemed to delight in her faults as well as in her achievements. The stories could be a bit fanciful. 'That's just Aunty June for you,' Mum would say.

When I told Aunty June gleefully that I had heard a song on the radio called 'Oh! Carol', Aunty June shook her head sadly and said that Carol didn't like it, and looked so serious we might have thought the song had been written specially for her, and that Aunty June herself had had to break the sad news to Neil Sedaka.

'And you've got a perfect mother,' Sarah said, as I passed Carol the book we were reading tonight and we snuggled up on either side of her.

Carol laughed. 'Mam's got a good heart, I know. And she spoils you lot. But it's different being her daughter. Guess who she volunteered to do all of Mrs Foster's shopping every week? Yours truly, that's who. And guess who spends her weekends baking for other people? The sergeant major will have nothing on my mother! The Army's going to be like a holiday camp after living with her.'

Could this be the same Aunty June who let us stay up late, gave us money to run along to Tait's for sweets (Charlton's closed early, but Tait's, over the road, run by the affable George and his wife, was a tobacconist's too and open all hours) and even allowed me to tap the ash from her cigarettes into the ashtray?

'Oh, not this again.' Carol groaned good-naturedly as she saw what I'd handed her. *Folk Tales of the World* was a present from Dad's brother, Uncle Peter. The stories came from exotic-sounding countries – Madagascar, Persia, Russia – and had long foreign names in them that were difficult to pronounce. We all laughed together as Carol attempted them before shortening them to something more manageable. We read stories of hill-sides that opened up to reveal whole worlds of little folk living inside them, women who changed into seals and animals that could speak. The pictures were as evocative as the stories. I gazed longingly at the beautiful fairy with her long yellow hair and butterfly wings and wished I could be a fairy, too. I hoped, if I was quiet, that I might catch sight of one, sitting on a toad-stool in one of the darkest corners of the garden, but they had eluded me so far. Tonight Carol read us the story of the Red Indian who brought his beautiful dead wife back to live with him, though he could only see her shadow. One night she revealed herself to him in her human form, but a jealous rival, hiding outside their tent, sneaked a look inside and thus destroyed the magic. With a cry and the sound of the rattling of bones, the young brave died and his wife disappeared. They had both gone to the Land of Ghosts.

Some of the stories had happy endings, but an awful lot of them did not. I wasn't quite sure if this one was happy or not, but it was one of my favourites, and being a Red Indian bride, even a dead one, seemed desirable in my eyes.

Being invisible, seeing fairies, flying – they were all things I felt I might be able to do if I just tried hard enough, or could stumble into a world of magic myself.

*

Mum said the change would do Carol and her mother the world of good.

'Aunty June and Uncle Andy might get to do some of the things they've always wanted to do,' she pointed out. 'They love their travel. And Carol will get to see the world too if she plays her cards right.'

Mum was a great believer in people living their dreams before they settled down, and thought she was the luckiest person in the world for having had her career in nursing, however short-lived. Kathryn's mum, Rita Egdell, had also wanted to be a nurse, an idea reinforced by spending time convalescing at a sanatorium in Switzerland after catching TB, and she and Mum enjoyed chatting about medical matters together. Rita had been working as an auxiliary at Ashington Hospital when she met her future husband, and marriage had put an end to further training. Bill Egdell, too, had seen his hopes dashed. He had told Dad at the parish party how, at the age of twenty-one, he had been offered a job as a staff photographer for the *Daily Mirror* in London, but his father had refused to let him go.

Could an adult be told what to do by their parents? Twenty-one was grown up, surely. But Mum said something about duty and obligation, and different generations having different ideas.

'So Papa could have stopped you from being a nurse?' I asked her.

'He wouldn't have dared!'

'But if he had?'

'Well, I suppose secretly he would have liked me to get a job in the bank like him. You know how he's always telling you what a good career it is. Lots of people go into jobs to please their parents – or people of my generation did. Think of all the family businesses that are called "So-and-So and Son". And it used to be common for sons to follow their fathers into the Church as well.'

'I can't imagine Mark being a vicar, can you?' I said.

Mark was bombing up and down the hallway on his sit-on truck. Bob and Mary Ann had left us, but he was still yelling the 'yee-hahs' that Bob had taught him.

'No, I don't suppose I can,' she said.

When Mum had come home from America, she had had all sorts of plans – to open an American-style milk bar, to run a hotel, to marry a farmer and ride horses all day. She had certainly not expected, within two years of her return, to find herself married to a man who was training for the priesthood. The irony of the situation was not lost on her friends. During the long, hot, dusty hours she and Pat, Molly, Maureen and Celia had spent in Flatus, their old Ford, when the scenery might not change from one day to the next, the girls had talked and talked. They wondered what they might do in the future, when they were back home in England, Scotland or Ireland, and whether they would marry or have children. During one of these conversations, the other four had laughingly predicted that Mum would marry a vicar on her return to the UK, and serve tea and cucumber sandwiches on the vicarage lawn wearing her jeans (they had all purchased a pair in America but women were rarely seen in trousers back home) and cowboy hat (another purchase) – not because it seemed like a possibility but because the Gwenda they knew was the most unlikely vicar's wife they could think of. She was not just the most daring among them – the one who insisted they stay a second night at a deserted ski lodge, even after drinking tea at gunpoint the night before – but the biggest joker, too. So when she told them that she had met a man who wanted to be a priest, they thought she was kidding at first and refused to believe her.

'People here settle down too young,' said Mum, shaking her head sadly after answering the door to 'a couple of kids' wanting to see the vicar about getting married. She looked at me and Sarah. 'There's plenty of time for that, you hear?'

Or peeling potatoes at the kitchen sink, she would say, 'Poor lass,' as Paula-from-round-the-corner strutted by on Newbiggin Road with her pram.

Paula was a few years older than me. On our way home from school one afternoon, Sandra and I had stopped and peeked in the pram. I wasn't really that interested in anyone else's babies as there had always been plenty of them in our lives, but Sandra wanted to see and I thought it would be rude not to show some interest as well. Paula stood back proudly and popped her bubblegum as we looked at the sleeping infant. I had heard Mum say to Aunty Beryl that there wasn't a father, but that was a stupid thing to say because everyone knew that a baby had two parents.

Paula was living at home with her parents and younger brother and sister. When Mum said to her one day that it would be lovely when she got a place of her own, Paula agreed, saying, 'Yeah, I'd love to live next door to me mam.' I could tell by Mum's reaction that she didn't think it a very lofty ambition, but she smiled and agreed that it would be smashing.

Paula was the first person I saw wearing hotpants, which were a big craze that summer. Sarah and I had to make do with a pair made by Grandma. No matter how much I tried, I couldn't love mine quite as much as the ones my friends and Paula wore. Theirs even had stretchy straps that they could twang.

Ashington might have been famous for its coal, but some of its sons and daughters were famous for other things. One Sunday at church I noticed a smartly dressed lady sitting in the choir stalls beside Uncle George and Miss Templey. Everyone seemed to know who she was, and nodded or said hello as they walked past. During the hymns she sang in a voice that could be heard above Miss Templey's, reaching all the high notes and holding them for longer. After church she came back to the vicarage, and Mum settled her in the sitting room to talk to Aunty Beryl while she went to make the coffee.

'Why were you talking all posh?' I asked her.

'*Tsk*, I wasn't at all. But that's Sheila Armstrong, the opera singer. I've told you about her.' She watched me as I tipped the biscuits on to a plate. 'Oh, for heaven's sake, don't put them on without a doily!'

'Divvent be daft,' said Uncle George, who had come to fetch an ashtray for another guest. 'You don't need to stand on cere-mony for Sheila. She's Ashington born and bred.'

Sheila Armstrong was a soprano, and quite famous. Mum and Dad had gone to see her perform at the Theatre Royal and had a record with a picture of her on the sleeve that they wanted her to sign. While the grown-ups were chatting, another name kept cropping up – Maureen Williams, who, it seemed, was another Ashington-born soprano.

Following in their footsteps was Janice Cairns, a pupil at Ashington Grammar School, who came to church with her par-ents and younger sister, Colleen, who Sarah and I sometimes played with. Janice's voice had astounded her teachers and Mum said she would almost certainly be going to study at a prestigious music school. (Later, after training at the Royal Scottish Academy of Music, Janice would go on to study with the internationally famous baritone Tito Gobbi in Rome and Florence and, like Sheila Armstrong, would make a name for herself while never forgetting her North-Eastern roots.)

But Ashington had produced other stars whose fame eclipsed that of its singers, stars who were the talk of the whole country!

One day, Dad got home just as we were sitting down for tea. He had a big grin on his face.

'You'll never guess who I met today,' he said to Mum. 'Cissie Charlton!'

'Ah,' said Mum, 'the famous Cissie.'

'Who's she?' I asked.

'She's the mother of Jackie and Bobby.'

We had heard of them, of course. Even people who didn't know about football had heard of the Charlton brothers.

'I'll tell you what happened,' he said, laughing. 'I almost got my knuckles rapped, that's what! I went to see Mildred Davies, who's just lost her husband, and she had a visitor in the front room. She said to me, "You'll know Cissie, won't you," and off she went to make us a cup of tea. Well, could I think who this Cissie was? The lady gave me a great big smile as if we'd met before and as if she was expecting me to say something. I was searching my brain, and in the end I gave up and said, "Hello, how are you?" and hoped she would drop some clues.'

Mum was laughing now too, as if she already knew the punchline. She put the teapot down in front of Dad.

'Well,' he went on, pouring milk into the cups, 'I was about to ask her to remind me how we'd met when Mildred shouted through from the kitchen, "What's your Bobby doing with hisself while there's no football?" and then the penny dropped. Phew! I wouldn't want to upset Cissie, she's a legend round here.'

'What was she like?' asked Mum.

'Oh, she's a lovely person, and so proud of her lads. Well, she's proud of the whole clan. Her brothers were professional players, too, and of course Jackie Milburn is her cousin.'

Jackie Milburn, who now lived back in his hometown after a hugely successful career playing for Newcastle United and for England, had been Dad's hero. Dad had watched him play at the three FA Cup finals in the 1950s which Newcastle had won.

Dad went on, 'The men in her family always played football after a hard day down the pit. It's been a pleasure for her to see her own lads make a living out of it.'

'Uncle Andy works doon the pit,' said Ruth suddenly, making everyone laughed.

'I wonder who you've been talking to,' said Mum.

'Doon the pit,' said Mark, beaming. 'Let's gan doon the pit!'

'OK, that's enough,' said Mum. 'It might be funny the first time. Eat your bread up, or no cake.' She said to Dad, 'I hope you told her you were a football fan.'

'Of course I did. I told her I was there at St James' Park every week when I was a lad.' He looked at me and Sarah. 'I told her one of your great-grandpa's stories, do you remember it, about the day Newcastle bought the great Hughie Gallacher from Airdrieonians? The stadium was so packed, he said he'd paid a shilling to get in, but . . . ' He looked at us both.

'He'd have paid a pound to get out,' we chorused.

Dad laughed. 'By, he was a little powerhouse was Hughie, one of the best players Newcastle ever had. He was from a mining town, too, in Lanarkshire. He'd been down the pit since he was a lad of fifteen.'

'Doon the pit,' chorused Ruth and Mark, delighted at their own cleverness.

'Don't start that again,' said Mum, addressing Dad this time. 'Pour that tea, will you. It's going to be stone cold otherwise.'

Later, Aunty June came running down the path to tell us that her telephone had been installed that day and to give us her number.

'But you could have rung us up and told us,' said Sarah, puzzled.

Aunty June looked floored for a second, then Mum gave a shout over the banister and said if that was June, could she find Mark, who was hiding somewhere, and bring him up for his bath.

Her face brightened. 'But darlin', I wanted to see youse all. What would you do without your Aunty June?'

Chapter Fourteen

Sarah and I were sitting at the dining-room table. It was raining outside – one of those urgent, squally showers that seemed to come out of nowhere. We had been caught in one on Newbiggin Prom at the weekend, but minutes later the sun had come out. I was writing a play that I had decided Sarah, Krishna, Nicola and I would put on for the adults. We might even charge people to come and see it.

'It'll make a change from all those services,' said Mum, sounding relieved.

We sometimes put on a service for her and Dad and Aunty Beryl. It was one thing we knew a lot about. Every school day started with an assembly, Brownies started and ended with prayers and of course there was church every Sunday morning. Sarah and Nicola wrote out and decorated invitations, we arranged the chairs and brought the old prayer desk down from Sarah's room, told Ruth and Mark they could come if they behaved, then the four of us bombarded our small congregation with our specially written prayers and favourite Bible readings before announcing that we would all sing a hymn.

'I think we should cut out some of the verses,' Dad would say, looking at his watch. 'I have to go and write my sermon, and I've a couple coming to see me about a baptism in twenty minutes.'

'And I've just got five minutes before I get the bread out of the oven,' Mum would say, mouthing something at Aunty Beryl we couldn't quite catch.

We would sigh and agree reluctantly, it never occurring to us that they might not be totally delighted by our efforts.

'We see a circus setting up in the field when we're out for a walk,' I told Sarah, looking up from my writing. 'We've got our little sister, Julia, with us, but she's a naughty child and she runs away. When we realize that she's missing we go to the big top to try to find her. Some clowns are rehearsing, and they tell us that the lion tamer has kidnapped her and is going to use her in his act, but that everyone knows his lions aren't well trained. We have to hurry and find her before she gets eaten.'

'Can I play the lion tamer?'

'If you want. I'll be the trapeze artist. Krishna and Nicola can be the sisters.'

'You didn't say there was a trapeze artist.'

'Well, there is. She's practising on one of those high swings they use.' I looked through the rain-spattered window into the garden. 'Perhaps we can use the climbing frame. Do you think we could tie a rope between it and the swing and have a tightrope walker as well? Krishna could do that. She's good at balancing. Or maybe Nicola because she's smaller. Perhaps they can do one of their dances.'

'On the tightrope?'

'No, man! That would be dangerous. But we could—'

Sarah jumped up. 'It's stopped raining,' she said. 'Let's go and see Rip.'

Rip was a pit pony who lived on a plot of land behind Spedding's. A narrow path – known by Grandma as 'the Dogs' Toilet' – ran between the land and the churchyard, and a fence and high hedge bordered it for most of the way, blocking any view of what went on there. But there was a gap in the hedge at one point. One day, not long after we'd moved, when all six of us had been going for a walk between the showers – Mark on his reins, Ruth pushing her doll's pram, me and Sarah with our skipping ropes – a small horse had come trotting up to us as we'd reached this opening and stuck his head over the fence. Ruth screamed and let go of her pram, Mark jumped and looked as if he was going to cry.

Mum laughed. 'He's only being friendly. Wish we'd known he was here, I'd have brought him a treat.'

He was a rust-coloured Shetland pony with a matted coat and mane and a pleading look in his large eyes.

A man walking past with his dog heard her, and said in a friendly way, 'That's Rip. His whole life's a big treat now. He's an old pit pony, ya knaa, retired, like.'

Mum and Dad looked at the horse with something like admiration. 'What a life,' said Dad, stroking his nose. 'All those years in the dark. Poor old chap.'

Sarah and I copied him, cautiously at first, then more confidently. He had a strong but not unpleasant smell. 'You mean, he lived underground?' I asked Dad.

'I should think so. I don't think they brought them up. Not much of a life, is it?'

'What would he have done?'

'Oh, pulled wagons, that sort of thing.'

'How old is he?'

'I don't know. Old in horse years, I should think.'

'Twenty?'

'I've no idea. You'll have to ask his owner. Or someone like Uncle Andy might know.'

We'd never seen his owner, but we often took Rip bits of apple. Even if we couldn't see him, he would usually appear when he heard us.

Today there was no sign of him. We stood there for a while and called his name. We could hear chickens clucking somewhere on the land, and a crow was hopping over the tussocks of grass, but there was no Rip. Instead we carried on towards what we called the Ghost Town, which lay between the churchyard and the black waters of the River Wansbeck. The Ghost Town was all that was left of the former mining village of North Seaton and its colliery, which had closed several years before our arrival in Ashington. I had a feeling we weren't really allowed to go there without Mum or Dad; there were potential dangers, like mine shafts and unsafe buildings, and the unexplained threat of 'strange men' – though it was hard to know who could be stranger than some of our parents' friends.

The derelict colliery was protected behind a high-wire fence. The two remaining terraces were practically crumbling in front of our eyes, yet wisps of smoke still came from a couple of chimneys. Grass grew tall around piles of rubble and through cracks in the pavement, and rusting machinery poked up through the weeds and bushes that were slowly taking over the old colliery buildings. A dog came running up to sniff us – luckily, only a small one – and a man walking with a young boy who might have been his grandson called out roughly, 'Howway, Sandy!' and it left us alone.

In the lane was a row of toilets – known as netties in this part of the world. A few, to be shared by the whole street!

The clouds were speeding across the sky. It looked as if it might rain again soon. We peered through the fence at the mineworks, wondering how deep the mine was and what would happen if anyone fell into it. I was fascinated by the idea of danger, but I liked to know that there was a way out of it too. I shuddered and stared.

Just when we decided it was time to go back, we saw old Mrs Hepscott waddling out of her back yard and coming towards us, head bobbing up and down as if it was on a spring. She was the smelly lady from church, and we had heard that she had no intention of leaving her home until she was carried out. 'Poor soul,' Mum always said when her name was mentioned. Nod, nod, nod went her head. Sometimes I imitated her in the service to make Sarah laugh.

I felt a giggle starting. 'Stop it!' I said to Sarah, even though she hadn't said or done anything. Surprisingly, she didn't argue, just nudged me. The old lady was saying something to us. Her harsh, guttural voice seemed to come from the back of her throat. I thought she might be telling us off at first, perhaps for being here on our own, but it soon became apparent that she was inviting us into her home. I remembered now how Mum had politely declined her offer on an earlier occasion, pointing at the number of children and laughingly saying that we couldn't possibly impose on her, but how very kind, and that she must come to us sometime instead. But it seemed difficult to refuse when it was just Sarah and me, and though our first instinct was always to say, 'No thank you,' she was already walking back into her yard, beckoning us and muttering to herself at the same time.

'Father Gofton's lassies ... aye ... grand man he is ... grand ... ' She sounded as if she was going to spit something out when she said the word 'grand'. 'Howway inside, hinnies, howway inside.'

There was a smell in the yard, something strong and unpleasant. It couldn't be the toilet because there wasn't one. But the smell of a toilet would have been better than this smell. It was even worse in the kitchen. I looked at Sarah. I could see her nose twitching, and when I caught her eye she pulled a face and mouthed something at me. I frowned and ignored her. I wondered if a smell could be so bad it made you sick, but told myself that was impossible.

It was dark in the kitchen. A pile of blankets lay in a heap on the table, but as we got closer they seemed to come to life and three, four, maybe five cats shot in the air and swept past our legs. Sarah and I both jumped and she grabbed my arm. We didn't know anyone with cats, and were nervous of most animals. As my eyes grew accustomed to the dim light, I could see there were cats everywhere, some curled up in corners, one stretching by the doorway, another leaping on to the newly vacated table and eyeing us suspiciously. They gave me the creeps. I wished we were outside again in the bright afternoon air.

'Can we go?' Sarah whispered to me, but Mrs Hepscott was pouring something from a bottle into two glasses.

With her hunched figure and old-fashioned long dark dress, her pinny fastened round what might have been her middle, the old lady looked as if she had been sewn into her clothes. It was hard to imagine a body inside, made up of separate arms and legs. She handed us a glass each.

'Lemonade, hinny,' she said, and made a clucking noise when we thanked her.

She watched us expectantly, her head still nodding, and shot us a smile that showed a row of brown, stumpy teeth. I loved lemonade, and it was a treat at home, so against my better judge-ment – and trying to overcome my nausea – I took the tiniest sip I could. If it was lemonade it had lost its fizz long ago, but I was more worried about the glass, which didn't look or smell very clean.

Sarah took a mouthful of hers and started to say something. I shushed her, and when Mrs Hepscott disappeared into the larder, I grabbed Sarah's glass and tipped both our drinks down the sink.

One of the cats walked towards us and began to wrap itself around my leg. 'Ugh, I can feel all its bones,' I whispered, shud-dering. 'And it's tickling me.'

Mrs Hepscott came out of the larder with an unopened packet of biscuits.

'For the bairns,' I managed to make out. She patted her hand on imaginary heads, as if Ruth and Mark were standing in front of her.

'Thank you very much. We've got to go now,' I said, and she nodded – or perhaps she was nodding anyway.

'Ta-ta, hinnies,' she called as we went.

We tried to save our horrified laughter until we were out of earshot.

'It stank!' I cried.

'Did you see that dead bird?' said Sarah.

'No. Where?' I was annoyed to have missed it.

'On the table. Where those cats were. And there was mess everywhere. Uggh!'

We ran all the way back to the churchyard, then slowed down to catch our breath. I remembered too that we had been told off for charging round the churchyard by a lady who had complained to Dad. Perhaps it had been the same lady who had told us off when we had been with Michael and Jeremy that day. Over by the path we could see that Rip had now appeared, but a crowd of children were gathered round him so we decided to come back later.

We told Mum about our encounter with Mrs Hepscott.

'What a couple of nincompoops. You'll get hydrophobia going in there.'

'We only had a little drink,' I said.

'You didn't drink anything!' exclaimed Mum.

'Just one sip,' I said, feeling foolish now. Then I added petulantly, 'You always say we can't be fussy when we're out.'

'Well, you have to use your common sense sometimes. You could have been poisoned. Have you heard this, Alder?'

'Isn't she generous,' said Dad, looking at the biscuits. The packet was so faded it might have come from Spedding's window. 'It's always the ones who have so little . . . ' He shook his head.

'Alder, you've seen inside that place! Can you believe they went in?'

'You hold your nose when she's not looking, then hold your breath when she is. That's what I do anyway. You've probably made her day. She'll be inviting you for tea next.'

We shrieked at the thought of this.

'Talking of which, you can set the table,' said Mum.

'How many for?'

'Just the six of us.'

Later that evening, watching *Stars on Sunday*, a man read from the Bible while a cat sat on his lap. 'Remember Mrs Hepscott's,' said Sarah, as if it had happened a long time ago. The Poole family, who were regular guests on the programme, sang a song together. Sarah said, 'Imagine if our family could all sing like that and be on the television!'

Mum popped her head round the door and pulled a face. She thought *Stars on Sunday* was a lot of sentimental nonsense. Next, a pretty lady sang a song about four angels, each guarding a corner of the bed while you slept. I liked the idea of having angels to protect me, though I hoped I wouldn't see them if I woke up in the middle of the night.

Chapter Fifteen

A few days before the end of the summer term, Sarah and I got home from school to find the house unusually quiet. On the sitting-room door someone had stuck a piece of paper.

Person sleeping. Do not disturb.

'Who goes to bed at a quarter to four in the afternoon?' I said sulkily. 'And it's *The Partridge Family* on telly.'

'It might be Brother Kevin,' said Sarah hopefully. Brother Kevin, one of Mum and Dad's Franciscan friends, sometimes came to stay.

'Or Uncle Doug,' I added, though doubting that he would be in bed at this time.

Mum was in the back garden with Ruth and Mark. Ruth was walking her dolls around the tennis court in their pram, talking to them as she did so. Mum was pushing Mark on the swing.

'Who's that in the sitting room?' we both asked her before she had time to say hello.

Mum looked towards the sitting-room window as if we had surprised her with the news. The curtains had been pulled across, though rather messily.

'Oh, that's just Jackie,' she said breezily. 'You'll see her later.'

'But why is she in bed now?'

'Yes, and why is she there and not upstairs?'

'Oh, I'll put her in the attic later.'

'Not in Sarah's room?'

'She'll be fine up there.'

'We want to watch telly.'

'Television.'

'Well, we want to watch it anyway and now we can't.'

'There's plenty of time. And television's not the be-all and end-all.'

'Yes, but it's *The Partridge Family*.'

'Well, she'll probably be up soon.'

'Do we know her?'

As we waited for her to answer, Mark leapt off the swing in mid-air. Mum gasped, but when he picked himself up and got back on she just laughed and shook her head.

'What a daredevil! I'm glad you girls weren't like him.'

'You haven't answered the question.'

'Well, no, I mean, yes, your father knows her. I can't remember the whole story. Remember how sometimes we have to share our house with others.'

'You could have put her upstairs,' I grumbled.

'She's set the table for you,' said Mum. 'Wasn't that kind?'

*

Jackie joined us at the tea table. She was small and thin and had dark hair pulled back in a tight ponytail. She smelt suspiciously like the apple shampoo I had got for Christmas but hadn't used yet as Mum insisted on washing our hair with a lethal anti-nit shampoo. Her face, which had a naturally sulky expression, lit up when she saw the spread on the table. Mum was considered an exotic cook – spaghetti bolognese and chicken curry were two of her specialities, and she was always trying out new recipes – but we ate our main meal at midday and tea was a simpler affair, usually bread and jam followed by cake, or at this time of year, salad. Today bowls of tomatoes, cottage cheese, coleslaw and hard-boiled eggs finely sliced in a mandolin were laid out beside a larger bowl of iceberg lettuce.

'What's this?' cried Jackie, picking up the coleslaw and bringing it close to her face, though not quite sniffing it. We all looked at Mum, knowing that if we had done that we would have been told off.

Mum ignored her misdemeanour by starting on one of her America stories, telling Jackie that she had never seen coleslaw until she went there, and how the salads they had eaten in their hospital canteen had contained a mixture of sweet and savoury that had seemed alien to her and the other British girls.

'And my father couldn't believe that we ate corn on the cob. He said it was cattle food. But I soon converted him.'

Jackie looked at her wide-eyed, as if she'd never heard such a thrilling tale before, then turned her attention to the rest of the table. 'Cakes!' she cried out. 'You've never made these, Mrs Gofton!' When Mum confirmed that indeed she had, she looked round the table at the four of us and said, 'Eeh, isn't she the clever one!'

She had quite a deep, crackly voice which sounded incongruous coming from such a tiny body. Her accent was North-Eastern, but not as broad as some of the people we knew.

I tried to pretend not to be interested in her, but couldn't help sneaking glances every so often.

Dad, who had been delayed at a meeting, made an appearance a few minutes later and Jackie leapt up from her seat and ran towards him, throwing her arms around his neck. 'Father Gofton, you're my saviour,' she said, and Dad laughed, sounding embarrassed, but she added, more seriously, 'No, I mean it.'

Dad patted her hand and said, 'Sit down and enjoy your tea, Jackie.'

I watched her with even more interest now.

At tea, Jackie was as chatty and familiar as if she'd known us all our lives. When Sarah said she had been told off by a teacher for talking when it hadn't been her fault, she became so indignant I half expected her to get up and set off to confront the teacher there and then. But when Mum told her that some battles weren't worth fighting, and it was best to save up energy for the ones that were, she said, 'You are right there, Mrs Gofton,' and nodded vigorously.

When we had eaten, she helped me and Sarah to clear the table and exclaimed over our dishwasher, saying she had heard of them but had never seen one before.

'It's not that good,' I told her. 'We still have to load it and unload it. It takes ages. I like going to Grandma's and washing up in hot soapy water.'

Jackie laughed and said I was a funny lass, and Mum said there was no pleasing some folk. She wanted me and Sarah to show

her our rooms, but Mum said we had to sit down and learn our
spellings first.

'We'll go and make up your bed in the attic,' she said to
Jackie. 'Then it won't be long before we pop the little ones in
the bath. You can chat to the girls later.'

I had finished my spellings and was practising handstands on the
tennis court against the sitting-room wall. I had put down my
cardigan to protect my hands from the gravel. Ruth wanted me
to play chasey before her bath, and Sarah joined in too. Then Ruth
suggested we ask if Jackie wanted to play the bears game with us.

With Ruth granted fifteen more minutes before bathtime, the
three of us stood at the top of the attic stairs, whispering about
who was going to do the asking.

'I think I can hear some little mice out there,' came that dis-
tinctive voice that sounded like a scratched record. 'I'd better
find a broom so I can sweep them away.'

Ruth laughed loudly. Sarah tapped gently on the door as if
we had just got there and poked her head round. 'Do you want
to play with us?'

'It's a special game that we sometimes play with visitors,' I
added, wanting it to sound more enticing.

'Come in, all of you, I'm not Greta Garbo,' Jackie said, and we
trooped into the attic where she sat, legs crossed, in the middle
of the large bed, looking as if she was about to take off on her
flying carpet.

We told her the story of the boy who had been killed by the
mother bear, and how we had turned it into a game.

'You are a gory lot!' she exclaimed, patting the bed to show
that we could sit beside her if we wanted. 'Tell us more.'

I shrugged. We didn't know what happened next, but I always wondered about it. The story Mum had told us was just the beginning. I pictured the child's mother standing at the roadside with her camera, the father – was he there too? – getting out of the car to see what was going on. What did he say to his wife? What did she do next? Did the bears take the body away? Were there any other children in the car, and if so, had they seen what happened? Mum could never answer these questions to my satisfaction. She had told us the story, and as far as she was concerned, that was it. She thought my imagination was a bit overactive at times.

We told Jackie she would be the mother bear and had to chase us.

'Thought so,' she said, jumping up. 'Let's go then, the bairns are having their baths soon.'

'Dad sometimes plays with us,' said Ruth as we went downstairs. 'But he's usually too busy.'

It was true. Dad was hardly at home these days, or, if he was, he would be stuck in his study writing sermons or having meetings. Mum might have five minutes free while something was in the oven or she was waiting for the dough to rise. But visiting grown-ups were always more amenable. Few took the role more seriously than Brother Kevin, whose brown Franciscan habit only added to his bearlike appearance.

Jackie proved to be an acceptable mother bear. Though she was very slender, her arms were strong and difficult to escape from. And with her husky voice she sounded quite fierce. At times, when you got close to her, you could detect another deep-rooted smell that wasn't my apple shampoo, a smell I recognized vaguely but couldn't identify. But it wasn't unpleasant.

After half an hour of running and shrieking round the lawn, taking refuge on the climbing frame and teasing Jackie into chasing us round the rosebeds, Mum came outside to call the little ones for their bath. Mark had joined us by then too.

'Are you our aunty?' asked Ruth as she took Jackie's hand and led her inside.

I think Ruth thought everyone was our aunty in those days. I didn't hear Jackie's reply as Mum was saying something to her about another pair of hands always being welcome at bathtime, and there being only so many times she could read *Tootles the Taxi* to Mark without going round the bend.

'Do you like her?' asked Sarah when we were alone on the lawn, the July sun still shining. We hung upside down on the climbing frame, seeing whose face got the reddest.

'She's quite nice,' I said. 'I wonder how long she's staying.'

'I wonder why she's not sleeping in my room?' said Sarah. 'We could have had a midnight feast in your room tonight. Shall I tell Mum she can sleep in my bed?'

'You can try, but I think she'll say no.'

'I wonder if she could turn the rope for us when she's finished bathing Ruth and Mark,' said Sarah. 'Shall we go and ask her?'

Jackie was still with us the next day, and the one after, and we grew used to having her around. She was the first person we wanted to see when we got in from school. When Mum thought it funny that I had been picked to be a scraper in September, and said it sounded like a job you would choose to avoid, I rushed to tell Jackie instead. She seemed to understand the importance of

it. After school one day we took her to see Rip, and carried on
to the Ghost Town. Ruth was with us, pushing her doll's pram,
but Mark had stayed at home. Though Jackie had protested, Mum
said Mark could be a bit of a handful, but we girls were always
very well behaved, and she had looked at us as she had said it, to
make sure we understood.

'I'm surprised this place is still standing,' said Jackie.

'We know the lady who lives there,' said Sarah, pointing to
Mrs Hepscott's house. Although it was a hot day and we had
changed into shorts and T-shirts, a whisper of smoke was coming
from its chimney.

'She stinks,' I said.

Jackie put her hands on her hips. 'Now that's not kind,' she
said. Then she added childishly, 'What does she smell of? No!
Don't tell me. I don't think I want to know.'

'Mum says it's not her fault,' I carried on, 'because she's never
had a bathroom, and she's old so she probably can't see all the
dirt everywhere.'

'Well, I know plenty of folk who don't have bathrooms, and
they don't stink,' said Jackie.

'She's got cats, too,' said Sarah. 'About a hundred.'

'Well, that might explain things,' said Jackie, and I wished I'd
remembered the cats.

'She gave me and Sarah a piece of cake, and do you know
what the icing was? Bird poo.' I stole a look at Sarah to see if she
would go along with it. She nodded her head, but was unable
to hide a grin.

'More fool you if you ate it,' said Jackie.

'And we had cat's wee to drink,' giggled Sarah.

'You two don't half come out with some tripe,' said Jackie.

We walked along the cobbled lane. The row of houses opposite Mrs Hepscott's was fenced off now, and work had begun on demolishing them. Some of the walls were gone, revealing peeling wallpaper.

'Doesn't this place make you sad,' Jackie said. 'Think of all the people who used to live here. All the men setting off for the pit every morning, the women hanging the washing out, the bairns playing football, or with their dollies, like madam over there.' She nodded towards Ruth, who was fussing over her pram. 'It's like looking inside a doll's house. Just think, someone used to wake up there and the first thing they saw was that wallpaper.'

I gazed at the houses in silence, and realized I had been thinking the same thing.

'You could write a good story about it,' she added, giving me a nudge. I had read her part of one of my stories the previous night, and she had proved to be an appreciative audience. 'I don't know why anyone needs to make things up in books,' she added, 'there's enough real stuff going on that would make your hair curl. You want to see my family, for a start.'

I was going to ask her about her family when she said, 'Here, what's your sister up to?'

Ruth had nipped into one of the netties, her knickers discarded on the way, and was clambering on to the seat.

'Ruth, no!' I cried, but we were all laughing too much to stop her.

'Well, it's better than wetting herself,' said Jackie. 'Clever lass!'

'It can't be very clean,' I said anxiously. 'And she's had her hands all over it.'

'Never mind,' said Jackie. 'We'll stick her in the bath when we get back.' She sounded as if she was our mother; as if she had lived with us for ever. I looked at her curiously, admiringly. I didn't know very much about her. I didn't have any real idea how old she was, whether she was a girl who was almost fully grown up, or already a woman. When she and Mum talked together, sometimes they sounded like friends, the way Mum and Aunty Beryl did, but more often Mum was slow and patient with her as if she were talking to a child.

'She likes toilets,' explained Sarah. 'Especially different ones.'

'It's easier for men, isn't it?' I added, hoping to make her laugh. Mum always made that remark when we went on walks, and Dad and Mark could pop behind the bushes with far less drama than when we girls needed to go.

But Jackie didn't laugh. 'A lot of things are easier for men,' she said bitterly. 'That's one of the problems of life.'

Chapter Sixteen

On the last day of term we were allowed to take games to school. I looked enviously at the girls who brought in Barbies. I had a Sindy at home, and one of Mum's friends had knitted her a wardrobe including a red-and-white-striped ski outfit with a matching pompom hat that I had thought was quite fetching, until now. I was glad I hadn't brought her; she looked like Second Hand Rose compared to Barbie. In fact, I wasn't even sure that my doll was a real Sindy. Mum was quite good at pretending sometimes. Elaine had brought in Coppit, one of the Susans had brought Buckaroo and someone else had Operation. The classroom was filled with screams and laughter as Miss Stewart took down displays from the walls, gave some girls the jobs of collecting pencils, jotters and exercise books, emptying the pencil-sharpening machines and putting chalk that was worth keeping back into packets, and occasionally pretended to be angry at the noise we were making. We had been embroidering needle cases in our sewing lessons, and these were ready to take home. I was proud of my simple cross-stitch and running-stitch geometric design, though some girls had produced far more intricate ones than mine. Alison had sewn a vase of flowers on the front of hers, and Sandra's depicted a cat seated on a cushion. I knew it was Mum's fault that mine would never be as good as theirs as she was almost proud of her lack of skill with a needle, though at least she could knit.

I went running up to Jackie's room to show her my handiwork as soon as I got home, but she wasn't there.

I shouted for her, and expected to hear her husky voice replying.

'Where's Jackie?' I asked Mum, who was in the kitchen.

'Nice to see you too!' she said. Then she added, 'She's gone away for a few days, hopefully to get better.'

'What's the matter with her?'

Mum looked at me for a few seconds, as if wondering whether I could be trusted with the information. 'She likes a drink,' she said, hesitantly.

'Oh.' I didn't really know what she meant. An image popped into my head of an old man sitting in his armchair nursing a glass of whisky.

Mum continued, 'She's gone to stay with some people who can help her, so hopefully' – she said that word with a hint of jollity in her voice – 'when we next see her, she'll be fine.'

'When will that be?'

'Well, I've invited her for Christmas.'

'Christmas! That's months away.'

Mum just smiled. 'Do you want salad for tea?'

I was amazed that Mum could be so casual about it. Jackie had inched her way into our lives in a matter of days, and it was hard to imagine the house without her. She had sat and combed my hair for me one night, read Ruth and Mark their bedtime stories and even hemmed a skirt for Mum. And I had never seen her drink anything other than a cup of tea. Sarah and I went up to the attic later, looking for clues. She hadn't brought many things with her, and she had left nothing behind, except the faint whiff of apple shampoo and a slight singeing smell.

Krishna and Nicola were going to Wales for a few days to visit their grandparents. Kathryn and her parents were going to stay in a hotel in Scarborough. I'd never been to a hotel before, or even out to eat in a restaurant, but I couldn't have been more excited about our own holiday if it had been to a five-star hotel with a swimming pool. Shepherds Dene was a retreat house for clergy that belonged to the diocese of Newcastle and lay on the edge of a village in the Tyne Valley, about an hour from home. Every summer it opened its doors for a week to clergy families wanting a sociable, affordable holiday. It was an Edwardian building, originally built as a weekend retreat for a wealthy local family, but to us children it felt and looked ancient. The huge wooden front door had surely been taken from a castle, while the main staircase and oak-panelled lobby seemed to belong to a house lit by torches rather than electric lighting.

For children – even clergy children used to big homes and gardens – the house was huge and mysterious and exciting with its three sets of staircases, three floors and grounds that included several lawns, a grass tennis court, a grasshopper field and a rounders field (the latter two names being our own invention and only applicable to the time we spent there), a wooden summer house, a sundial and a long tarmac driveway for ballgames. It was the best place in the world for hide and seek – Sarah and I would probably have said it was the best place in the world, full stop – and yielded new curiosities every time we visited. The previous year, in a bathroom in the attic, we had found a bath so large we thought that this top floor must surely be inhabited by giants. We ran away quickly before we could find out.

Outside the dining room – a light-filled room overlooking the back lawns and the valley beyond – ran a passageway that smelt of polished floors and lingering cooking smells. Doors led off it into kitchens and sculleries – so many! – each one lined with giant pots and pans, brown mixing bowls and containers holding implements for patting butter and other old-fashioned tasks. We were served four meals a day, so the kitchens must have been in almost constant use, and yet, if you wandered along that corridor between mealtimes, they seemed unusually still and silent, as if waiting for the house's original inhabitants to return from a day's fishing or shooting.

Other rooms included a Common Room that we congregated in on rainy afternoons and before we were chased off to bed at night, a Quiet Room that no one ever went into with shiny armchairs and a bookcase of serious-looking books, a Wardens' Room where the wardens, Mr and Mrs Millican, lived in what was basically a bed-sitting room, a Speaker's Room that was always locked and a small chapel where one of the fathers took the Sunday service. In the recess below the stairs was a sweet shop, really just a table covered in a red-checked cloth. The cloth was briefly removed by a supervising adult after dinner –

served at midday, as was the norm in this part of the world – and, when it was lifted, the most wonderful smell wafted upwards.

Apart from the appeal of the house and grounds, we loved going to Shepherds Dene because we had friends who went too. As children of clergy, we all had something in common, and though we may have been as different from each other in other ways as we were from our non-vicarage friends, our fathers' common profession was enough to bind us together for this holiday, and, in some cases, for far longer. We had known Michael and Jeremy Parker – now with a baby brother, Adam – for all our lives, as Dad and Uncle David had been trainee priests together, along with David Smith, father of Rebecca and Christopher. Colin and Wendy Rogerson, parents of Catherine and Jane, were Ruth and Mark's godparents. Newer to the Shepherds Dene holiday were the Scott family, whose girls Jeanette, Hayley and Julie were similar ages to me, Sarah and Ruth. The Beniams were a family of six children, five of them boys, most of them older than me, who acted like kindly older siblings to us all and who we all adored.

Our parents enjoyed this holiday because they were away from the parish, away from ringing doorbells and telephones and being at everyone's beck and call. And they, too, were with people who understood them and their lives, people with whom they could share their frustrations and tell funny or cruel stories without having to be wary about what they said.

The house wasn't visible from the road. As we turned into the winding driveway, passing cottages in the grounds that were used by the staff, seeing a tall chimney appear then disappear, I would get an excited feeling in my stomach. What if none of our friends were here this year? What if there was no one to play with? But even though there would usually be some changes – a new family to get to know, a regular family who hadn't been able to make it or whose children had grown out of it – the holiday was always a success.

As soon as we arrived, after finding out where we would be sleeping and helping to unload the car, we did what we always did on arrival and ran off to see who else was here, checking that nothing had changed and familiarising ourselves once more with the gardens. Did the grasshopper field still click with the sound of grasshoppers? It always did, and off we went to the kitchens to beg for jam jars to house our new pets. We held grasshopper Olympics on the top lawns, where the grass was more neatly kept.

'Guess what, Michael, we've got a pit pony living next to the churchyard. We'll take you to see him when you next come,' I told our friend when we found him loitering by the main door.

'Can we race him?' he asked. Michael was even more competitive than we were.

'I don't think so. He's old.'

'We've brought our tennis rackets,' said Sarah, skipping up to us, 'and I found loads of balls in the garage.'

'I've got a new cricket bat,' said Michael. 'Let's go and play now in the rounders field.'

'Hey, they'd better not be my new balls with the demon on them,' said Dad, overhearing the conversation as he passed by.

Dad liked to play tennis with Uncle Colin while we were here, and was always in demand to play with us, too, something he rarely had time to do at home.

'Uncle Alder, Uncle Alder!' Michael was chasing him down

the corridor now. 'Will you come and play cricket? I've got a new bat and stumps! Pleeease! We'll get me dad!'

'Not now, we've just got here. But I promise to give you a game sometime.' Dad gave him a playful punch and pretended to be doubled over in agony when Michael gave him one back.

By day two, Mum and the other mothers were engrossed in a competition from *Family Circle* magazine. They had to see how many words they could make from the word 'unbelievable'. At morning coffee (always served on the veranda overlooking the flowerbeds and the top lawns) and after lunch, they sat throwing new words at each other. Later, as the list of words grew and their competitive spirit sharpened, someone produced a dictionary from the Quiet Room.

'We've got to win, surely,' said Aunty Cathie as she totted up the latest figure. 'No one will have put in the effort we have.'

Sometimes we came back from our wanderings to find our mothers in hysterical laughter, only stopping long enough to tell us that the tennis balls were wherever we last had them, or order us to wash our hands before the mealtime gong went, or to take the younger children with us when we went off to play again. We roamed the grounds like a pack of animals.

On hot afternoons or mild evenings, the fathers took us through the gate that lay at the bottom of one of the lower lawns, across the farmer's field – leaping over crusty cowpats – to the river, which was actually a burn that ran into the River Tyne. The air under the canopy of trees smelt mossy and slightly pungent. We paddled and floated sticks, and Dad was always in charge of building a dam. Now and again the mothers came too, and dangled their feet in the icy water as they held the little ones' hands.

We had begun a new ritual the year before: a game of rounders after tea, played on a field overlooking the farmer's land. An air-raid shelter with slippery damp steps and an echoey interior ran along one side of it, but we were only allowed down there with an adult. We took turns picking teams. Dad would usually be chosen first, especially if Michael or Jeremy were captains. He had a competitive streak that he had passed on to me and Sarah, and took seriously his aim to ensure victory for his side. Along with Michael, who always got overexcited, he was probably the most vociferous player. He cheered on every runner as if they were competing for an Olympic medal, and kept up a running commentary worthy of a live radio broadcast. 'He's hit it for six, well into the trees. He can do it, he can do it! They're looking for the ball, but will they find it? Oh, Jeremy's got it, he's thrown it to Hayley, but – oh, no! – she's missed, and Michael's up to the third bay now, Sarah's streaming home, and – can he make it? – yes, he's done it! Another rounder!' Mum, if she'd come down to watch – the mothers didn't usually play, though they occasionally helped to field if they were standing in the right place – would roll her eyes and wonder aloud who the biggest child was.

We were all louder and wilder and more boisterous when we were there, and we were usually left to our own devices, so I wonder what it was like for the family of three who arrived halfway through our stay that year. The father was a priest from the Durham diocese, close to retirement and unknown to the rest of the party. Mum, who got on well with the wardens, had been told of the misunderstanding that had occurred when he was booking the holiday. He had spoken to Mrs Millican by telephone, telling her that he and his wife would be bringing their daughter with them, but as it was a rather late booking, added helpfully that it wouldn't be a problem if all three of them slept in the same room.

'Will she be requiring a cot to sleep in, or is she old enough for a bed?' asked Mrs Millican.

On the other end of the phone the priest cleared his throat. 'A bed will be fine,' he answered. 'She's thirty-six.'

And so she was christened 'the thirty-six-year-old daughter' before we'd even met her. We all thought it was a great joke. We wondered endlessly what she would look like. Thirty-six wasn't much younger than our parents, perhaps even older than some of them, but it had become in our minds an amusing age that belonged purely to this poor woman.

'What if we call her that to her face?' said Michael.

'You'll do no such thing,' said Aunty Cathie.

'But if it just slips out.'

'You never mention a lady's age,' Mum said to him. 'I mean, your mother wouldn't like everyone to know she was fifty-seven, would she?'

'Get away with you, Gwenda,' Aunty Cathie said.

I don't think we ever spoke to the thirty-six-year-old daughter, though she did throw a ball back to us in a good-natured way when we were playing on the driveway and she was passing. But she and her parents seemed normal enough, and got on with the other adults. She looked rather like a schoolteacher – which she probably was – with sensible bobbed hair and glasses. I had heard the mothers say that she could be an attractive girl if she made a bit more of her appearance and dressed less frumpily.

I can't remember whose idea it was to write her a love letter.

We had played this trick before on one of the mothers, signing the letter from one of the fathers, and enjoying watching their over-acted responses. We sensed it was a bit more dangerous this time, but once we had decided to do it, we were unable to stop ourselves.

We slipped into the dining room before the gong for supper was rung and placed the letter, written in Sarah's best writing, at her place at the centre table where all the grown-ups sat. We children were allowed to sit at the long window table, as long as we behaved. Today there was more of a scramble than usual to sit at the window seat and thus be facing the adults.

We sat down promptly and waited for her arrival. Most of our parents were already seated when she entered, and we saw to our surprise a strange man walking beside her. She looked happy, slightly sheepish, as she pointed towards the table and said something to him.

Mrs Millican came up behind them. 'I've set you a place beside Elizabeth, Professor,' she said, and both he and the thirty-six-year-old daughter thanked her profusely.

'Have you seen that man?' I whispered to Jeanette.

'Maybe it's her brother. They look a bit alike.'

'What, with a beard and moustache!' snorted Michael. 'Nah, you can tell she fancies him.'

'Don't make me laugh!' I felt slightly hysterical, my hysteria tinged with fear. My heart was beating fast.

From across the room, Mum gave me one of her questioning frowns. I knew she was wondering why we kept looking at their table.

There was a new family at Shepherds Dene this year, the Stallards. Charles Stallard was short and jolly with expressive bushy eyebrows and a wheezy laugh that started with a shaking of his shoulders and gradually convulsed his whole body. Knowing what a good sport he was, we had signed the letter from him.

Now at her place, the thirty-six-year-old daughter noticed the letter, propped up against her water glass. She picked it up and looked at it for a few seconds, as if not able to believe it was addressed to her. We had written just 'Elizabeth' on the envelope, even though Michael had suggested we write 'Thirty-Six-Year-Old Daughter' in brackets underneath. Then she placed it on her lap and appeared to be opening it. She had her back to our table, so we couldn't see her face. Her head stayed bowed for what seemed like ages. Her companion, who had been talking to her father, looked at her and said something in her ear. Suddenly her shoulders began to tremble.

'Bloody hell!' said Michael. 'She's not bubblin', is she?'

Now some of the adults had stopped their conversations and were looking at her.

On our table we all froze, except for the younger children, who hadn't been part of the game and who were tucking into their bread and jam as normal.

'Elizabeth, is everything all right, dear?' asked her father, who was sitting opposite her.

It seemed like ages before Elizabeth looked up, and when she did she was wiping her eyes. Then she held the letter in the air, fluttered it for a few seconds, and said, 'Charles, I never knew you cared.'

'She really thinks it's from him!' whispered Hayley.

'Don't be stupid, man,' said Michael. 'She'd never have said that if she did.'

Charles, at the other end of the table, looked bewildered for a second, then, as if guessing what had happened, began his wheezy chuckle. His head shook up and down and his eyes seemed to disappear into his eyebrows. We all started to laugh, relieved. Elizabeth passed the letter to her friend. He read it and didn't seem to understand, because she then pointed behind her with her thumb and said something, and he turned round to look at us all.

'I'd heard about children of the clergy,' said the professor to the adults, but in a voice that was clearly supposed to be heard by us all, 'and I see it's all true.'

Mum did tell us later when she popped into the bathroom with our towels that we'd gone a bit far, and that it was best not to tease people we didn't know well.

'But she thought it was funny!' I protested. 'Everyone did!'

'You're lucky that she has a sense of humour. And her fiancé, too. But it was going too far putting that line about her "pretty titties". Honestly!' She swallowed a laugh and looked stern again.

'You're laughing!'

'No, I'm not. And I think I know whose idea it was.'

After Shepherds Dene, we spent a week in a cottage on the sand dunes at Embleton, the beach a short scramble below us. Fag End belonged to Mum's childhood friend Aunty Barbie, and had no running water or electricity. We filled our water container from a tap nearby, cooked on a stove fired by a gas cylinder and lit a lamp at night. The view from the front door was of the North Sea and Dunstanburgh Castle, which stood on a cliff at the end of the bay, its ruined towers like prehistoric

creatures. Our playground was the beach. We had a few visitors –
Grandma and Papa one day, our friends from Gosforth, John and
Betty Reid, who were staying in a caravan nearby, another. John
and Betty brought us bags of sweets, and one day John arrived
on his own with a cardboard tray full of cans of fizzy drink. As
it was a mile-long walk from the car park to Fag End, this was
a mark of true friendship and we children welcomed him like
a returning hero. Mum always said our stay at Fag End was her
favourite of our holidays, for the peace and seclusion, but though
I loved it, I missed the magic and camaraderie of Shepherds
Dene.

On rainy days we read or played board games and wrote postcards to everyone we knew. This was also the time for the
dreaded visits. Mum and Dad had both accumulated people
from their pasts to whom they felt some sense of duty, and this
was the ideal opportunity for the annual visit to those who lived
in this part of Northumberland. These visits were always unan-
nounced, but it was rare to find the person not at home. Sarah,
Ruth, Mark and I would sit, squashed together on a settee, while
the adults talked about things that meant nothing to us about
people we had never heard of, politely declining – following
Mum's instructions – any offer of food and drink.

'Otherwise we'll never get away,' she would warn us in the car
beforehand, and I'd wonder why we were going if it was such
an ordeal for her too.

In these rooms clocks would tick loudly, there would be a
smell of furniture polish or yesterday's dinner and even Mum
and Dad seemed to be on their best behaviour, talking in their
nicest voices, commenting on how well this person looked,
saying something else was a tragedy but didn't things always turn

out for the best. If we were lucky, we came away with a coin each or a note to share to buy an ice-cream. If we were unlucky it was a faded box of candied fruit that had lain for too long in a drawer, or something flavoured with almonds.

One evening, Dad decided to visit an old priest who had given him guidance earlier in his career. He went on his own, to our relief, as he thought this man might not be used to children. On his return he told us how they had sat in semi-darkness as an owl rested on a perch, staring at Dad as if sizing him up for his next meal. He had been glad to get out.

Even though it was sad when it was time to come home, there were still three more weeks of the school holidays left and we had guests coming to stay and days out to look forward to.

As Mum pulled into the drive, the half-pulled curtains in the kitchen window gave the house a sad, shuttered appearance. The sticky weed we liked to throw at each other was going wild in one corner of the vegetable patch. We jumped out of the car.

'Ooh, what a lovely smell of smoke,' said Sarah, sniffing the air.

Mum and Dad laughed, and even Mum agreed that it was nice to be home.

Mum had set a load off in the washing machine within five minutes of getting inside. The rest of us were helping to unpack the car when the phone started ringing.

'Oh, for pete's sake,' said Mum. 'Answer that, will you? And remember, your father's still on holiday.'

I went to pick up the phone in the cloakroom. 'Is the vicar in, pet?' said a man's voice, followed by a name I didn't catch.

'Er, what's it about, please?'

'It's about Mrs Wilkinson over the road from youse,' said the man. 'She'll not let the lads in to install her bathroom, and she's getting herself in a right tizz. She says it's unhygienic to have the netty in the house. And now she's thrown everyone out and won't do nothing until she's seen Father Gofton.'

'Just a minute, please.'

Mum took the phone, and I heard her alternating between tuts and sounds of sympathy.

'Poor old soul,' she said to Dad when she had hung up. 'I'd never really thought about it like that, but I suppose if you've always had your toilet in the yard, and then someone comes to put it on the end of your kitchen, you might be forgiven for thinking it's not the best place for it.'

'And very disruptive for an old lady,' said Dad. 'I'll pop over and see what I can do.'

'But don't invite her to live with us while she's got the work-men in, whatever you do,' said Mum with an anxious laugh. As if to make sure that didn't happen, she added, 'Hang on, and I'll get her a loaf out of the freezer.'

A loaf of Mum's home-made bread appeared to be the answer to many of life's problems. I was surprised how grateful people always were to receive one. I far preferred the white bread that came out of colourful waxy packets that we ate at other people's houses, and I loved the advert for Nimble with the flying girl. Mum insisted her bread was healthiest, even when I told her that Nimble made you slim.

'Maybe they can go and give Mrs Hepscott a bathroom instead,' I said, as Dad set off clutching the loaf. 'Her and all the cats can have a bath together.' I giggled, picturing the scene.

'*She* and the cats,' murmured Mum, filling the kettle and

looking to see if she could detect any signs of the disruption, for Mrs Wilkinson lived almost directly opposite. 'You wouldn't say, "Her can have a bath", would you?'

'Who's she, the cat's mother?' trilled Sarah, emptying her dirty washing on to the floor. This was a favourite saying of Grandma's.

'She's the cats' mother, all right,' said Mum. 'Twenty cats, by the sound of it. Poor soul.'

Chapter Seventeen

At the vicarage, pipes burst into life at odd times of the day and night, floorboards creaked when no one was there and sometimes someone seemed to brush by you, leaving a slight unsettling of air in their wake. I thought all big houses must be the same. If we ever heard a strange noise, it was always 'just the pipes', according to Mum. All sorts of things set them off – hot days, cold days, windy days, parties, returning home from holidays.

The attic still had that slightly creepy atmosphere that Sarah and I had felt on our first visit to the house. There was a feeling of being sealed off from the rest of the building when you stepped inside, and there were shadows on the walls that didn't seem to match what was in the room.

Yet on the nights when we had visitors, and Sarah and I had to vacate our bedrooms and move up there, the attic became cosy under the yellow light bulb and all day long the sight of our sleeping bags laid out on the mattress made us long for bedtime. The sleeping bags were a reminder of holidays, for they had been purchased specially for staying in Aunty Barbie's cottage on the dunes.

We were up there tonight because Aunty Pat, Uncle Ian and their sons, Iain and Alastair, were staying for a few days. Visits from Aunty Pat meant lots of reminiscing between her and Mum about their nursing days in Newcastle, London and America and lots of shared jokes and laughter, but also days out, Mum trying new recipes and special treats.

We had smuggled a bowl of Sugar Stars up with us, a breakfast cereal we were only allowed in the holidays. Sugar Stars were crisp and sugary, as nice as sweets. We hid the dish when we heard Mum coming up the stairs to say goodnight.

'Uh-oh,' she said almost as soon as she walked in, and I thought she must have seen them somehow. But she had noticed something else. 'Why are you doing that?'

Sarah was scratching her head. In fact, now I thought about it, I realized she'd been doing it all day.

'Let's have a look.'

Mum was expert at finding nits. She had found them in other people's hair, but she was adamant that she would never find them in ours. She could have got a job as the school nurse, who lined us all up in the hall looking for 'dickies', as the girls called them. Anyone who was harbouring the offending visitors was singled out and made to form a new line, then given a letter to take home to her parents. Nits were one of Mum's biggest fears about living in Ashington. I'm sure we could have caught them anywhere, but as most of our friends were yet to have indoor bathrooms, she probably reasoned that it would be harder to eradicate them – and keep them away. Mum had bought a shampoo that promised to render our heads unattractive to head lice with regular use. Hairwash night was a military operation in our household, with Sergeant Major Gwenda rubbing the shampoo into our scalps with the vigour she used when she was kneading dough. It smelt strong enough to disinfect public toilets. I longed to start using my apple shampoo – if Jackie had left any of it – but that was only allowed when I went swimming.

'I don't believe it,' Mum said as she foraged. 'I just don't believe it.' She tilted Sarah's chin and looked into her eyes. 'After all that palaver, as well as expense. Your head's full of them. Let's take a look at your sister.'

It was my turn to have my hair divided into clumps and my scalp peered at. Mum couldn't see anything at first, but when she started lifting the hair from behind my ears, she wasn't so sure. 'Hmm, think that might be one there. Oh yes, definitely one or two. Well, that's this evening taken care of. Good job Aunty Pat's here to help. I just hope you haven't passed them on to the little ones and to everyone else. Heaven forbid that Iain and Alastair go home with them!'

The little ones were asleep, and would have to be checked in the morning. Sarah and I sat at the feet of Mum and Aunty Pat in the sitting room as they went through our wet hair with toothcombs, a basin of water between them. I loved having my hair combed, and it felt even nicer with the toothcomb. I could have happily sat there all night.

'My worst nightmare,' Mum kept saying. 'And I pay a fortune for that shampoo.'

'You'll have to write and tell the manufacturers,' said Aunty

Pat. 'But are you sure they don't just say that it *helps* to fight nits? I can't believe they would actually guarantee it.'

'No, really, they do.' She went to fetch the bottle from the bathroom to prove it. 'You see? *Clinically proven to prevent nits and head lice with regular use.*'

'Well, that deserves a letter,' said Aunty Pat.

'I'll be writing, no fear,' said Mum.

'How many dickies have I got?' Sarah asked Mum.

'How many what? Oh, Sarah, where did you get that word from?'

Aunty Pat was laughing.

'Aye, the dickie nurse comes every term,' said Sarah, and Mum and Aunty Pat collapsed into helpless giggles for a few minutes and had to stop combing.

When they had resumed their work, Aunty Pat said that she certainly hadn't expected to find herself visiting Mum in Ashington. She told me and Sarah that during the war she had been evacuated from Wallsend, in the east end of Newcastle, to the mining village of Ellington, staying with a woman she was told to call Aunty. Every Saturday they used to catch the bus to Ashington to visit the lady's aunt, and the aunt always cooked rabbit pie for them. Sarah and I pulled faces and wondered how anyone could eat rabbit.

Aunty Pat said, 'I was a bit suspicious, too, as I'd never had rabbit before, but it was quite tasty. I think the miners went out and shot them to eke out the meat ration. And they had the most marvellous allotments.'

Dad and Uncle Ian came in from the garden, where it was starting to get dark. Dad fetched liqueurs for the adults. We were going to the beach the next day. My mind wandered back to our holidays. Papa had joined us in the sea one afternoon – we were always impatient to get in, but had to wait an hour for our dinner to go down before we were allowed to – and a wave had knocked him over. Whenever he tried to get up, another wave had done the same. We had all been laughing too much to help him.

'Do you remember that little man we shared our packet of soup with on the Alaska Highway?' Aunty Pat said suddenly. 'You should have seen him, girls! I thought about him today, Gwenda, when you had the gravedigger and your gardener friend in for lunch.'

'Looking for gold, wasn't he?'

'Uranium rings a bell with me. But I couldn't believe you invited him to eat with us! There was barely enough for us, never mind one extra!'

'He was half starved!'

'So were we! Well, it was all good training for demonstrating your Christian charity. Your gravedigger looked quite at home with you all.'

'Oh, Alan's like one of the family.'

'He seems a nice chap. Mind, I don't know how you put up with the doorbell going all the time. And all those people in and out.'

'We even had someone staying with us,' I piped up. I hoped Mum might start telling Aunty Pat about Jackie and I might find out what had happened to her, but it didn't work.

'Life's never dull, that's for sure. When did you last see Molly?'

Mum and Aunty Pat combed and recombed our long hair as they talked.

'Yuck, I swear this one was playing dead and now it's moving. Don't they just turn your stomach?'

'We were on the Kyle of Lochalsh,' Uncle Ian was saying to Dad in his rich Scottish accent that made every word sound exotic. 'We did a lovely walk from ...'

'Some of the girls' friends are the fussiest eaters,' Mum was saying now. 'Kathryn seems to exist on meat buns.'

'Meat buns? What are they?' laughed Aunty Pat.

'I'll tell her, I'll tell her, she's my friend!' I cried, and explained that Kathryn's favourite food was a white bread roll, split in two, with a slice of ham on each half.

'Not a sandwich,' added Mum. 'And not on my brown bread. I had to send her home for her tea as there was nothing she would eat.'

She gave my hair a yank. 'Right, missus, you're done.'

'Are you sure?' I asked, and added hopefully, 'I'm starting to feel all itchy.'

'Nice try, now get to bed.'

The next day we went to Druridge Bay. Even Mum and Aunty Pat put their costumes on, though they didn't go in the water other than to wet their toes. We played French cricket and jumped over the waves. Another large group arrived on the beach as we were eating and set out their things about fifty yards away from us. The adults wore dark clothing, and even the children had an old-fashioned look about them and kept their clothes on when they went into the water. The men and the boys wore little caps on their heads. Dad said they were Orthodox Jews. They seemed to be having as good a time as we were, even though they didn't get undressed.

After lunch, Dad and Uncle Ian went for a long walk down the beach and when they came back, Dad said he had greeted some parishioners walking their dog, but that they had looked at him blankly and just nodded.

'Probably didn't recognize you without your dog collar on,' said Mum. 'You'll have to wear it next time.' She and Aunty Pat laughed at the thought of him in his swimming trunks and dog collar.

'I don't suppose Canon Morton ever paraded around in his trunks,' she added.

That night, Mum washed our hair again and she and Aunty Pat combed it through. The comb came out clean every time. I knew it was a stigma to have dickies, but it would have been nice for this special treatment to have lasted a while longer. I wondered if Jackie would have helped with the combing if she had still been with us. She would have either performed the job with great ceremony, I thought, or pulled a face and refused point blank.

Both my grandmothers liked to brush my hair when I stayed overnight with them. 'One hundred brush strokes,' they both insisted. No one but they had time to do that.

We weren't really supposed to play in the attic when we had our own bedrooms plus a playroom and a big garden, but it wasn't exactly forbidden, either. When Krishna and Nicola came round the next morning when their mother was at work and Aunty Pat and Uncle Ian had gone to visit some relatives, we took them up there. Pushed up against one wall were two trunks, the sort I imagined the children in my books took to boarding school with them. I expected them to be locked, but they both opened easily. One was full of clothes that looked as if they might have belonged to our grandmothers – things made of fur and tweed. But there was also a pair of embroidered blue silky pyjamas and some summery skirts and blouses. We tried them on, holding the skirts in place with wide plastic belts and scarves. The other trunk was filled mainly with packages of letters and postcards, tatty-looking brochures and guidebooks, some with names we recognized from Mum's American travels. We opened a bulging brown envelope and saw that it was full of tiny little matchbooks, most of them bearing the name of a restaurant or hotel. *The Summit Café, Alaska Highway Mile 392. The Goofy Gal. Hotel Moana, Honolulu.* Was there ever a word as exotic as Honolulu? I didn't think so. The Alaska Highway may not have sounded exotic, but it too seemed to promise endless adventures. Perhaps it was the word 'highway', so much more evocative than 'road' or 'motorway'. These names gave me a funny feeling inside. I wished I was eighteen and old enough to leave home and visit these places for myself.

I picked up one of the packages of letters and saw that the top one was addressed to my grandparents – Mum's mum and dad – in Ponteland. A quick flick through revealed that they all were. I knew it wasn't right to read other people's letters, so I put them down again. Besides, they didn't look very interesting.

In the same trunk as the letters was a faded cowboy hat. Nicola put it on but it was too big for her. It fitted Sarah better.

'Bob Jones would have liked that,' said Krishna, admiringly. She carefully opened out a string of miniature postcards that were attached to each other. 'These are pretty ... the Grand Canyon and Arizona.'

'What do you think this is?' I picked up a bottle that was standing in the corner of the trunk. Inside it, something black and squiggly floated in a dark liquid.

'It's a snake!' cried Sarah.

Nicola screeched.

'It's not,' I said.

'Well, what is it then?'

None of us knew. In fact, it looked more like a snake than anything else. We had heard Mum's stories of bears, of hearing coyotes in the night, of chipmunks who came up close to eat their crumbs, but I didn't remember any encounters with snakes. Yet there must have been snakes too, surely.

'Perhaps one attacked her and she fought it off, then had it pickled in a jar to show everyone,' said Krishna. 'I wouldn't put it past your mum.'

She had a point. It wouldn't be the strangest story, if it were true.

'I wonder why she hasn't told us about it before,' I said. 'Perhaps we should try and get it out of her, but not tell her what we've found. I'll put it back for now.'

Downstairs, Aunty Pat and her family had returned. 'Let's go and see what they think of our outfits,' said Sarah, tucking the strap of the hat under her chin. 'Last one down stinks!'

Aunty Pat and Mum were in the kitchen. Iain and Alastair had gone outside to find Ruth and Mark, who were riding their bikes round the tennis court.

'You look like hippies,' said Aunty Pat as we wandered in, our skirts trailing the floor. 'Oh, is that your original hat, Gwenda? Trust you to have it still!'

'Well, haven't you got yours?' asked Mum, pretending to be shocked.

'Somewhere, no doubt. Unless I chucked it out.'

'I could never get rid of it,' said Mum. 'Have you seen the

bullet hole, girls?' She removed the hat from Sarah's head and pointed to a hole close to the brim that we hadn't noticed before.

'You were shot at?' asked Krishna.

Mum and Aunty Pat laughed. 'He did have us all at gunpoint later that night. But this was earlier in the evening.'

'When he was sober,' said Aunty Pat. 'Well, soberish.'

'He decided to show us what a good shot he was and put a bullet through each of our hats. We all had one. Molly's was red – she liked to be different. We really looked the part with these, didn't we?'

'Didn't we just,' said Aunty Pat.

Mum put the hat on her own head. 'Howdy, y'all,' she said.

We looked at her, incredulous. For once, Sarah and I were as impressed as Krishna and Nicola. To think of Mum, Aunty Pat and the other three standing in a line wearing their cowboy hats and trusting someone enough to fire a bullet at their heads!

We were so smitten by this story that by the time Mum asked us to set the table for dinner, we had forgotten all about the snake.

Chapter Eighteen

Towards the end of the holidays, Sarah and I went to stay at Other Grandma's (as we usually called Dad's mum when we were talking about her, to distinguish her from Mum's mum). In some ways, this was the biggest treat of all because Grandma spoilt us terribly, fed us things we wouldn't have been given by Mum – oranges stuffed with sugar lumps, glasses of Lucozade – and allowed us to do things we wouldn't have been allowed to do at home, like go out on the streets with our scooters. Our scooters were presents from Grandma and stayed at her house. As we had had them since we were quite small, Sarah's had three wheels but mine was a bright blue two-wheeler with curved handlebars and a brake on the back. Whitley Bay, where Grandma and Grandpa lived and where Dad was brought up, was our main seaside town and resort, and while not as busy as it had been in its heyday, it still felt like a holiday town, especially

down by the seafront with its ice-cream sellers and amusement
arcades and the Spanish City funfair with its whitewashed walls
and Moorish-style dome. As long as we kept popping back to
Grandma's, and waved at her through the kitchen window, she
was happy for us to go where we pleased.

In the afternoon, if it wasn't a work day – for Grandpa was
still running R. A. Gofton & Sons, his building company – we
might go out for a run in the car. When we were small we took
it in turns to sit on the armrest. One of our favourite trips was
to the fish quay at North Shields where, if we were lucky, the
ice-cream van was parked. But even if it wasn't, Grandpa always
had a tin of Black Bullets in the glove compartment, and
Grandma and Grandpa didn't know or care about fillings or
about sweets spoiling your appetite.

When it was raining, and in the evening before the television
was switched on, we listened to music from Grandma and
Grandpa's cassette collection. Our parents loved music, too –
classical composers, musicals, James Last and his orchestra,
Tijuana Brass – but it was at Grandma's that I fell in love with
some of the great male vocalists: Perry Como, Nat King Cole,
Frank Sinatra and the French singer Gilbert Becaud, in whose
voice you could hear smiles and laughter. Their songs seemed to
contain the promise and wonder of adulthood. Listening to
them, I felt, as I so often did, an impatience to grow up and discover this world for myself. And in Grandma's home, with its
thick carpets, velvet settee and twinkly lights on the sitting-room
ceiling, that world felt closer than it did anywhere else. I imagined living here with Gary Hunt, one of the servers at church,
who sometimes blew his long fringe from his forehead when he
sat listening to the sermon.

Uncle Peter, Dad's younger brother, had his own flat, but once he had lived with Grandma and Grandpa in a secret room in the roof which could only be reached by pulling down a retractable staircase. The room, though almost empty now, contained a few fascinating items that had belonged to him, and it was a treat to be allowed up by Grandma just to have a peek. Some pictures he had left behind were stacked up against the wall beside a strangely shaped guitar. On a shelf were ornaments that looked as if they came from foreign countries, including tiny dolls in colourful costumes. Peter and Grandma and Grandpa went on holidays abroad and brought us similar dolls on their return. In a built-in cupboard were shelves full of hard-back children's books that I was allowed to read while I was staying. How funny to think that when he was a boy, Uncle Peter had read some of the authors I liked! That was where I first read Enid Blyton's Adventure series. They were hardbacks with dust jackets, and it felt like a privilege just to open them and see Uncle Peter's name printed neatly inside.

Uncle Peter was so different from Dad it was hard to believe they were brothers. He was seven years younger and unmarried. All Sarah and I wanted was for him to find a nice wife, partly so that we could be bridesmaids at his wedding, and also so that we could have another aunty. We only had one aunt, Aunty Marina, the wife of Mum's brother, Doug, and she lived Down South. My friends in Ashington had aunts who lived next door or up the road or in Blyth or Newbiggin. Luckily, Uncle Peter was funny and flamboyant enough to make up for his deficiency. He came to Grandma's every day for his dinner – Grandpa picked him up at one o'clock from the fancy-goods store he owned – and ran him back an hour later. He might come by at other times, but he was always in a rush and either Grandpa or a taxi would be summoned to whisk him home or to some social engagement. But in the few moments that we had him to ourselves, we followed him around and crept up behind him and made him laugh with our newly cultivated Geordie accents.

'Uncle Peter, Uncle Peter, when are you getting married?' we cried if we felt he was in the right mood, but he simply turned round and tickled us until we had to beg him to stop.

'Ciao!' he called out when he arrived. 'So long!' when he left. Grandpa often called him Pedro, perhaps because they had been on lots of Spanish holidays together. He was the most exotic person we knew.

He had a quick, jaunty walk and a habit of rhythmically stroking the underside of his chin. We watched him doing it at the kitchen table and copied him. When he saw us, he just laughed.

As Peter had suffered badly from asthma as a child, he had missed many months of school and spent more time with his parents than Dad had. During that time he had read every book in the house, including all of Dad's, so he knew something about everything. He was also an accomplished pianist and a good dancer. Sometimes he whisked Grandma around the kitchen floor when he arrived; she would pretend to be annoyed with him for dragging her away from her pans, but you could tell she was secretly pleased.

Grandma and Grandpa didn't go to church, so we had Sunday off. They were even slightly suspicious about church-goers in the way some non-church people are, and wary of people they felt were 'a bit too religious'. So how had Dad come from this family to be the person he was?

Dad had attended Sunday school as a boy and he and Grandma had been confirmed together when he was eleven years old, perhaps encouraged by the local vicar, Father Jackson, who was a good friend of Grandpa. Grandma had rarely been inside a church after that, but if it was the end of something for her, it was the start of something for Dad. The church became more and more important in his life, and St Peter's – which Grandpa had built in 1938 – was full of people he liked, people to drink and socialize and chase girls with as well as worship with. When Norman Taylor, the young man who had led his Bible class, left to become a priest, it was a revelation to Dad that someone as down to earth as Norman would make that choice. By the time he left home at eighteen to do his National Service, his faith was so deep that whenever he moved to a new camp, one of the first things he would do was find the local church.

I'm sure Grandpa would have liked Dad to go into the family firm. He had founded the business with his father and brother, Liddle, and though it had stagnated during the war, it was booming again, thanks mainly to the long hours he put into it. But he and Grandma supported Dad when, after the Army, he went to university to study modern history, and asked no questions when several years later, after four years as a history master at Cannock Grammar School in Staffordshire, he decided to be ordained.

Peter may well have wanted to go to university, too, but whether he had the opportunity, I don't know. He was certainly as clever as Dad. The brothers had both gone to Tynemouth School, which was owned by its headmaster, a man who liked to remind his pupils what a superior establishment they were attending. Although Grandma and Grandpa believed in the value of a good education – having left school at fourteen themselves – the reason for their choosing the fee-paying Tynemouth was more prosaic. The family had gone to live in Allendale in the South-West corner of Northumberland soon after the start of the war, as Grandpa had built several houses there and kept one for the family. But when his sisters and their families also decamped to the country, Grandma decided she would rather come home and risk the bombs than be cooped up under the same roof as them all. In Whitley Bay in early 1941, most of the local schools had been evacuated, but Tynemouth had stayed open thanks to its having cellars which could be used as air-raid shelters.

So Grandma's sons received the education she felt she had been denied. She was chatty and charming and good company – our friends all loved her too as she was kind and generous, and any who happened to be present when she was visiting would receive the same treats as we did – but she felt insecure in certain social situations and could be sharp-tongued.

She had gone into service after leaving her home in Prudhoe in the Tyne Valley where she was the youngest child of a miner. They had moved to Prudhoe from Gateshead on account of her sister Anne's weak chest when Grandma, whose name was Margaret, was a very young girl. Her father was at work when his wife and children took the train to Wylam, the nearest station, along with all their furniture. At their destination the boys loaded their belongings on to a handcart and went ahead. Little Margaret, her mother and older sisters began the walk to their new home a few miles away. Kitty, the eldest of the girls and like a second mother to Margaret, carried her when she got too weary.

They were all tired, and relieved when they reached their new home. The boys had already arrived and were unpacking their furniture. But their mother froze when she saw the house, and shouted at her sons to stop. 'We're not living in this place, it's little better than a stable!' she cried. It consisted of just two rooms, with a ladder leading to the upper floor. The boys tried to reason with her, but she was adamant. They had not left their respectable home in Gateshead to live in this hovel. She sent the boys to the colliery to fetch their father from work.

It seemed like ages before they reappeared with a colliery official. The man was sympathetic, but he said there was nothing he could do at present. He promised my distressed great-grandmother that a bigger house would be found for the family as soon as possible. It was getting late now, and the two youngest girls had fallen asleep out there in the open on top of one of their bundles of belongings. There was no other option but to carry on with their unpacking and move in.

They did get their new house eventually, but Grandma's mother never felt that she belonged in Prudhoe and was considered a 'townie' by the locals.

Grandma had met Grandpa when she was working for a doctor and his family in Whitley Bay. Now she lived in a beautiful Dutch bungalow that Grandpa's firm had built and that was the envy of many in Whitley Bay. Grandma's life since her marriage had been spent looking after Grandpa and her sons, and as Grandpa had been so preoccupied with the business, she had brought up Dad and Peter almost single-handedly. She was a proud housewife, and produced a roast dinner every lunchtime (including the best roast chicken and bread sauce anywhere) and ham or tongue salad for tea. When Sarah and I were looking for her we would usually find her in the kitchen, singing along to the radio as she worked – she liked the cheeriness of Tony Blackburn and knew more about modern music than Mum and Dad. Or, occasionally, with her feet up, reading a book. Music and books were her escape.

Sometimes a friend of hers would pop round to see us, the granddaughters, and she and Grandma would smoke a cigarette from her silver cigarette box after we had said our hellos and answered any questions. Or we might be taken to the local shops to be introduced to the people she knew there. We weren't sure why we were so interesting, but I think now that people like her and her friends simply loved children and liked to be in touch with modern childhood, which must have been so different from their own.

Our maternal grandma sometimes told us what we would need to do if we were ever to find a young man – this mainly involved not biting our nails and looking after our cuticles – but Other Grandma thought we were already perfect. While I was at her house, I had no doubt that the men who sang those romantic songs were singing them just to me.

I returned to Ashington with Perry Como singing 'Snow Bird' in my head, and visions of handsome men sweeping me away with them across the snowy meadow.

Chapter Nineteen

That summer, we seemed to spend most of our time in the garden. When Krishna and Nicola were with us, or when school-friends came to play, we constructed circuits on the lawn. We might have to run a figure of eight round the rosebeds, touch the top rung on the climbing frame, crawl under the swing, do a hop, skip and a jump taking off from a line marked out with a skipping rope, then finish by touching the post – possibly from some ancient washing line – in the corner of the tennis court. On hot days we filled the paddling pool, the cold water becoming warm and grassy as the afternoon wore on. When there were a few of us we played 'What time is it, Mr Wolf?' using the whole length of the tennis court, trying not to give ourselves away as we stepped closer and closer to the wolf.

I spent ages practising my cartwheels. I longed to turn a perfect cartwheel, but I knew, even as my legs sliced through the air, that I did not look as graceful as my friend Joanna, whose compact body could whizz across the lawn doing one after the other, like a proper gymnast. Other times, Sarah, Joanna and I tied a rope between the swing and the climbing frame and practised high jumps with the scissor kick we had learnt at school.

With Krishna and Nicola, Sarah and I had formed a society called The Secret Four and kept a selection of mysterious possessions in a Ross's ice-cream tin, as if that alone might cause exciting things to happen to us. Sarah and Nicola had made each of us a badge with our name on it which we had to wear to our meetings. Ruth wanted to join too, but we said she was too young. In the end, we made her a badge just to keep her quiet and sometimes let her sit in the room with us, if she promised not to tell Mark, while we discussed whether to put on a circus act or a play. In the tin were some coloured stones we had collected from the gravel on the edge of the tennis court, topped up with the odd one that Sarah and I pinched from the fancy graves – shiny green or white crystals that we were sure must be valuable – along with a book on how to be a spy, an empty Jif lemon that we used as a water pistol and an old pair of Mum's sunglasses that we thought would make a good disguise. We passed messages down to each other from Sarah's bedroom window, she and Nicola always one team, me and Krishna the other. They might kidnap one of my dolls and hold her to ransom, and the note would tell us what we had to do to win her back – a silly dare, or find a four-leaf clover, or make up a rude limerick about someone. But most of the fun was in them dangling the message down in a tin and us retrieving it.

*

Kathryn and I continued to swap our Enid Blyton books, and wish we had mysteries to solve like The Famous Five and The Secret Seven. Mum had enrolled me in the Puffin Club and was trying to steer me towards some new authors, telling me I was getting too old for Enid Blyton, but I wasn't ready to give her up quite yet. The children who lived on Willow Farm rode to school on donkeys and knew a wild man called Tammylan who lived in the hills and could be relied on to come to their aid when they needed him. Kathryn and I longed to find a Tammylan of our own. One morning we tailed an untidy young man in the churchyard whose long hair and sideboards gave him a friendless appearance. He went from grave to grave, throwing away dying flowers from one, weeding at another. When he sat down, took a swig from a bottle in his knapsack and made a cigarette out of a piece of paper, we were convinced we had found our man.

'He probably filled his bottle in the river,' whispered Kathryn as we hid behind a tall gravestone at a safe distance. 'You see, he can't even afford to buy proper tabs.' We decided that his family were all dead – his father and brothers killed in the mine, his mother dying of grief a few weeks later – and he was now living rough on the banks of the Wansbeck. If we could find his camp, we could leave him food. We would start with the odd sweet, but if we were crafty enough we could smuggle some of our meals into a napkin on our laps (children in Enid Blyton stories were always doing this) and leave him something more substantial. When he found out it was us he would be eternally grateful and always come to us when we needed him.

After he had put his bottle back in his knapsack, our wild man sauntered off to see Rip. Tammylan had a special way with animals, and had healed a sick horse belonging to the children's father when no one else knew what to do. And now it looked as if our own wild man might have the same gift! He stood there for a while, stroking the pony's nose and feeding him Polo mints. When he half turned and we thought he might have seen us, we decided it was best to walk purposefully past him, talking as nonchalantly as we could manage.

As we came almost level with him, he caught sight of us. 'Eeh, hello, bonny lass,' he said to Kathryn. 'Yer mam and dad all reet?' She muttered something in reply.

When we were far enough away, I looked at her for an explanation.

'I didn't recognize him,' she said, shrugging. 'His dad works with my dad in the butcher's.'

So that was the end of that. He was probably going home for his dinner just like we were.

Some afternoons we packed the Morris Traveller with bats and balls, rugs and the windbreak, Mum made squash and filled a flask with hot dogs and we went to Druridge Bay for a picnic tea. The car popped and banged down the grassy lanes leaving a fine trail of blue smoke behind us. Birds leapt ahead of us along the tangly hedgerows as if they were showing us the way. The air that blew through the open windows began to smell of the sea.

'What a lovely afternoon,' Mum would say as we cut through the marram grass and the wind picked up. It was always colder and breezier on the beach. I didn't know if she was trying to convince herself or us.

On days when we could see the sea fret hovering at the top

of the hill, we would change direction and go to Grandma's instead. 'The sun's always shining in Ponteland,' was Grandma's favourite saying, and it usually was. Her sheltered back garden was hot and sunny, and Papa would sprinkle us with the garden hose.

On one of those afternoons, Sarah and I went inside for a drink and found Mum and Grandma in the kitchen doubled over with laughter.

'You've got to tell,' I protested when Mum wiped her eyes and said it wasn't for our ears.

'We'll not say anything. Cross our hearts,' said Sarah.

'Brownie's honour,' we both said at the same time, putting our right hands into the three-fingered salute.

Mum relented, slightly reluctantly. She told us that one morning when Aunty Pat was staying and we had all been playing in the garden, Aunty June had come to help with the cleaning as usual. Uncle Ian was in the downstairs loo, 'No doubt hoping for some peace and quiet,' said Mum. (I wasn't really sure why peace and quiet should matter, but had gathered by now that some men did seem to shut themselves away for an awfully long time during this activity.) He heard Aunty June open the door to the cloakroom and push her mop over the floor, and hoped she would realize the toilet was occupied and go away quickly, especially after she tried the handle of the lavatory door and found that it didn't open. Instead, not even considering that it might be locked, she tried it again, more forcefully this time. Aunty June was as strong as an ox – Mum was always telling us that – and the lock was no match for her strength. The door flew open, the lock fell to the floor and one of the screws that had been holding it in place landed in Uncle Ian's hand. Aunty June didn't say a word. She closed the door almost as quickly as she had opened it, picked up her bucket, shut the cloakroom door and went away. It was Uncle Ian who related the story to Mum and Aunty Pat, and who mended the lock after she had gone, along with the other jobs Mum had given him during his stay.

'I thought about holding on to the handle after her first attempt,' he had said, 'but she did it with such force I think I would have gone flying off the seat if I had.'

'Did Aunty June tell you about it later?' I asked, when we had stopped laughing.

Mum shook her head. She hadn't said a word.

'But why can't we say anything?'

Mum said we all knew that Aunty June had a good sense of humour, but if she wanted to keep it to herself, then that was her business. She turned serious. 'People have a habit of surprising you sometimes,' she said. 'You have to learn to respect that. It's unkind to embarrass someone.'

Just before it was time to go back to school, we had another guest, one whose summer visits would become a part of our lives for many years to come.

Margaret Falconer was a friend of Mum and Aunty Pat's from America. She came from a suburb of Glasgow originally, and sometimes still sounded Scottish, though she also sounded very American when she called us 'honey'. She had gone to work as a domestic in America when she was a young woman, eventually becoming housekeeper for a wealthy American family in Cleveland, Ohio. Margaret had been Aunty Pat's patient in Mount Sinai Hospital and had befriended her and Mum, inviting them to visit her at home in one of the nicest suburbs of

Cleveland whenever she had the house to herself, which seemed to happen quite frequently. She enjoyed spoiling the young nurses – she must have been getting close to fifty by then, so was nearer in age to their parents than to them – and used to feed them delicious meals. As most of Mum and Aunty Pat's money went on maintaining their car and travelling, slap-up meals were a luxury they could seldom afford. Aunty Margaret liked seeing their faces as she put giant steaks, potato salad and buttered corn on the cob on the table. They were also grateful recipients of items that Margaret's employers, the Waldman family, were throwing out – their cast-off curtains, lampshades, bits of crockery and old Christmas decorations all found their way to the pair's Cleveland apartment. They never left Margaret's home empty-handed, and she never arrived at theirs without bearing gifts.

Now Aunty Margaret lived in New York City, having moved in with Ronnie, one of the boys she had helped to bring up, and his wife Lee, to look after them and their two daughters. Elizabeth was a few years older than me, and Margot somewhere between me and Sarah.

In her neat dresses and cardigans, proud demeanour and slightly sharp manner, Aunty Margaret brought with her an air of wealth and privilege from the Upper West Side she inhabited, though I'm sure her own background must have been a more humble one. Not surprisingly, she arrived at our house laden with gifts, including clothes for me and Sarah that Elizabeth and Margot had either grown out of or no longer wanted.

'Look at the label in this!' Mum marvelled, as Aunty Margaret presided over the pile of clothing that had been emptied on to her bed.

Aunty Margaret whistled to herself at the sheer extravagance of it. 'I know for a fact that this cost a small fortune, but would the little madam wear it? *Ffff.*' She gave a little jerk of her head and shoulders in disgust as she picked up a checked dress, not unlike our school summer uniform but made of far more substantial material.

'Saks Fifth Avenue, girls,' said Mum, a breathless note to her voice, and when we asked her what she was talking about she shook her head at Aunty Margaret to absolve herself of our ignorance. 'Girls, that's the best shop in Manhattan! We didn't even dare step inside when we were in New York, we were so scruffy.'

'Only the best is good enough for Ronnie's girls,' said Aunty Margaret with a hint of pride.

'Some of these are as good as new, Margaret,' said Mum, holding up a white tunic with contrasting colours on the pockets. 'Girls, you are so lucky.'

Grandma made a lot of our clothes, so it was indeed a luxury to have so many new things to choose from. I was still pining for some shop-bought hotpants, but knew that battle was lost. At least, after much pleading, I now owned a pair of brand new Dr Scholl's, as did several of my friends. I thought I was the bee's knees as I clomped around in them. The clothes in front of me now were different from the clothes anyone we knew dressed in. There were also two sailor tops with embroidered boats on the pockets, a white linen jacket with a strawberry pattern, a yellow shift dress and two funny pairs of trousers with a bold, brightly coloured design.

'These trousers are too short,' I said, holding them up to my waist.

'Get away with you, they're Bermudas,' said Mum. 'They're

shorts, not trousers.' When neither Sarah nor I looked convinced, she added, 'They're supposed to be that length.'

Sarah refused to try them on. Mum said everyone knew that
Bermudas were the in-thing this summer. Not in Ashington,
they weren't. A battle raged for the rest of Aunty Margaret's stay
as Mum tried to get me and Sarah to wear them: 'Just once, to
please Aunty Margaret.'

Aunty Margaret brought us books as well – a chunky hardback
called *Mystery Stories for Girls*, with a female sleuth on the cover,
and several paperbacks, some of which had won a prize called
the Newbery Award. I spent a sunny afternoon under the
mountain ash tree reading *Roller Skates*, about a young New
Yorker called Lucinda left in the charge of two elderly school-
teachers for a whole year while her parents holidayed in Italy.
Children in books were so lucky to have parents who were so
careless over their welfare. I couldn't really imagine Mum and
Dad sailing off somewhere and leaving the four of us with
Grandma or Aunty June, even for a month, though I quite liked
the idea of it. I imagined becoming best friends with Margot
and skating the streets of New York City with her, befriending
the people we came across, just like Lucinda did, so that our
day-to-day lives became an adventure.

I lent it to Kathryn as soon as I had finished it. She looked
less than impressed when she read the title and saw the old-
fashioned picture on the cover. I managed to change her mind
by telling her that there was a murder in it. She took the book
home and read it overnight, and we decided the next day that
New York was really the place to be.

*

Mum took Aunty Margaret on days out, but she seemed equally happy to sit and read in her favourite seat in the sitting room by the window. She didn't say much. She clucked at Ruth and Mark whenever they burst into the room, smiled benignly at me and Sarah and would ask us the odd question or tell us something about Margot and Elizabeth, then went back to her reading. At regular intervals she pulled her cardigan closer around her and let out a long shiver. 'Brrrr!' she would say, before picking up her book again. Whenever she got up to leave the room, or sat down for a meal, or anyone asked her how she was, she would first of all give that trademark shiver. 'Brrrr!' Mum told Dad he should put the heating on, just to take the chill off the place in the evenings. Dad said there was no way he was putting the heating on in August.

'She's not used to these temperatures,' pleaded Mum.

'Get away with you, she comes from Scotland,' he replied.

Sometimes a visitor to the house would ask her about herself, and she would become more talkative and tell them about the Upper West Side apartment where she was treated like one of the family, had her own bathroom and ruled the roost in the kitchen. How she walked several blocks every day as she shopped for groceries – steak one day, salmon the next – took her coffee in such-and-such a coffee shop and always had brunch at the diner opposite the apartment on a Sunday, which was her day off. She told them about New York winters ('Brrrr!') and the thick, exhausting heat of summer.

She went to stay with Aunty Pat in Edinburgh for a week and we met her at the station on her return. 'Brrrr!' she said as she got off the train. 'It's sure turned cold since I left.'

*

One day, Aunty Margaret answered the door while Mum was busy upstairs and came face to face with Mrs Russell. Mrs Russell had been a regular caller ever since her appearance that first day. I had been rather afraid of her back then, with her abrupt manner and superior air, but felt a sort of respect for her now, having called round on an errand for Mum one evening and seen the white L-shaped leather settee in her living room. I couldn't believe such a piece of furniture existed – a chair that went round a corner! I thought it was the most luxurious thing ever, more special even than the velvet sofa at Other Grandma's that I liked to stroke, one way then the other, and watch the colour change. Nobody had been sitting on it. Ernie was in his favourite armchair by the fire, and Mrs Russell's cardigan was laid out over another armchair. The settee was big enough for all of our family to sit on quite comfortably and still have room to spare. I couldn't help thinking that it would be more useful in our house than in hers. Of course, Mum had laughed when I told her about it and begged her to buy one. Why anyone wanted a piece of white furniture was beyond her, she said, and how long did I think it would stay white in our house?

I heard Mrs Russell's voice, and then Aunty Margaret say, surprisingly sharply, 'Who do you want to speak to?' with the emphasis on the word 'who'.

'I'd like to see Gwenda,' said Mrs Russell.

'I think you mean Mrs Gofton,' said Aunty Margaret.

I put my head round the playroom door and listened.

'I asked for Gwenda,' said Mrs Russell.

'She's Mrs Gofton to you,' said Aunty Margaret. 'And if you address her properly, I'll call her for you.'

Thankfully Mum came downstairs at that moment.

'Oh, thank you, Margaret. I see you've met Mrs Russell. She lives in the nice house at the top of the road.' I was sure she gave Aunty Margaret a little wink when she said that.

'The big house with the Venetian blinds,' said Mrs Russell.

'Huh,' said Aunty Margaret, as if she didn't care two hoots about Mrs Russell's blinds. She went back to the sitting room and her book while Mum saw to her visitor. I had no idea why she took exception to Mrs Russell's familiarity. Perhaps she felt that in Mum's role as a vicar's wife, only certain people earned the right to call her Gwenda, though as Mrs Russell was much older than Mum, Mum certainly would not have objected. However, most of Dad's parishioners at that time did use formal terms of address. Dad was Father Gofton to almost everyone, Mum was Mrs Gofton. The familiarity with which people address their clergy today was a long way off, especially in places like Ashington.

I don't believe Aunty Margaret took against anyone else. She liked my grandparents, she admired the way Aunty June threw herself with such vigour into whatever she did, she enjoyed her little chats with the miners and miners' wives she met while she was staying with us. But even years later, long after we had left Ashington, she still referred to Mrs Russell as 'that woman'.

Chapter Twenty

I was in Mrs Pickering's class now. Mrs Pickering was young compared to some of the other teachers in the school, good fun and fierce-tempered. I was sure that she wouldn't have disbelieved me about Dad teaching 'Cushie Butterfield' to Bob and Mary Ann, like Miss Stewart had done. I felt sure she would have tipped back her head and laughed and wanted to know more. While some of the other teachers seemed to discourage the individual quirks of their pupils, she took pleasure in them. At least, she did when she was in the right mood. Girls who could do the splits or bend their fingers all the way back were allowed to show the rest of the class; Karen Critchley was asked to do her Doris Day impression for another teacher who popped into the classroom during one of our light-hearted interludes. She confessed to us her infatuation with the singer Cat Stevens and we competitively scoured our comics and magazines for his

picture and presented our cuttings to her, which she pretended
to be delighted with. But she also got angry quickly: her face
would redden, and something that she could laugh over one day
would vex her the next. One day forgetting your homework
would merit the reprimand, 'You'll be shot at dawn!' with an
imaginary gun pointed at our heads, but on another it might
earn the culprit a demerit or even a smack.

The first day of the new school year began as usual with assembly in the hall. Back then in the early 1970s everyone in our school
was white – apart from one Chinese girl whose family had
opened a takeaway on Newbiggin Road a few months earlier –
and almost all were Protestant (there was a Roman Catholic
junior school for those who weren't). I'm sure some children
came from families of little or no faith, but everyone attended
assembly and there we all worshipped God, the same God some
of us worshipped in church every Sunday. Every girl in the
school knew the most popular stories from the Bible and most
of them knew by heart the words of the most popular hymns.

We had a new pianist, Mrs Brown, a plump, smiling lady with
an infectious love of music who played the piano with a vigour
that took us by surprise. We had become used to old Mrs
Simpson, who plodded away so slowly it sounded as if she was
hitting each note with a stick. Now that we were in the third
year, a few of us left our places to help the first-years find the
hymn in their hymn books. The first one was 'For the Beauty of
the Earth', and we were surprised to find that it was actually a
jolly, uplifting hymn and not the dirge it had been with Mrs
Simpson. But old habits died hard, and Elaine let her voice go
deeper and deeper into the chorus so that the last word was
almost a growl. I smiled but I didn't want to laugh and get into

trouble on our first day back, and hoped that Elaine wouldn't either. Elaine wasn't really a naughty girl, just lively and more fearless than the rest of us, the sort of girl who put up her hand to answer a question without caring if the answer was wrong or if people laughed at her. Miss Templey had a soft spot for her at Brownies, where she was always quick to volunteer for any jobs, and Dad liked the way she cried, 'Hello, Father Gofton!' whenever she saw him.

We had a new head now, too, Miss Snowdon, who had been the deputy before. She had a long neck – which looked even longer thanks to the polo-neck sweaters she wore – and when she swivelled her head, which she did frequently, I was reminded of a goose.

We all sat on the floor cross-legged for the address. Miss Snowdon told us a Chinese parable about a man who wanted to know what heaven and hell were like. He was taken to a room where a table was piled high with delicious food, but was surprised to see that the people in the room, who each had a set of three-foot-long chopsticks, were thin and hungry. The chopsticks were simply too long to reach their mouths and so they failed every time they tried to eat. He was shown another room, identical to the one before and with an equally well-stocked table, but in this one the people were happy and well fed. Then he saw why. The people in the second room were looking after each other and feeding their neighbours with the chopsticks, rather than themselves. Miss Snowdon told us we should all help each other and be mindful of each other's needs, and by doing so we, too, would be happy. She led us in a prayer where she thanked God for our friends and neighbours, before we all sang another hymn then recited the Lord's Prayer.

In the classroom Mrs Pickering chose new pencil monitors, PE monitors and blackboard monitors. There was a monitor chosen for each of our four houses – George, Andrew, Patrick and David, after the saints – whose job it was to collect all the merits and demerits at the end of each week for their own house. The demerits were subtracted from the merits and the figure given to the house captains, who gave them to Miss Snowdon, who would later announce the winning house for that week. There was a cup at the end of term for the best house. We were probably more competitive, however, about which house won on sports day. (Sadly, my house, Andrew, was always last.)

Today we had PE. Mrs Pickering gave us exercises to do, one of which was cycling in the air. Sarah and I often did this at home, playing an old record of Mum's called 'Wheels Cha Cha'. We would cycle one way then do it in reverse, quickly and slowly. We had decided that this would be a good opening act for our circus. To our astonishment, Nicola could walk along Krishna's spine, and Krishna even seemed to enjoy it. This spectacle would have to be the main act. After some stretching exercises, we picked teams for dodgeball. Picking teams was one of the hardest things to do. You naturally wanted a good team, with some of the most athletic girls on your side, but you also felt compelled to choose your friends early – after all, a good friend wouldn't leave you standing right until the end like an unclaimed bit of luggage. But suppose your best friend wasn't very sporty (Kathryn wasn't), what did you do then? It was one of life's dilemmas. We had the same problem when we picked teams for games at Brownies. It was better, really, not to be the captain at all.

'Me, me, me!' some of us yelled, sticking our hands high in the air and bouncing up and down. Mrs Pickering told us to stop and stand like soldiers, and we pushed our arms into our sides and stretched up as far as we could, elongating our necks (like mini Miss Snowdons), top lips stretched over the bottom one. One of the Susans slouched sulkily across to one of the Julies, who had chosen her for her team. Susan wanted to be in the other team where her best friend, another Susan, had already been chosen. Mrs Pickering told her she would send her back to the classroom if she didn't stop behaving like that immediately, and she straightened herself up and gave a thin smile.

It was playtime straight after PE, and I was late getting dressed as I had to help tidy up. When I went to my bag to retrieve my new skipping rope – actually a washing line, but perfect for tying to the post on the edge of the tennis court so that only one turner was required – it wasn't there. My face went hot as I wondered what had happened to it. I knew I had brought it to school. Someone must have taken it. Kathryn and I had fallen out a couple of days earlier – I wasn't even sure why, now – and I had a feeling it might be her. When I had whispered something to her in PE, thinking we were friends again, she had scowled and moved away, so I told her she wasn't coming to play any more and that I would have the book back I had lent her, please. We seemed to have quickly forgotten the lessons of Miss Snowdon's assembly.

In the playground, I saw that my suspicions were correct. Kathryn and Angela were turning the rope. Kathryn looked at me, smiling to herself, daring me to say something. Joanna was jumping and some of our other friends were standing to the side, singing and performing the actions along with Joanna. Whose skipping rope did they think it was? I wanted to cry – I knew that some girls would have done – but I was determined not to, especially not in front of other people. I quickly composed myself and decided to act as if I didn't mind at all. I joined in the rhyme, reluctantly at first, then more wholeheartedly:

Not last night but the night before
Twenty-four robbers came knocking at my door
I went out
To let them in
And this is what they said to me:

Spanish lady turn around
Spanish lady touch the ground
Spanish lady do the kicks
Spanish lady do the splits

And as we sang, Joanna performed the actions. She could even do the splits, and she was beaming when she jumped out of the rope at the end. Kathryn and Angela stopped turning.

'We thought you might be late. You didn't mind, did you?' said Kathryn.

A lot depended on what I said next. 'No, man. I was gonna tell you to take it anyway.'

Kathryn nodded across at me. That was it. We both understood we were friends again.

'Can we do "All in together, girls", then I'll turn for a bit,' I said.

'Ah, man! I wanted to have a go at "Spanish lady,"' moaned one of the Susans.

'It's her rope,' said Angela, and she and Kathryn began to turn again, and we all chanted:

All in together, girls
Never mind the weather, girls
When I call your birthday
You must jump in

And we all skipped together – me, Alison, Elaine, Joanna, one of the Susans and two Julies. As we went through the months of the year we each jumped in on our birthday month and stayed in until we had gone through the whole year and started the rhyme again, except that this time we had to jump out on our birthday month.

I was a scraper now, and had hardly been able to wait for dinner-time. Mrs Neal kept a strict watch over us. Sarah had been right about the slop bin; it was disgusting. It had a stewed-vegetable and gravy smell, not really that obnoxious except that it got stronger every time you went back to it and even started to linger in your nostrils. And as the bin got fuller, the sight of globules of mashed potato floating in a sea of everything else could have turned the strongest stomach. But nothing was going to distract me from this task, the most responsible posi-tion I had held in my life and one to which I had aspired since my first day at Hirst South school. I wished that I looked as grown-up as the third-years had looked to me back then. If Mum would let me wear nylons and have a heel on my shoe when I stopped wearing my summer dress and sandals, then there might be some hope.

The fourth-years had the honour of serving the puddings, and one special girl had to serve Miss Snowdon, who was the only member of staff to sit with us in the hall. Today's pudding was chocolate sponge with a pink sauce. I hated it. School puddings were far worse than the dinners, which I usually enjoyed, though at least we didn't have tapioca or semolina today, the worst of all. But as I had heard one girl have her position as a scraper threatened for asking the dinner ladies for only one scoop of potato, I ate my pudding without a murmur.

'You already knew – it's the rules – that you had to be a two-scooper,' Mrs Neal told her sternly. She looked at the lady who had served her, who gave a shrug, and Mrs Neal softened. 'I'll tell you what, pet, if you have two scoops from now on, we'll forget about today. But divvent tell no one else.' She went away muttering to herself that she was too soft with us all.

I swallowed the last spoonful of pink sauce and pretended it tasted of strawberries instead of a weird mixture of bubblegum and cherry. Across the hall, Sarah looked as if she would die if she ate another mouthful.

When we got home after school, Aunty Margaret was reading a Ngaio Marsh mystery in her favourite seat. It had been a hot day and the sun was streaming through the window.

'How was school, honey?' she asked, putting the book down for a second. I told her that I was a scraper now and got to wear my own apron. Aunty Margaret said she would buy me a nice apron when she went into Newcastle with Mum, so that I had a spare one.

Mum was in the kitchen, telling Dad, who had been out all day, that she had received a reply from the manufacturers of the anti-head lice shampoo. 'Listen to this,' she said. 'You'll love it.'

We were concerned to hear that your daughters were found to have head lice after regular treatment with our product. During rigorous tests, the shampoo has been found to make hair unattractive to head lice and to the laying of their eggs (nits). However, it has recently come to our notice that in Durham, Sunderland and other parts of North-East England, the head lice are developing immunity to our product.

She lowered the letter and looked at us. 'Well,' she said, 'what do you think of that? It takes some beating, doesn't it? In case you needed proof that we live in another world up here, you've got it.' And she gave a slightly crazy laugh.

Dad chuckled. 'I always knew we were a brainy lot.' He wagged his finger at me. 'You see, even our head lice are cleverer than they are in the rest of the country. Tell that to your teacher.'

He went back to his study whistling 'The Blaydon Races', then began to sing the chorus in one of his funny voices.

Mum and I laughed.

'Aunty Margaret will be glad to get home,' said Mum.

Chapter Twenty-one

'The swallows'll be gannin' soon,' said Alan. He leant on his spade and looked up at the sky. It was a beautiful autumn day, with just the slightest breeze fluttering down Newbiggin Road from the North Sea. A few leaves had fallen from the trees in the vicarage garden, but there were still more green than golden ones.

All I could see was a pigeon, its wings making a snapping sound in a nearby tree, and two crows hopping over a grave. 'Which ones are the swallows?' I asked.

'Them ones up dead high, flittin' around with the forked tails. Watch them swoopin' and divin'. You don't see them land much but, mind, they're handsome little chaps if you do see them up close.'

'Where are they going to?' asked Sarah.

'Ooh, Africa I should think.'

Sarah and I, perched on a gravestone, squinted into the sun. Africa sounded a long way from Ashington, a long way from England. It was on my map of the world on my bedroom wall, a satisfying, easy-to-recognize shape with a bulge at the top.

'Why are they going to Africa?' asked Sarah.

'It'll be summer there when we're having winter.' Alan hesitated for a minute. 'Warmer than here, any road.'

'I'd love to go somewhere really hot,' I said. It was hard to imagine the heat Aunty Margaret had told us about, and how they needed fans that blew icy air at them to keep them cool during the New York summer.

'Aye, but not too hot,' said Alan. 'Look at me.' He pointed to his reddish hair and white skin, now lightly tanned and smattered with freckles. 'What do you think would happen to me if I went to Africa? I would turn into a lobster, that's what would happen. I would gan bright red.'

I looked at my own arms. I didn't go very brown either, which seemed most unfair when I played outside so much.

'Look, there's your mam,' said Alan, with so much enthusiasm you would think he hadn't seen her for months. Mum was coming out of the side gate to cut through the churchyard, which probably meant she was on her way to Spedding's. 'She's got the bairns with her,' he added fondly.

Mum approached us and I thought she was going to tell us not to pester Alan, but instead she asked us to keep an eye on Mark, who had been refusing to go into Mr Spedding's shop ever since an incident a few weeks before.

'Did you hear what happened?' she asked Alan, who shook his head. Mum loved a good story, and even though I'd heard this one several times recently, I still liked to hear her tell it. She told Alan how she and Mark had popped to Spedding's to buy a card for an elderly relative who wasn't well. After looking at several, she found one with a pretty floral design that looked just right, and opened it up.

'I don't suppose you've got something like this, but without the soppy words, have you?' she asked Mr Spedding, pulling a face.

Mr Spedding kept a box in the shelves behind the counter with yet more cards in it.

'I'm sure I can oblige,' he replied. Mum began rooting through the small chest of drawers on the shop floor which also contained cards, while Mr Spedding hunted for the box. Mark stood at Mum's side. He had been given strict instructions not to move, or to touch anything, though it was unlikely he could have done much damage. But he was a real live wire these days, the sort of boy who was at your side one second and up the nearest tree the next.

The box wasn't in its usual place. 'Have you seen it, Mary?' Mr Spedding asked his assistant.

Mum looked up from her rummaging and shared a smile with Aunty Mary. 'It's a wonder you find anything in that mess, Jack,' she said, indicating with a dip of her head the shelves where he was hunting.

Mr Spedding stopped what he was doing. 'Any more calling my shop a mess and I'll jump over the counter and give you a wallop,' he replied. They often spoke to each other in this jokey, almost flirtatious way.

Mum chuckled. 'I'd like to see you try,' she said, picking up another card and reading it. 'Oh, for heaven's sake, who says things like, "You are always in my heart, I hold—"'

The next thing she knew, Mr Spedding had done a magnificent leap over the counter – more spectacular, it seemed, than the time he vaulted over to greet me and Sarah on our first visit to his shop. He was at Mum's side in a flash, rearing up as if ready to pounce, all six foot three of him.

'Now, do you still think my shop is a mess?' he asked in his most menacing voice as Mum made a mock dash for the door.

Mum was helpless with laughter. When she had pulled herself together and Mr Spedding had gone back behind the counter to serve a startled customer, she said, 'I didn't know you were so athletic, Jack. Don't go doing yourself an injury, will you.'

But the whole episode had been too much for Mark, a few weeks shy of his third birthday. He burst into tears and cowered against Mum's legs.

'See what you've done to my son, you big brute,' she said, picking him up. 'Never mind, it's only Mr Spedding having a bit of fun. You should know what he's like by now. What a funny man, he is. Look at him! What a funny old thing!'

Mr Spedding was pulling faces now to make him laugh, but Mark buried his head in Mum's shoulder and kept it there. And now he was refusing to go into the shop belonging to 'the big nasty man' unless he was absolutely sure that Aunty Mary was there on her own.

I took Mark's reins and let him lead me down the churchyard path. He started running. 'Giddy up, boy,' I said.

He veered off on to the grass. 'Hey, I never said "right turn", but go on then.' He careered along, dodging the gravestones and leaping over the kerbs. A lady arranging flowers in a stone urn turned and smiled at us.

'Mind, he's a bonny lad,' she said. 'Hello, pet.'

'Hello,' said Mark, beaming.

'Eeh, doesn't he talk nice, and all,' she said.

Mum would be pleased to hear that. Now that Ruth had started school – and come home on her first day saying that she had a *spelk* in her finger, instead of a splinter – Mum had begun mourning the nicely spoken children she used to have. Mark was the only one left who wasn't so open to outside influences. But I already knew I wasn't going to tell her.

I steered Mark in the direction of Alan, and by the time we reached him, Mum was back from the shop and was looking at us as we approached. 'I don't know what we're going to do with this one, though,' she was saying to Alan. I looked at her questioningly, but she waited until I had let go of Mark's reins and he had run down to join Ruth by the gate before she explained.

'We've been invited for tea by Jack Spedding. Do you think your brother will come?' She didn't seem to expect an answer, and directed her conversation back towards Alan. 'I said to him, "You can't possibly want the whole family, Jack, we've got four kids, remember!", but he said he's had four sons of his own, so our lot will be nothing compared to them.'

'He'll be champion, Mrs Gofton,' said Alan.

Mum looked at Mark, now trying to climb over the gate instead of waiting for her to come and open it. 'Oh well, at least it might mean he'll be on his best behaviour.'

The last Saturday in September was an unusually quiet one for weddings, so that was the date set for our visit. We dressed smartly, but Mum didn't think we needed to go 'over the top'. Mum had on a denim hand-me-down pinafore dress from

Murial Swinton, and I wore my blue Ladybird skirt with a white blouse that had come from Margot and Elizabeth.

Mr Spedding lived in Newbiggin-by-the-Sea in a terraced house, though it was a different sort of terrace from the colliery rows in Ashington; smarter, and built of stone rather than the smoke-stained red brick of our neighbouring streets. I knew that he closed the shop and went home at the end of the day – I had seen him locking up, and he had dropped in at the vicarage on a couple of occasions on his way home, once allowing us to hold a bag of money that he said contained several thousand pounds – but I preferred to think of him as living there. It was where I thought he belonged. I pictured a flight of stairs leading steeply from the back room to an upper floor and a warren of tiny rooms, each one dark and cobwebby and piled high with dusty items, just like the shop was. And Mr Spedding would be sitting in one of them in a high-backed rocking chair, presiding over a table set for tea.

It was cooler today, with a feeling of autumn in the air, but bright and sunny. Newbiggin was full of people taking dogs and children for walks. In Victorian times it had been a popular holiday resort; later it had its own coal mine. Today, though its heyday as a big maritime centre was over, it was still a fishing port and the traditional high-bowed boats, known as cobles, were always resting on the sand when we visited. As we drove I glimpsed the sea, shimmering with streaks of silver.

We were all slightly wary as we walked up the path to the front door. I felt as if I didn't know the Mr Spedding who lived in this house. I had asked if his sons would be at home and Mum said she didn't think so; she thought they had all left home or were at university. I hoped she was right. The thought of four large boys like Mr Spedding was quite exciting, but made me feel nervous too.

When the door opened I could sense Mum's surprise in her reaction, though it was only just discernible. In front of us stood a tall, dark-haired man who, though he bore a resemblance to Mr Spedding, was also quite different from him. This man was clean-shaven, his hair neatly combed. Gone was the scruffy shirt with the open collar and the rolled-up sleeves. This man was smartly dressed in a jacket and tie. Was it really our friend? Mum gave a start and looked quickly at Dad, perhaps wondering if his polo shirt was quite the right attire for the occasion. Dad always wore what Mum told him to when he wasn't in his clerical garb, as he had no interest in clothes. She was therefore responsible for any mistakes.

She recovered her composure almost immediately and turned into the polite guest, greeting our host quite formally as if she didn't see him several times a week and share regular jokes with him. She seemed almost bashful as he welcomed us to his home, counted us all in and ruffled heads. Mark was so in awe of the situation he didn't make a sound, and if he had recognized Mr Spedding, it was impossible to tell.

We were shown into a light-filled hallway that smelt of the flowers that stood in a large vase on a rather ornate table. An equally ornate clock ticked loudly behind it. Mum grabbed Mark, who was standing too close to it for her liking. A smell of baking wafted from the kitchen.

And then a lady appeared. Though I had suspected that there must be a Mrs Spedding, I had never – unusually for me – thought to visualize her. And if I had done so, it would not have been a lady like this one. For Mrs Spedding was, indeed, a lady –

a slim, smart lady with carefully coiffed hair that looked as if it had just returned from the hairdresser's, rather stern spectacles, but a smiley face. When she spoke, it was with a voice I heard on the programmes Mum listened to on Radio Four, which was usually playing in the kitchen.

'Hello, I'm Hazel. Jack has told me so much about you all. It's absolutely lovely to meet you.'

Mum had one or two friends who spoke in similar crisp, well-enunciated voices – Sarah and I always imitated them when they had left – but we had never come across this sort of accent in Ashington or Newbiggin.

'It's a pleasure to meet you, as well,' said Mum, and I noticed that she had switched to her own posh voice. 'It's so kind of you to invite us. And with four children – I mean, there are limits, aren't there!'

I sometimes wondered why Mum had chosen to have four children when she often apologized for how numerous we were, as if we had been foisted on her through no fault of her own.

'Nonsense,' said Mrs Spedding, ushering us into the sitting room. 'Jack has done nothing but talk about you all since you arrived at Seaton Hirst. Now, do sit down. Or perhaps the children would like to have their squash in the garden? It seems quite a pleasant afternoon. But don't worry, I don't mind mess.'

Mum, who had seen the nice furniture and carpets, almost pushed us out of the open patio doors.

Mr Spedding brought us a jug of squash and some beakers and put them on a garden table. He asked Sarah and me about The Secret Four and what our latest mission was, and told us some stories about the things he and his sons used to get up to when they were younger. Then he went inside to join the adults.

After about half an hour, we went into the dining room for sandwiches, scones and cakes, but we were happy to be allowed to leave the table early and go outside again. We played a game in which Ruth and Mark pretended to be rabbits, then we decided it was more fun for us all to be rabbits and we had races doing bunny jumps from one end of the garden to the other. When Mr Spedding came out and saw us, he asked if we knew how to do wheelbarrow races and held each of our legs in turn as we raced each other, then dangled us in the air until we screamed to be put down.

Mum and Mrs Spedding came outside, shivering slightly in their cardigans, and Mum asked Mark to do his latest party piece.

'He sings so beautifully,' said Mum.

Mark hung his head at first and pretended to be shy, then, with some cajoling, gave his rendition of 'Christmas is Coming'. Mum and Mrs Spedding clapped their hands when he'd finished, and Mum said, 'He's like Little Lord Fauntleroy when he sings. You'd never think he was such a horror,' while Sarah and I squirmed and rolled our eyes at each other.

Later, after we had all thanked them profusely and were back in the car, and Mum had told Mr and Mrs Spedding not to stand and wave goodbye, she and Dad looked at each other as if waiting for the other to speak.

Dad was first. 'Well, would you credit it?' he said. This was one of his favourite expressions. 'Heh-heh,' he chuckled.

'Unbelievable,' said Mum, shaking her head as she started the engine.

'What is?' I asked.

'And working as our postmaster!' Dad continued. 'Our newsagent! In that scruffy old shop!'

They sat there shaking their heads in disbelief, ignoring our questions.

'I didn't recognize him either,' I said, wanting to be part of the conversation and thinking it had something to do with Mr Spedding's smart appearance.

'Did he tell you about his gun?' asked Sarah.

The word 'gun' made Mum take notice. 'Don't be silly,' she said.

'It's true. Him and his boys used to shoot rats down by the tip at North Seaton Colliery. And they go fishing. And they've got beehives.'

'*He* and his boys,' corrected Mum before looking at Dad, as if he could verify the story.

'They used to have a horse called Sweep. I think we should get a horse, one big enough to ride. He could keep the grass short for us.'

'We've gone through all that before,' said Mum. 'Now, listen to this: do you know what your father and I found out when we were talking? That our friend Mr Spedding was decorated in the war.'

I didn't know what she meant. I pictured Mr Spedding on a battlefield, war raging all round him, adorned like a Christmas tree with lights and baubles.

'What was he decorated with?' piped up Sarah.

'It means he was a war hero,' said Dad. 'He was a pilot and flew some very brave missions and won lots of medals. Of course, he's an incredibly modest man. I don't suppose we would have heard any of this if it hadn't been for his wife letting the cat out of the bag. Did you see his face, Gwenda?' Dad laughed. 'But he was a bit more forthcoming when he saw how interested we were. Hey, I wonder how many people in Ashington know about this? Not a lot, I bet.'

Mum glanced at us in the rear-view mirror as she pulled out into the road, a satisfied smile on her face. 'I always sensed there was something special about him – not just your run-of-the-mill postmaster,' she said.

'Oh, come off it,' laughed Dad. 'You hear this, kids? Your mother knows everything. She probably knew the second she saw him that he was a squadron leader, didn't you, dear?' He patted her hand playfully.

Mum ignored him. 'He just has that way about him.'

'Well, we've always known he was a character, I'll give you that. But as for his illustrious record . . . ' He shook his head. 'It's a miracle he even survived the war . . . Ninety-six missions in a Mosquito – that's a wooden plane! It's almost unheard of.'

'I'm telling you,' said Mum, 'I thought he had that military bearing.'

'Yes, dear,' said Dad.

'Don't you remember, I said after that first time I went into the shop, it wouldn't surprise me in the least if—'

'Oh, stop arguing, you two,' said Sarah.

'Yes, stop it,' said Ruth.

'Your mother's a genius,' said Dad. 'That's why I married her.'

'I suppose he just wants a quiet life now,' said Mum. 'These people often do.'

Though we didn't know the whole story then – and as children we didn't appreciate it anyway until much later – this is what my parents learnt about our postmaster that afternoon and during a friendship that lasted many more years.

Jack Spedding first applied to join the RAF in 1934 when he left college, but as he was recovering from bronchitis at the time, he was found to be unfit. He was called up in 1940 and eventually became a pilot and flying instructor, going on to specialize in instrument landing systems.

As a Mosquito pilot in Pathfinder Force, he marked targets for the main bomber force with coloured pyrotechnic flares. By the end of the war he was Acting Squadron Leader commanding B flight, 109 Squadron and had flown ninety-six missions.

At the end of hostilities, he found himself in Berlin, and with a handful of RAF colleagues walked to the Führer's headquarters, the Reich Chancellery, which was now guarded by the Russians. They tried to talk their way in, but when this proved unsuccessful they simply walked around the back and climbed over a wall. (This part of the story was Mum and Dad's favourite.) They all took some souvenirs away, and Mr Spedding's included one of Eva Braun's wardrobe doors which he took from the bunker beneath the Chancellery, and letters from the composer Richard Strauss pleading that his chauffeur be spared war service.

He was awarded the DFC and the DSO.

That night Mum was on the phone to Grandma telling her about our visit. There was that word again – she and Dad had used it non-stop since we got home – *decorated*. This time I pictured Mr Spedding in goggles and flying suit, rather like the hero of a film we had seen on a recent Sunday afternoon, but with medals pinned all over him. I wondered if he would seem different when I next saw him in the shop, grander and more deserving of respect. I didn't want him to change, and wished we had never found out about his war record. But when I saw him hunched over some figures in the dimness of the post-office booth, sprouts of beard poking out from his chin, I promptly forgot all about his illustrious past.

Chapter Twenty-two

For most of my childhood, Sarah and I were known as 'the girls' and Ruth and Mark 'the little ones'. It wasn't until Ruth was an adult too that 'the girls' began to include her as well. Sarah and I – only fourteen months apart – shared friends and toys, planned exercise routines and secret assignments and went on our own holidays to stay with our grandparents in Ponteland and Whitley Bay. In the same way, Ruth and Mark – eighteen months apart – were treated as a team, even though Mark was a typical boy who had been born with a lust for rough and tumble, toy guns and wild behaviour, while Ruth loved her dolls and books and make-believe. Ruth probably suffered the most from this, having to endure being beaten up by her little brother while missing out on the big girls' treats, one of which was going to the shops in Newcastle on a big yellow double-decker bus when we stayed with Grandma in Ponteland. One day when she came back from school saying that she had never been on a bus before, while her friends caught buses all the time, Mum said wasn't it lucky that we had a car, and she didn't need to wait in the cold and then sit on a dirty old bus with sweet wrappers on the floor breathing in all the horrible cigarette smoke? But Aunty June understood that this was an omission that needed to be put right, and the pair of them took the bus to Newbiggin one Saturday afternoon.

Ruth came back full of excitement, not just about the bus trip but about what Aunty June had bought her when they were there. The list included a pack of notelets with rabbits on them, a bar of Caramac, an ice-cream, a snowman pencil case and a gold chain with an apple pendant on it. Not real gold, of course, though Ruth was sure it was.

Mum raised her eyes and said she didn't think it was Christmas yet. Aunty June said it was nice to treat the bairn, and they had both had a nice afternoon, so that was all that mattered.

A few days after this, Aunty June stayed the night when she was babysitting as Mum and Dad had gone to a party some distance away and were going to be back very late. She slept in Sarah's double bed while Sarah came into my room. Early the next morning, I woke to find Ruth and Mark at my bedroom door, giggling and telling us to get up and follow them. They led the way along the landing and stopped at the entrance to Sarah's room. We could hear Aunty June's snores building to a crescendo every so often, then subsiding, and though they were funny, I didn't think this a very good reason for dragging us out of bed. But Ruth put her finger to her lips and crept into the room. When we were all inside, she and Mark pointed to the bedside table, hands to their mouths to stop their laughter erupting. In a glass was a strange object. It looked like, well, it could only be, a set of teeth. Mark was giggling so much now he had to run out of the room. Aunty June stirred and muttered something in her sleep. We had never seen a set of dentures before, though we had once seen Aunty June without any teeth and she had spoken in a funny, muffled way that alarmed me, as if there were an impostor in her body. But it hadn't occurred to me that taking them in and out was a regular occurrence, nor that they would be displayed so prominently.

'Urgghh!' said Sarah, and as Aunty June rolled over and opened her eyes, we all scarpered.

We celebrated harvest in church, and at the end of the week it was the school harvest festival. Everyone was asked to bring in food to be given away to the less fortunate in our town. Some girls brought cardboard mushroom baskets, the metal handles proudly hooked over their arms, as they showed off the beautifully arranged assortments of tinned and fresh produce.

'From me dad's allotment,' said one of the Susans proudly. There was a huge vegetable like a giant cucumber, which she told us was a marrow; carrots, potatoes and shiny red tomatoes still on the vine.

'Ooh, can you really grow tomatoes?' someone asked, awestruck at the perfection of them. 'Or are they pretend?'

Our own garden hadn't produced much yet, but Dad said we had arrived too late to get anything properly started this year, which was why we had only harvested the potatoes that Dougie Lewins had put in before our arrival, plus some gooseberries from the already established bushes. Mum had made a gooseberry crumble but Sarah and I preferred them raw. Mum and Dad kept suggesting we help in the garden, too, but I didn't much like the idea of eating anything we had grown and couldn't believe it would be as good as something from the shops. I hoped nobody would notice that I put down only a couple of tins when we placed our offerings at the front of the school hall. Mum said there were three of us taking in contributions, and we had all done the same thing at church on Sunday, and that we weren't made of money so it was quite enough.

Dad came to school to take the service. I saw how proud Miss Snowdon looked as she introduced him, and how most of the teachers were beaming. Some of the girls began to whisper and nudge each other. Further along the row where I was sitting, one of the Julies whispered to me.

'Psssst, Barbara.'

When I looked at her she pointed to the front of the hall. *Your dad*, she mouthed, as if I might not have noticed. I nodded briefly and turned away.

Sandra nudged me, but I decided to ignore her.

Dad began by asking if anyone had a favourite vegetable. Several hands shot in the air. He picked a girl near the front.

'Tatties!' she shouted. Dad and some of the teachers laughed, while Miss Snowdon told the girl she didn't need to be heard in Newbiggin.

He chose a few more girls. Carrots were popular. Corn from the Green Giant raised a laugh. Someone said she loved Brussels sprouts, and the girl beside her said 'Yuck!' very loudly.

He moved on to fruit, and there ensued a short discussion about whether a tomato was a fruit or a vegetable. He asked the teachers what they thought, and Mrs Pickering, smiling broadly and looking a bit pink, said she was sure it was a fruit.

Then we had to name our favourite flowers. Angela was standing high on her tiptoes, her right arm stretching into the air, her whole body wriggling with anticipation.

'Chrysanthemums,' she said, looking pleased when Dad knew her name.

Dad said she clearly knew more flowers than he did, and that he'd have trouble naming anything other than a rose or a daffodil. I wondered if it was really Angela's favourite flower, or if she was just showing off.

Then Dad told us that God had provided us with these fruits and vegetables to make us strong and healthy, and he had given us flowers to make us happy and to surround us with beauty. 'Look around,' he said. 'The earth is full of beautiful things, not just now but at other times of the year. Appreciate every season for what it gives us, but at harvest time in particular, let us thank God for farmers and for our food.'

As we waited to file back into our classrooms, a girl I didn't know in another class called to me from her own line. 'Eeh, that was your dad there!'

'She does recognize her own father,' said Kathryn sharply.

The girl stared at her. 'I wasn't talking to you. Anyway, I was just saying.'

'Yeah, well, don't bother,' said Angela, joining in.

'How'd he know your name?' asked the girl suspiciously.

'Because I go to St Andrew's,' Angela said proudly.

'So what, who cares?' replied the girl.

Our line was moving now. Angela put her hands on her hips. 'Don't bother asking if you're not going to listen to the answer,' she said, and tossed her long ponytail over her shoulder before marching into class behind the others.

Back in the classroom, someone asked me what it was like to see my dad standing there in front of us all. I shrugged. I didn't really know what the answer was. Until today, it hadn't seemed strange. I was so used to seeing him conducting the service in church that I didn't even think about it. In fact, it was more unusual when we were on holiday and trooped along to another church to have Dad beside us in the pew, wearing trousers and a shirt and tie, while some stranger stood at the altar in his robes. But now I could see that what I took for granted was not normal. A lot of things about my life were strange compared to other people's. Friends commented on how there were always lots of people coming and going when they came to play – one of them had stood, speechless, in the hallway as Dad showed a young couple out of his study to the front door just as Mum was showing another couple inside. 'Who are they?' she had whispered to me, and been even more surprised when I told her I had no idea. But my friends were right – *they* were the normal girls whose fathers did normal jobs, while I was the odd one. Having a father who stood up in public telling us all about God and Jesus in a voice that was clearer and louder than his normal voice was a very odd thing indeed.

'Does he wear that white collar thingy when he's in bed?' asked one of the Susans with a snigger, and when I told her she was stupid she replied that at least her dad didn't go around in a dress.

I had heard Dad saying recently that he hoped to get a curate to help him in the parish one of these days, and I hoped there and then that the curate would take these assemblies in future.

*

There was another thing bothering me. But this was something I could put right myself. That night I declared to Mum, 'From now on, I'm calling you Mam.'

'So am I,' said Sarah.

She started to protest that she didn't like 'mam', but in fact she didn't have a leg to stand on. She had called her own mother that when she was younger, and Dad called Other Grandma 'Mam'.

'You used to be such nice little girls,' she said, as if we had suddenly started swearing or being unkind to old ladies.

We slipped up a few times in the early days, but eventually it became a habit. We now had a mam and a dad, just like everyone else.

Chapter Twenty-three

Mrs Hepscott had continued her solitary existence in the Ghost Town, but everyone knew that her days there were numbered. One day two men came to the door to speak to Dad. They were supposed to be moving her to her new council accommodation in the centre of town, but having seen the state of her old home they had refused to touch anything.

'Wor meant to be shiftin' hor, but we'll nivvor get a job again if that lot gans on the van! I've never seen anything like it in all me life!'

'I don't think there's much worth taking,' said Dad. 'Can't most of it go to the tip? And the new place is furnished, isn't it?'

'That's what we've telt her, but she says it's all gotta come.' He blew out noisily through his mouth and shook his head.

'If she was just moving down the road, we could shift her

with a bogey, like,' said the other man. A bogey was like a wardrobe door on wheels, and was used for conveying things over short distances. We had seen someone move house with one, steering it down the back lanes like a gondola in the canals. 'But that's not an option here,' he continued. 'I'm not really sure what you can do, mind, vicar. I wouldn't want you touching anything either. There's no knowing what you might catch. There's deed mice, deed bords. Caca everywhere.' He coughed. 'It's a health hazard. But she's gotta gan. The place is coming doon next week.'

Dad went to speak to her, armed with a loaf of Mam's bread. He managed to convince her to leave a lot of things behind, but there were some things she insisted on taking. After several phone calls, Mam arranged for the local rag-and-bone man to transport her most prized possessions in his horse and cart. I pictured Mrs Hepscott sitting proudly in the midst of it all, her cats crawling all over her, but in fact Dad took her in the car. The RSPCA came to take the cats away as she wasn't allowed animals in her new place – they counted twenty-two – though on Dad's next visit he saw a bowl of water on the kitchen floor and the time after that, there were most definitely two cats curled up on the only decent armchair. And somehow, the numbers went on increasing.

Every Sunday morning Dad picked up the organist and Mrs Hepscott and took them to church. Whatever the weather, Eric Perkins would sit with his head out of the car window, unable to bear the catty smell in the car.

The drama group started rehearsals for their first production and met every Wednesday evening in the vicarage. Sarah and I helped Mam get ready for their arrival. Ashtrays were put out, flasks filled with boiling water to speed up coffee time later, cups and saucers were laid out on the trolley and doilies put on plates ready for the biscuits. Mam hadn't been sure how many people to expect. A notice had been put in the church magazine and she had twisted several arms, but even she was surprised at the turnout. Most of them came from St Andrew's Church and included all of the Bennett family apart from Cecil; Wilf Kirkup; Doris Smith (the wife of Uncle Jim and the enrolling member of the Mothers' Union, of which Ashington had the biggest membership in the whole of Newcastle); Sylvia Lewins, the wife of our gardener Dougie, all softness and giggles to her husband's more brittle demeanour; Joan Stoker, Don Pirt, Joyce Turner, Lorna Beadle and Jean Wilkinson, the director.

The noise from the sitting room grew louder and louder as the evening wore on. Sylvia Lewins had a chuckle – actually, it was more of a shriek – that set everyone else off. Wilf's deadpan delivery did the same thing. When Mam came out of the sitting room to pour the coffee, she was wiping her eyes.

'I don't know how we'll ever manage to keep a straight face when we do it for real,' she said.

Joyce Turner came up behind her to give her a hand and said something in her ear, and the two of them collapsed with laughter again.

At half-term we went blackberrying at Longhirst, where Dad's old friend David Smith was vicar. The Smith family lived in a huge vicarage, far bigger than ours. I liked his daughter, Rebecca. She was a bit younger than me and Sarah, good-natured and happy to join in whatever games we chose. Her brother Christopher was younger still and played with Ruth and Mark. We picked pounds and pounds of blackberries that day, and compared our purple mouths and tongues. I didn't like them as much when they were cooked, but raw they were even more tasty than strawberries. So sweet and tart at the same time, our tastebuds seemed to be exploding!

'Mmm, these are delicious,' said Aunty Mary, Rebecca's mother. 'Blackberry pie, tonight, I think.'

'Mine are going straight into the freezer if I can find any room,' said Mam. 'Have you got one yet, Mary? Honestly, I don't know what I would do without mine.'

Mary confessed that she hadn't, but that it was on her list. She just had to talk David round. 'You know what he calls you, don't you? Slender Gwenda the Mind Bender. Every time we've been together I come home telling him I need a new gadget.'

Another question I had become used to being asked at school was whether I was scared living beside the graveyard. And once again it was a question I didn't understand. Why should I be scared? The churchyard was an extension of our garden – in fact, the fence around the tennis court had only been erected after we had moved in when Dad had insisted that it was necessary on account of having young children. In the graveyard we chatted to Alan and rode our bikes, Kathryn and I looked for characters to incorporate into the tales our feverish imaginations dreamt up and we would sometimes pocket the odd coloured stone for The Secret Four tin. I certainly didn't associate graves with ghosts in the way some of my friends did. I'm not sure that I even associated them with the dead.

'I'd be terrified, me,' said one of the Julies, shivering. 'You never know what might get you. And on Hallowe'en they all come out, you know.' She fluttered her hands in the air and rolled her eyes.

'When our Gavin was there last year he saw someone rise from the grave,' she continued. 'And if you don't believe us, just ask him.'

For Hallowe'en, we had a small party at home with a few friends – Krishna and Nicola, Kathryn, Sandra and Sarah's friends Dawn and Linda. We had made lanterns from turnips which we were also going to use on Bonfire Night five days later. Nicola had brought some 'spooky cookies' she had made from a recipe on *Blue Peter*. She gave a gappy grin as she proudly opened the tin to show us. Mam said they were far too good for our party and that – didn't we know? – she was feeding us slugs and snails and bats' wings. Dawn had brought a broomstick that her Dad had made and I wished I had one, but one that really flew. I wondered if rich children might have such a thing.

We bobbed for apples in a bucket, and Mam had tied some on strings as well and hung them in the kitchen doorway. With our hands tied behind our backs we had to try to take a bite out of one, which was harder than it looked.

We also played a game that we played at all our birthday parties, where we sat in a circle and each took a turn to shake the dice. If we got a six, we went quickly into the middle of the circle, dressed up in the clothes that were laid out – today these consisted of a witch's hat, a warty plastic nose and a pair of mittens – and only then were we allowed to tuck into a Mars Bar with a knife and fork. But as soon as another person got a six, it was their turn in the circle, so you were lucky if you got as far as a mouthful.

Mam's new friend, Trudy, called in for a few minutes and

ended up staying far longer and lending a hand. Trudy was an Ashington lass who had recently moved back to her hometown after a few years in London. She had taken a shine to Mam, and though Mam seemed to despair of her at times, and said there was only so much she could take of her love life – which was Trudy's main topic of conversation – they got along well. Mam was trying to persuade her to join the drama group, telling her it was a good way to make new friends. Trudy hadn't been a churchgoer before, but now there was no stopping her. She wanted to be confirmed, she wanted to go on the rota for reading and taking the offertory up to the altar and she spent an awful lot of time at our house, drinking coffee. Dad said that he'd come across people like her before, and that in a few months' time she would have lost interest and we probably wouldn't see her any more, but he seemed to enjoy her company as much as anyone when she was around.

'I'm not sure I belong here any more, Gwenda,' Trudy was saying, as we tucked into our cakes and cookies with just the flickering turnip lanterns for light.

I pricked up my ears and caught Krishna's eye across the table.

'No?' Mam was only half listening as she helped Mark down from his chair and told him to find Dad and ask him to run his bath. 'Wait, wait! You've got chocolate all over your fingers. Don't move until I get a cloth.'

Trudy put a restraining hand on him while Mam disappeared into the kitchen. 'I'll give you a hand with that, Gwenda,' she called after her. 'I love bathing the bairns. I must say, I thought I'd have my own by now. I always swore I'd never be the oldest mam at the school gates, but just look at me.'

We all looked at Trudy, then at each other. I didn't know if she was trying to be funny or not.

Mam came back into the dining room. 'Heavens above, Trudy, you've got years ahead of you.' But she said it with too much conviction and I wasn't sure if she meant it.

Then Ruth suddenly pointed to the window and said there was a fire in the churchyard. Mam told her it was the reflection of the lanterns in the glass, but Ruth insisted. Mam went to the window but she couldn't see much because of the trees, and moved to the sitting room where the view was more open. When we heard her shout, we all scrambled down from the table and ran to look. The churchyard was flickering with light, and we could make out lots of shapes moving around there.

'It's just torches,' said Mam, then corrected herself. 'No, I think she's right, there are some fires as well. In fact, that looks a bit too close to our back fence for comfort. Alder! Where are you? Have you seen this?'

Dad came dashing out from his study. He didn't seem as worried as Mam was, but he said he would go outside to check. Trudy said that he mustn't go on his own and went to get her coat, but Dad said it was probably only kids and not to worry. He said he'd yell very loudly if any devils tried to grab him.

He came back about twenty minutes later, looking both amused and exasperated. As he had suspected, it was some youngsters getting overexcited and trying to scare themselves and each other. Mam wondered if we should call the police, but Dad said he had asked the kids to put the fires out, and as long as there was no criminal damage there was no point in bothering the police.

'Well, I'm keeping an eye on our fence,' said Mam, looking unimpressed. 'I don't fancy waking up dead tomorrow morning.'

Our friends went home, and we were all rather disappointed that there would be no visit from policemen, as that would surely have been the highlight of the evening.

'I would have liked that too, girls,' said Trudy, winking at Mam.

'I bet you would,' said Mam.

We had always celebrated Guy Fawkes Night in our old house, and now that we had a big garden our celebration would be bigger than ever, with a proper bonfire and fireworks. Mam and Dad invited our friends and parishioners from St John's and St Andrew's. Dougie Lewins was in charge of the bonfire, and had been building it for the past couple of weeks. Mam served soup and hot dogs and cakes.

The night was cold and misty, and the air smelt smokier than ever. Trudy turned up in a long purple coat and high-heeled boots.

'Come and give me a hand,' Mam said bossily as Trudy poked her head round the kitchen door. 'Ooh, you're nicely dressed for an outdoor party. Are you sure you can walk in those?'

Trudy assured her that she could walk in anything.

Mam pointed to a tray of soup. 'In that case, you can take this round for me. Don't break your neck, will you?'

Later, when I went into the kitchen to look for the ketchup, Mam was saying to her, 'I would hang on if I were you. Don't throw yourself at him.'

Trudy gave me a shrug and an apologetic smile. 'Your mam always knows best,' she said. She looked too old to me to be having this sort of conversation. I thought she should be married and have children by now.

As I was going back outside, I heard Mam say, 'And for heaven's sake, leave Alan Murray alone. He's a confirmed bachelor. And the poor man's terrified of you.'

Alan Murray was the priest-in-charge at St Andrew's Church; tall, dark and pipe-smoking, with a nervous habit of clearing his throat.

Trudy snorted. 'Oh, you heard about that, did you?' and I left them both chuckling over whatever she had done.

Ted Nichol and Simon stood a few yards from the bonfire. Mrs Nichol wasn't there. She was never there. Ted was holding Simon's hand. I had never seen Simon so still. He looked mesmerized by the flames. When Trudy came out again and chatted so nicely to them both, directing her conversation at Simon as much as at Ted, I thought what a lovely mother she would make for Simon. Perhaps Mrs Nichol would die and she and Ted would get married. By all accounts, Mrs Nichol spent a lot of time going to bed on account of her nerves. Some people said it was Simon who had made her like that. I wondered how some people found husbands and wives easily – even when they looked odd or weren't very nice or clearly didn't deserve them – and others never did. Old Mrs Hepscott with her cats and funny smell had once had a husband. And the girl up the road whose teeth stuck out had managed to find a boyfriend. Mam always said there was someone out there for everyone, but what if you were unlucky and never found that person? Older women we knew with no husbands were either sweet and shy or dragons, and women like Mam seemed to pity them.

Mam asked Trudy if she would pass her fruit crunchie round, and she flitted through the crowd to deliver it, as graciously as if she were the hostess. Mam had said to her once, only half jokingly, that she would make a good vicar's wife, but unfortunately most vicars already had wives, or they were like Alan Murray and didn't want one.

I spotted Dad, in his element as he chatted and listened, sharing himself out as fairly as he could with each group for everyone liked to have their bit of time with the vicar. Ruth and Mark were with Aunty June and Uncle Andy and Ruth was clutching Paul Lewins' hand. Mark had been given strict instructions not to go anywhere near the fire if he wanted to be allowed to stay up. Earlier, Aunty June had been showing everyone the photos of Carol's passing-out parade in Guildford which she and Uncle Andy had attended.

We all stood as far back as we could when Dougie began to light the fireworks. The sky fizzed and crackled with light and the air around Dougie filled with pungent green and purple smoke. Simon looked into the sky with wonder, even too engrossed to do one of his dances.

'He's never seen anything like this,' said his dad.

'Be careful, Dougie,' said Mam every time she came back outside with another tray of cakes or biscuits. She seemed to have spent most of the evening in the kitchen.

'I'm all rect,' said Dougie, jumping back as a spark shot out of a firework he had gone back to examine after it failed to go off. It started to hiss, then turned into a multicoloured fountain.

We had been told the rules for Bonfire Night at school, one of them being never to return to a lit firework, but grown-ups were allowed to do what they wanted. Dougie did, anyway.

'Set an example to the children, at least!' said Mam, pretending to be angry.

Dougie just laughed.

'You cannot tell him anything,' said Sylvia, his wife.

Trudy watched as a firework sent streamers of light back to earth.

'Beautiful, aren't they?' she said.

'Mind nothing lands on you,' said Dougie. He winked at her. 'What gans up has to come doon.'

Trudy giggled. 'A good job, too.'

I wondered if finding Trudy a man could be one of the missions of The Secret Four, and I resolved to ask Sarah, Krishna and Nicola what they thought about this when we had our next meeting. Perhaps we could write a letter, pretending it was from someone she liked! Memories of Shepherds Dene and the thirty-six-year-old daughter came flooding back. Perhaps, if we were successful, she would ask all four of us to be bridesmaids at her wedding. I smiled to myself at the thought.

Chapter Twenty-four

For as long as I could remember, my parents had been friendly with the Franciscan friars who lived on a hilltop in the village of Alnmouth on the Northumberland coast, a few miles north of Ashington. Dad had been interested in the lifestyle of the Franciscans since he was a young man, and had gone with a friend to visit a community of them in Dorset in the days before the North-Eastern house was established. Later, he had done his training for the priesthood in a religious community, the Community of the Resurrection, in Mirfield, West Yorkshire. He had toyed with the idea of joining one himself, but had opted for married life instead.

In 1961 the Franciscans established the house in Alnmouth, and by the time we were in Ashington, some of the brothers had become regular visitors to the vicarage. Dad would invite them to preach or to lead courses for the parishioners of St John's and

St Andrew's Churches, and such an invitation always included a meal or two with our family as well. The brothers, who were led by the charismatic Father Edward, led a simple life – they spurned personal possessions, grew their own vegetables, took their turns with daily chores and worshipped together several times a day. But they also helped out in the community and welcomed visitors to the friary, where they often had people staying. In fact, all of the friars we knew were very sociable.

Brother Kevin was the first one we got to know, and he was Ruth's godfather. Mam and Dad had first met him when we lived in Newcastle, and he had come to speak at the Ladies' Club. At the end of the session, when he had invited questions from the floor, one lady had asked him what happened to the friars when they grew old, as all the photos they had seen showed young or middle-aged men. Without a smile on his face, Kevin told them in his melodious Irish accent – no one's voice sounded more sincere or caring than Brother Kevin's – that they had planned long and hard for that event, and that when the friars reached the age of seventy they were put into a wheel-chair, wheeled to the cliff at the far end of the garden and pushed over the edge. There was a deathly hush in the audience, followed after a few seconds by a roar of laughter.

I think Brother Kevin and the other friars must have looked forward to leaving behind the austere monastic life every so often for the pleasures of the outside world. In our home they could enjoy different company, eat home-cooked meals, lie in a hot bath and enjoy a tot of whisky – or whatever their favourite tipple might be – before bed. When we had been younger, Sarah and I would creep into Kevin's room in the morning and rudely awaken him with our singing or whatever other entertainment we had thought up for him. Kevin told Mam later that it was the only time he ever had a woman in his bed.

All the friars we knew seemed to like children. Kevin, in particular, was enormous fun, chasing us round the garden, squirting us with the garden hose on summer days, unprotesting when we dragged him from his armchair asking him to pretend to be a bear. During these games he usually ended up laughing as much as we did.

We knew that the men who lived in the friary were special in some way, but I couldn't understand why anyone would want to live that way of life. When we dropped in on the brothers while holidaying in nearby Embleton, they were always welcoming, but the refectory was bare and chilly and the invitation to join them for Evensong not very appealing. Sarah and I pre ferred to play outside in the large garden, which looked out over the bay. We couldn't think of anything more boring than having to go to church several times a day. Once a week was quite enough.

Brother Kevin came to preach on St Andrew's Day at our sister church. He had just got up into the pulpit when there was a banging on the big double doors at the back of the church, which weren't often used. Cecil Bennett rushed to open them and an old lady, Bessie Naylor, who lived nearby, manoeuvred herself inside in her wheelchair. It was a monstrous contraption, more like a Victorian bath chair with two large wheels and a smaller one at the front, driven by Bessie with two handles. Slowly, she began to squeak her way up the aisle, refusing any offer of help. In the pulpit, Kevin looked down at his congregation, smiled, then leafed through his notes, clearly deciding that it would be best to wait until she was in her place before beginning. She carried on towards the front. The squeaks grew louder. Bessie was mumbling under her breath and sounded as if she was having trouble. Mam, sitting beside Vera Bennett and Sylvia Lewins, began to get the giggles. The three of them had to look down to hide their smiles. Someone behind them got a tickly throat and spluttered into a handkerchief.

As she got close to the front, the old lady came to a stop, turned to Cecil and said in a hoarse whisper – loud enough for everyone to hear – 'I've got a puncture, will you pump me tyres up?' Cecil shook his head in disbelief and said something in Bessie's ear before grabbing the back of the chair and pushing her into a space beside the front pew. As he kicked out the footrest, the chair shot back with a jerk and an audible intake of breath rippled through the whole congregation when it appeared that Bessie might be catapulted out of her seat and across the shiny floor, cleaned so lovingly by Annie Jobson every week. But the brake was on, and instead the wheelchair shuddered to a stop. Bessie gave Cecil a nod and he went to sit down. Mam said that by this time she had almost burst. Then somehow, mustering all of his dignity, Kevin began his sermon as if nothing unusual had taken place.

Brother John, our other favourite, was older, had a slightly lugubrious face, but was as soft as a puppy by nature. He didn't run around with us the way Kevin did, but we still found his company entertaining. He was a plain-speaking Derbyshire man and had been stone deaf in one ear ever since an overenthusiastic doctor had stuck an instrument too far down it when he was a boy. Perhaps the hearing aid and the hand he often held to his good ear as he asked you to repeat what you had said made him appear more severe than he actually was. He often complimented me and Sarah on our slim figures or on what we were wearing, and he had a soft spot for our mother, and used to say that if he had been ten years younger he would have married her. Mam, who looked on him as an old man, thought it should have been twenty years, at least, but lapped up his compliments all the same.

The Franciscans wore a long brown habit with a white rope belt called a girdle, which had three knots in it. These had been devised by St Francis himself to remind him of his three vows of poverty, chastity and obedience. Or, as Brother John put it, 'Got no money, got no wife, do as I'm told.'

Brother John came to preach one Sunday and had the congregation in stitches as he told them his funny stories. In our front-row seats, Krishna, Nicola, Sarah and I, not used to paying much attention during the sermon, sat up and listened. He looked straight at us when he told us how he had gone to stay at a vicarage one night and been greeted and shown to his room by the vicar's attractive teenage daughter. In the middle of the night he needed to spend a penny, but found himself confronted on the landing with four closed doors and had no recollection of which one the bathroom was. Afraid of ending up in someone's bedroom, he went back to his own room and relieved himself in a large vase he found there, smuggling it out the next day. (In later years, he grew forgetful when visiting us, too, and on one occasion Mam just managed to stop him from peeing in the airing cupboard.)

After dinner, Mam drove him to Alnwick where he had been invited to tea by the Duke of Northumberland's forester, with whom he had become friendly. She had washed his habit as soon as he arrived at our house, thinking that standards of hygiene at the friary left something to be desired, and he was fresh and clean. She popped to see a friend while he was there, then collected him from a very fine house on the duke's estate where she found a rather grey-looking Brother John. He had eaten well, he told her on the way home – not that the cooking had been as good as hers, he explained hastily, but he had enjoyed it. 'Though I'm not used to such rich food,' he added, rubbing his tummy, 'and after such a big dinner, too.' Mam asked him if he was feeling all right, and he said that yes, he would be fine. A few minutes later, somewhere on the A1, he was suddenly and violently sick all over his nice clean habit. Mam stopped the car at the side of the road, helped him out and stripped him down to his vest and longjohns, much to the bemusement of passing motorists. Back at the vicarage, the habit went in the wash again, and Brother John was plonked in the bath. He went to bed saying he still felt poorly, though he managed a plate of crackers and cheese before going to sleep. The next morning he declared he wasn't well enough to go back to the friary, but might manage scrambled eggs, which he followed with two slices of toast and marmalade and a pot of tea. He continued to recover as the day went on, and after school we took him to see Rip, whom he made a big fuss of. 'But I'd best stay another night, to be on the safe side,' he told Mam, when she asked if he wanted her to run him home after tea.

Dad dropped us off at school one morning and after saying goodbye to us, got out of the car to talk to someone he knew. As Sarah and I shuffled through the gates to join our friends, a boy's voice shouted out, 'Father Gofton! Father Gofton!'

I froze for a second, then looked back at Dad to see if he had heard. He had stopped talking and was looking around, a puzzled smile on his face. The man he was with pointed, and now Dad saw who had called out. On the other side of the playground, a boy was climbing on the bars that separated the boys from the girls, waving an arm in the air and grinning.

Dad waved and shouted back, 'Hello-o-o, Brian!' extending the 'o' in hello the way he did when he answered the telephone to an old friend, or just someone he was pleased to hear from. Then he turned his attention back to his companion. Fortunately parents weren't allowed to enter the playground – not that anyone would have objected to Dad doing so, but I was grateful at least that he stayed where he was. Yes, it could have been far worse, I realized later. He might have come bounding in, cassock billowing, causing girls to either gather round him or hang back and stare. But it was bad enough, as nobody could have failed to hear him. He had a loud, clear voice at the best of times, but the theatrical voice he had just used was a real show-stopper. It felt as if everyone in the playground had stopped what they were doing and was looking my way. Ropes stopped turning and balls stayed in their owners' hands. Dad, deep in conversation on the pavement, was completely unaware of this. I cringed. Why did he have to be so conspicuous all the time, not only in the way he looked but when he spoke as well?

However, one of my questions had been answered. So that was him. Brian Turner. My supposed boyfriend. He was still hanging on the railings, and I could feel him watching me. Well, he could watch as long as he wanted; I wasn't going to give him the satisfaction of looking his way. All around him boys were playing in that boisterous ways boys played when there was a large group of them. Boys at that age seemed so rough when they were all together, and so immature compared to us girls. It was no coincidence that Gary Hunt, who I still liked to sneak the odd glance at when he was serving, was a few years older than me. He looked like an angel in his surplice. For the reading of the Gospel, Dad and the crucifer and two servers moved down from their places near the altar and stopped almost level with the front pew where I sat. Gary was so close to me then that I was sure he must be able to hear my heart beating extra quickly. Though I longed to look at him over the candle flame, I kept my eyes glued to the Bible reading as if my life depended on following every word, not daring to look up until he was walking back to the altar. His hair was so long now that he had to wear it in a ponytail.

It was too late to join my friends in their games. I saw the teacher who was on duty look at her watch and go to pick up the bell, and then I couldn't help myself any longer. I looked across at the railings quickly, and saw him. He had a cheeky face, quite a pleasant one, the sort that looked constantly amused by something.

'Hello, Barbara!' he called out, then – quick as a flash – he let go and disappeared into the unruly swarm. I was relieved that he didn't seem to have any expectations of me. Perhaps he didn't care about being my boyfriend at all and it was only his mother who did. I wasn't sure if I was pleased about that or not.

Someone who did need a boyfriend was Trudy. When The Secret Four held their next meeting, I asked for any suggestions.

'Hold on, man,' said Sarah. 'The meeting's not open yet. We have to read a prayer first.'

She opened her pamphlet of Bible readings and turned a few pages.

'Here it is. Close your eyes, everyone.'

We all obeyed, though when I peeked through mine I saw Nicola doing the same and quickly shut them again.

'Dear God, thank you for the friendship we find here today,' she read cheerily. 'Please help us to be good friends in all our thoughts and actions.' Then her voice took on a more hesitant turn. 'Please help . . . your . . . daughter Trudy to find a boyfriend, or even better, a husband.'

Nicola giggled. 'It doesn't say that!'

Sarah carried on. 'In case you don't know who she is, she's the one with the—'

'Purple coat,' I said.

'I know, I was gonna say that. Before I was so rudely interrupted, God, she's the one with the purple coat who comes round here five times a week and eats all of Mam's ginger biscuits. We think she needs your help. Amen.'

'Amen,' we all said in unison.

'I've got a great idea,' said Krishna, now that we were ready for business. We sat cross-legged on the playroom floor, wearing our badges. She looked at our expectant faces.

'Father Murray!' she declared.

Sarah and Nicola looked pleased at the suggestion, but I shook my head. 'He's no good. Mam says Trudy's already tried him and he doesn't fancy her.'

'I wonder who he does fancy?' said Sarah.

'Your mum,' giggled Nicola. During the summer, at a particularly dull meeting, Father Murray had been seated beside Mam, who was wearing her new hotpants, and had whispered in her ear that he dared her to stand up and give all the men who were present a thrill. The story of the vicar's wife in hot-pants had gone through the parish like wildfire.

We thought of some of the men at church, but they were either too young or too old for Trudy, or had wives.

Mark came bursting into the room in the pedal car he had got from my grandparents for his third birthday, and decided he wanted to stay.

'Mark, geddaway, man,' Sarah said, and when he refused, she shouted to Mam to get rid of him. She was having coffee with Dorothy Dowling, an older vicar's wife from a neighbouring parish who liked to come and swap notes every so often.

'Come and do one of your lovely poems for Mrs Dowling,' said Mam. 'Come on, and I bet you can't steer your car in there without hitting anything. I bet you're not a good enough driver.'

That seemed to do the trick, and Mark carefully negotiated his way out of the playroom.

'What about Mr Spedding?' said Nicola, returning to our mission.

We all laughed at the idea.

'But,' I began, 'he's got four sons. I'll find out from Mam how old they are, then maybe we can introduce one of them to Trudy. I don't think they'll talk too Geordie, if they're like their dad, so that's good. Trudy says she's not fussy, but she likes nicely spoken men and they have to be at least five foot ten, slim, have their own teeth, and everything else in working order – that probably means their car.'

We had a good laugh at the thought of having a boyfriend with no teeth. One of Krishna and Nicola's grandad's friends had a wooden leg, and we imagined having a boyfriend who sat down and removed his teeth and then his leg, and wondered what other parts he might take off.

A few minutes later, Mrs Dowling put her head round the door to say goodbye to us, and added that our brother had been most entertaining. When she had gone, Mam burst into the playroom, a look on her face veering between amusement and embarrassment.

'Who taught him that rhyme?' she asked. 'Come on, you must have put him up to it.'

'How could we of?' said Sarah. 'We're having an important meeting here.'

The rest of us nodded.

'And when he knows so many lovely songs!' Mam carried on.

We all looked at her innocently. She touched her cheek as if to see how hot it felt, before carrying on. 'It started off so nicely at first. Something about Cinderella losing her shoe. But unfortunately it went downhill very rapidly when Little Jack Horner came along.'

We tried to keep straight faces, but none of us managed to. Even Mam was finding it difficult now. 'Well, you can imagine what a shock he gave us! Luckily Dorothy has got a good sense of humour, but imagine if it had been the bishop, or the archdeacon!'

'Well, it's nowt to do with us,' said Sarah. 'Ruth must have taught him.'

Mam didn't look convinced. 'We won't make a big thing about it this time or he'll carry on. Not a word, OK? But if you or any of your friends . . .' She tailed off as Mark drove back into the playroom looking very pleased with himself.

'Let's go and get dinner ready,' she said to him. 'The big girls are busy.'

I asked her later if she thought that one of Mr Spedding's sons would make a good husband for Trudy. Mam said, heavens above, we should do something more useful with our time, and that someone would turn up for Trudy when she was least expecting it. 'That's always the way,' she said.

Chapter Twenty-five

The weather was getting colder. One day the weatherman talked about snow, but nothing fell except for a few flakes that melted as soon as they hit the ground. We were desperate to build an igloo in the garden, which we had planned to do by stacking giant snowballs on top of each other. While we waited for the blizzard to start, we practised doing handstands up against one of the walls in the playroom. Dad came in to see what all the banging was, as he was trying to write a sermon. We decided to do a handstand display. Krishna, who was the strongest of the four of us, did the first handstand, spreading her legs apart against the wall. Then it was my turn, my legs going into the gap, followed by Sarah and finally Nicola. We timed how long we could stay up, then did it to music, beginning with a little flourish as we prepared to pounce and ending with an elegant skip back when we landed, like professional gymnasts. We often did our routine to the record 'Itsy Bitsy Teeny Weeny Yellow Polka Dot Bikini', an old single we had inherited from Mam.

Sarah and I had started going to Krishna and Nicola's ballet class, which took place every Saturday morning in St John's hall, and I hoped that I might be as good as they were one day, though the teacher, Margaret, expected a lot of us and I didn't think I could bear to carry on being such a disappointment to her. But I loved the soft pink ballet shoes with ribbons that tied around my ankles, the navy leotard and the wide headband I wore. And I loved watching the older girls as they walked across the hall on their points, holding our teacher's hand. Apparently you had to be at least eleven to be allowed to do this.

We learnt the five different positions for our hands and feet, and how to do *pliés* and *jetties*. Our teacher smoked as she explained things to us. She had a soft spot for Krishna and Nicola, who called her Aunty Margaret and attended a more senior class, but I didn't think she liked me that much, and Sarah was sure that she hated her. But that only made me more eager to please her, and I was delighted when one day she congratulated me on my point.

Towards the end of the year, she told us beginners that we were ready to take our primary examination. It wouldn't be very difficult, she said. We would simply have to demonstrate the positions and simple moves we had learnt and perform a short routine to a piece of music.

Aunty Beryl, who was used to preparing her daughters for dancing shows, pinned up our hair and covered it with a net. I thought I was the bee's knees, and resolved there and then to win a place at the Royal Ballet School. We even wore a frill round our waists, so that our leotards looked like tutus. There were six of us taking the exam, and we stood in a row in front of the examiner, whose large chest must have got in the way if she had ever been a proper ballerina. Margaret might have smoked a lot and was probably Mam and Aunty Beryl's age but she was slim and graceful and a good dancer. We followed the examiner's commands in unison, terrified in case we made a mistake, especially as our mothers were sitting in chairs down the side of the hall, watching. She walked in front of us, looking at our points, straightening some of them, clapping her hands if she thought we were being too sluggish, even sometimes nodding her approval.

'And now, gels,' she said in her strange accent, 'please demonstrate a *jeté*.'

We thought we must have misheard at first. What was a jeté? None of us had heard of one before. We stood there blankly, quickly looking to see whether anyone else had made a move. Sarah pulled a face at me and I pulled one back.

'A jeté, please, after three – a-one, two, three,' she repeated, slightly impatiently.

When it became clear that nobody had a clue what she was talking about, our teacher, who was standing watching, blew a puff of smoke into the air, coughed a couple of times and called out, 'Howway, you lot, do yer jetties!' and now we understood. A *jetty*! We knew what that was. Nobody had told us that jeté was a French word, and that today we had been hearing it pronounced properly for the first time. We began our little jumps from one foot to the other. We all passed the exam.

Mam thought it all very funny, and for weeks afterwards it was her favourite story – even replacing the one about Mark and the rude rhyme – and was regaled to every visitor.

*

We had been looking forward to the night of the drama-group play for such a long time now, ever since the first burst of hysterical laughter had escaped from behind the sitting-room door. I couldn't wait to see what Mam looked like. I had helped her learn her lines and knew that though her part was a small one, she was one of the funny characters. She told us it was going to be a hoot.

The play was taking place on two consecutive nights in St Andrew's hall, which, though a plain building from the outside, with its corrugated-iron cladding, had a proper stage. Tonight it felt like being inside a theatre, with a curtain drawn across the stage and lights rigged up. Cecil Bennett and Uncle Jim were fiddling around with wires and switches and making last-minute adjustments. From backstage I could hear the usual giggles – yes, that sounded like Sylvia Lewins, and Mam was hooting over something too.

'They're never going to do it without laughing,' said Sarah. 'I hope Mam doesn't make a fool of herself.'

Someone I didn't recognize streaked past us wearing what I assumed was a wig, their face a strange shade of orange. Joan Stoker chased after her. 'I want to see myself in a proper mirror,' the orange person cried.

'It'll look fine when you're on stage, it has to be exaggerated for the lights,' Joan was calling after her. When a shriek went up from the loos and the cry, 'I look like Dick Emery!' it felt as if the night's entertainment had started already.

Sarah and I were on the door. The production didn't start until seven o'clock, but people began arriving at six fifteen.

'We thought we'd be sharp and get a good seat,' said Aunty

June, arriving with Aunty Mary. 'Yer Uncle Andy's livid that he's on night shift.'

We had been told that there was a reduced rate for OAPs, but I had no real idea what an OAP was or looked like. I had a feeling that my grandparents might fall into this category, and that it had something to do with getting old and receiving a pension, but unless people were very old, it could be hard to tell the difference between fifty, sixty and seventy on some people.

Most of the audience had already bought their tickets and simply handed them in, as few people had wanted to risk missing out. But every now and then someone paid on the door. Up until now it had been quite straightforward, but then a lady appeared who was exactly the kind I had been afraid of. She had blondy-grey hair in granny-style curls, and lipstick painted in a large bow shape that missed most of her lips. She asked for one ticket and handed me a pound note. I felt panic-stricken. How much should I charge her? Something told me that it would be rude to ask her if she was a pensioner. It was surely almost as bad as asking an adult how old they were, something we had been told never to do. I would have to phrase the question in the most polite way I could think of. She stood there looking down at me, wondering, no doubt, why I was taking so long.

'Do you, er, pay the full price?' I asked her.

She looked puzzled. 'What do you mean, pet? Why wouldn't I pay the full price?'

'It's just that . . . ' I stopped, wondering what to say next.

Dougie Lewins, who'd been helping to set up and was standing keeping an eye on us, overheard the exchange. He chuckled and gave her a nudge. 'Heh-heh. She's asking if you're a pensioner, Audrey.'

The lady gawped at him, then looked back at me and with a smile that was a little clipped told me that no, she had a long way to go before she retired.

I felt very foolish. I wondered if everyone would get to know about my error. Grown-ups could be funny with the stories they chose to recount, laughing at things we didn't find that amusing. Sarah seemed totally unaware of what I'd done and was chatting to some new arrivals, who were asking if Mam was nervous. I was glad when it was time for the show to start and I could forget about it.

The production was the best entertainment we'd had for ages – a tale of mistaken identity called *Who Do You Think You Are?* Most people got a laugh when they walked on the stage for the first time and were recognized by their friends and family. Those who were unusually good or unusually bad in their roles caused great hilarity throughout the performance. Mam got one of the biggest laughs of the night before she even appeared, when her offstage cry, 'Keep your hands off me, young man!' reverberated around the hall and she burst on to the set carrying a crocodile-skin handbag and sporting a padded bosom.

'That's never Mrs Gofton!' I heard someone whisper loudly behind me, followed by, 'Eeeeh! It is, and all!'

Sarah and I nudged each other and tried not to laugh too much.

Dad, who had a loud laugh that he found hard to stop once it got the better of him, roared most of the way through the production and set off Sarah and me and several other people.

In the interval, Sarah and I sold raffle tickets while Mrs Kirkup and her ladies passed cups of tea along the rows.

When it was finished the cast got a standing ovation. The

biggest cheer went for Jean Wilkinson, the director. Then Dad jumped on to the stage to thank them all and said what an amazing night it had been, how quickly they had progressed from those early nights at the vicarage when he had truly wondered what on earth had been going on, to this polished and highly entertaining production. Then he drew the raffle, and there was more laughter when he picked his own ticket.

'I hope I don't win,' I whispered to Sarah. 'I don't want to have to walk on the stage in front of everyone.'

'I thought you wanted to be an actress,' she said scornfully.

'Well, I do. But not this sort.'

Then everyone put on their coats, lit their cigarettes and set off into the chilly, misty night while Sarah and I helped to tidy up and leave the hall ready for the next performance.

The audience had all agreed about one thing – it had been better than the telly.

Chapter Twenty-six

Apart from the Franciscans and clergy friends of Dad's – like John Dudley, Mark's godfather, who often turned up at teatime smoking flamboyantly, while his little dogs hovered round the edge of his cassock – the other men we knew the best were miners. Almost all of our friends' fathers, and all the men of working age in both the churches, bar the odd exceptions, were miners. Men like Uncle Jim, now training to be a lay reader and still one of the most frequent visitors to the vicarage; Aunty Mary's husband, Albert Sobey; Ted Nichol, seldom seen without Simon at his side and Uncle Andy, often surprised us with their talents and with the quiet way they accepted their dangerous occupation. 'They're the salt of the earth,' Dad used to say.

Although I knew that mining was a dangerous job, it was hard to relate this to the men I saw laughing with Mam in the kitchen, giving us piggy-back races in the garden or buying us chips on the way home from Brownies.

Even when Uncle Andy came round one evening hiding behind a pair of Carol's extra-large sunglasses and I heard Mam say, 'But Andy, you could have lost your eye!' I didn't really worry about him, or think for more than a few seconds about the accident he had suffered. He was Uncle Andy, he was bound to be all right. Miners were invincible.

As children, our worries were few. We knew we had to be polite to adults, to be kind to those less fortunate than ourselves, to pray for people in the poorer countries of the world. After a special report on *Blue Peter* before Guy Fawkes Night I had worried, briefly, about hedgehogs that might be sleeping in our bonfire. Sarah, Kathryn and I had poked around in it, clapping our hands and shouting at the creatures to urge them to escape before Dougie lit it later that evening. Dougie asked us what we were playing at and told us that he had personally escorted them all to safety.

But as Christmas approached, we sensed that there was something else going on, something bigger, something that was going to affect the lives of everyone in the town. We heard it in the adults' conversations – at first when they didn't think we were listening, later when they didn't care if we heard as well.

'Me dad says we're going to have lots more money and go on holiday to Butlins next year!' said one of my friends as we walked round the playground linking arms, inviting anyone who called herself a friend to link up too. 'But we might have to go on strike first.'

I didn't know that meaning of the word 'strike', and wondered what she was talking about.

'Has your dad ever been on strike?' she asked me.

'Um, maybe. Once, I think.'

She nodded as if that was the right answer.

'My grandad says the writing's been on the wall for our pitmen since the fifties, and this'll not help anyone,' said the cleverest of the Susans, but nobody took much notice.

The girl on the other side of me squeezed my arm and said, 'We'll be even richer than you when we win.'

I shrugged. 'You are already,' I said, thinking back to what Mam had told me. Dad didn't earn much. It was a job you did because you had a 'calling', she said, and not because you wanted lots of money. But then on another day she told me that we were rich, and that millions of people in the world had nothing compared to what we had. It was confusing sometimes.

The girl looked at me in disbelief. 'You must be richer,' she said. 'You live in a massive house.'

'Yes, but it's not ours.'

'So whose is it, then?'

'I think it belongs to the church.'

She thought for a few seconds. 'Well, you must still be quite rich, 'cos you need a lot of furniture to fill it, and lots of carpets and stuff. And Sandra says your mam puts fancy paper on plates at teatime.'

We did have quite a lot of furniture, it was true, but most of it had been handed down from grandparents or wealthier friends. However, I made a mental note to ask Mam to stop using doilies.

'And I bet you've got colour telly,' she added. 'Mind, we're getting one soon.'

I shook my head, thinking of our little black-and-white set

that took ages to warm up, though it was better than our old one, which didn't even get ITV. Mam had wondered what the 'twinklies' were that Sarah and I kept enthusing about. We shouted to her to hurry from the kitchen whenever they came on, and she kept on missing them. They were the best thing about our new television. She laughed when she finally came into the room just in time to see a star open out across the screen and the adverts begin.

One night, not long before Christmas, Mam was closing the curtains on the landing window halfway up the staircase when she gave a yell.

'Alder, quickly! Alder! I think the church is on fire!'

Dad came dashing out of his study. We children jumped up from the sitting room where we were watching television. Dad had a quick look from the window then went flying out of the front door, yelling at Mam to ring the fire brigade and to start filling buckets of water. Huge flames were leaping up into the air, then the biggest cloud of smoke I had seen rose up and blotted out everything else.

Mam had reported the fire and was now at the kitchen sink, shouting at me and Sarah to find more buckets in the garage.

We couldn't tear ourselves away from the window, and Ruth and Mark, too small to see out of it, had to be lifted up. Ruth scrambled from my arms on to the windowsill. 'It might be Spedding's,' she said, sounding worried. 'Will Mr Spedding be all right?'

In the panic about the church, it hadn't occurred to me that it might be the shops that were on fire. And now it was impossible to tell.

'He'll have gone home,' I said, hoping I was right.

Beside her, Mark gazed out with huge, frightened eyes. The smoke looked very black against the darkening evening sky.

'Let's go and look from the gate,' I said to Sarah, and we were in the porch, Ruth and Mark at our heels, when Mam came up behind us and cried out, 'No, you don't!'

We pleaded to be allowed to go closer to watch, but she said it could be dangerous and that we had to keep out of the way for the fire brigade.

'But what about the buckets of water?' asked Sarah, and she said we'd see what Dad said when he got back.

'What will happen if the church burns down?' I asked her. 'Will we all have to move?'

She shook her head briskly and said it wouldn't come to that, but I could tell she was worried and that she didn't really know the answer.

Just then the phone rang. Mam didn't have to ask me to answer it as I was already on my way, sure that this evening's drama had something to do with it. I was right. It was Aunty June.

'Did you know the Hipp's on fire,' she said. 'I just had a call from Mary. She can see it from her house. Yer Uncle Andy's gone to see what he can do, but it's probably too late. We used to gan to the pictures there, double bill on a Saturday afternoon. Mind, it needed pulling down.'

By the time I was off the phone Dad was back and con-firming, with a big smile, that it was indeed the Hipp, and not the church, or Spedding's.

'What a relief!' said Mam.

'You can say that again.'

'Anyone know how it started?'

Dad shook his head. 'Not yet.'

We had never known the Hipp in its heyday, like Aunty June had, but the smoking pile of rubble we saw the next day was still a sad sight.

Aunty Beryl was working on Christmas Eve morning, so Krishna and Nicola came to play. With the *Tijuana Christmas* album on the record player, we decided to set a test for Santa Claus. I still believed in him, and Kathryn's dad had seen him in his sleigh flying over Newbiggin Road the year before. When Sandra, who had an older sister, had told me as kindly as she could that it was my mam and dad who were leaving me presents, I felt a bit sorry for her. But just to be on the safe side, we had planned a way to prove his existence and I was looking forward to telling Sandra about it when the mission was accomplished. On the blackboard in the playroom, which was where he was going to leave our presents, we wrote a special message, wishing him a happy Christmas and asking him to sign his name on the dotted line to prove that he'd been.

The rest of the day took too long. I had wrapped my own presents for everyone – bought in Woolworth's in Morpeth, where Mam had dropped me and Sarah, Krishna and Nicola while she was having her hair done – almost as soon as I had bought them. We had to help Mam tidy up, clean the cloakroom washbasin and wrap some extra presents for unexpected guests.

'What have we got for Jackie?' I asked Mam, as I wrapped bags of her home-made biscuits and coasters with local scenes that she had bought from Uncle Peter's shop.

Mam didn't appear to have thought of her.

'We need to wrap something, just in case,' I insisted.

She agreed, and found a little make-up bag. 'I'm putting her name on the label,' I said. 'It's not for anyone else.'

The next morning, though I went straight to my sack of presents, I quickly remembered the blackboard. Shielding my eyes at first, I looked through my fingers. The space remained blank.

'I don't know why he didn't sign it, because he definitely came,' I told Krishna sadly after church. We looked at the blackboard together, willing his name to appear like magic before our eyes.

'Perhaps he can't write,' said Krishna, not sounding convinced.

Mam came up behind us. 'What did Santa Claus bring you?' she asked Krishna, hugging her. She saw our faces. 'What's all this about?'

When we told her, she seemed to see the blackboard for the first time. 'Ah,' she said, then added briskly, 'Well, I think Santa Claus is far too busy. Imagine if he had to do that in every house he went to.'

We couldn't believe anyone else would have had the same idea, but still, we were pleased with our presents. Sarah and I had dolls, Sasha and Gregor, which Mam said were the sort we could keep for the rest of our lives. Sasha was beautiful with her silky blonde hair, dark complexion and demure navy dress. I knew she was more special than other dolls, but I couldn't help feeling a little envious of Kathryn, who had turned up at church with Tippy Tumbles, whose advert I had watched longingly for several weeks. I wondered why Kathryn had asked for her, as she wasn't even that keen on dolls.

Our grandparents, a widowed great-aunt and a couple of lonely parishioners came for Christmas dinner, but not, to our disappointment, Uncle Peter – still unmarried – who had been invited to a friend's house and was perhaps in search of a quieter Christmas than one dominated by four overexcited children. Sarah said she was surprised Trudy wasn't coming when she came almost every other day. Mam told her not to be cheeky. There was no sign of Jackie, either.

Chapter Twenty-seven

The Christmas holiday passed as it usually did in our household. Once Christmas Day was over, Dad took a few days off and we spent time with family friends. It was our turn to visit the Parker boys, while Catherine and Jane Rogerson and their parents spent the day with us. Sarah and I were pleased that they were visiting us this time, as at their house earlier in the year, after a delicious tea, Aunty Wendy had gone to fetch her guitar and we all had to join in and sing songs about our Saviour. It was all right until she sang a new song into which she inserted our names and expected us to sing a line on our own back at her. I mumbled mine, and wished I was somewhere else, a long way from the arms of Jesus. Mam smiled and clapped her hands, frowning at me and Sarah until we did too. It was harder to tell what Dad thought. In between songs, he kept talking about the tennis match he and Uncle Colin had promised themselves when we had been on holiday at Shepherds Dene and hadn't yet got round to playing. On the way home, Dad said that Uncle Colin and Aunty Wendy were evangelicals. They made a bigger noise about their faith than the rest of us did, which was a thing to be applauded.

We also had Mam's brother, Uncle Doug, and his family to stay, all the way from Down South, to catch up with friends and visit Grandma and Papa.

The only disappointment was hearing Mam tell Aunty Cathie that she had discovered in her latest *Family Circle* magazine that they and the other Shepherds Dene mothers had not won the word competition they had spent so many hours working on the previous summer. The winner had found an incredible twenty-three more words than they had. They didn't even qualify as runners-up and receive a *Family Circle* apron and ballpoint pen.

'But that's impossible! You had every possible word,' I protested, and Mam said she quite agreed, and fancy them wasting all those hours when they could have been doing something more useful with their time! But she and Aunty Cathie didn't seem as bothered as I was on their behalf.

That twenty-five-pound prize, even shared among them all, had seemed like a small fortune.

We went back to school. There were icy patches in the playground which we hoped wouldn't melt so that we could skate on them at playtime. But there was still no snow. At the end of the week we were allowed to bring in our Christmas presents. Mam wouldn't let me take Sasha, but I took the label-maker I had got in my stocking and a new game, and Kathryn, who had brought in Tippy Tumbles, let me play with her for a while and showed me how to make her do a somersault.

A few days into the new term, after three months of negotiations, the National Coal Board withdrew its pay offer to the miners, who promptly walked out in their first national strike for almost fifty years.

The first thing I knew about it was when one of the Julies announced that her birthday party was cancelled. Her birthday was in the middle of January, but she had handed out invitations two weeks before Christmas. She didn't say why it was no longer taking place but most of the girls seemed to understand.

The other indication that things were different now was the adults' universal cry of 'Switch that light off!' if we were last out of a room and being constantly reminded to save electricity. Most of the country's electricity then came from coal-fired power stations, so when other workers supported the miners and refused to cross picket lines at ports, power stations and coalyards, it wasn't just coal for our fires that was in short supply – our whole power supply was threatened.

One day I heard Mr Spedding tell a customer that he was running out of boxes of matches. Someone asked for some candles, and he was short of those as well. It wasn't normal for Mr Spedding to run out of anything.

They were days of cold, days of darkness. Instead of feeling that winter was behind us and that spring might be just around the corner, it felt as if we were going deeper and deeper into a winter from which we would never emerge. The world had become an old-fashioned place of stillness and candlelight. Our routines vanished. No Brownies in the school hall. Posters on shop windows announced new, shorter opening hours and the cancellation of meetings and social events until further notice. But it was exciting, too. With fuel stocks getting low, the government announced power cuts for the whole country. We went to school in the morning, wrapped up warmly – we were even allowed to wear trousers – and we came home at lunchtime with work set by the teacher to complete on our own. The house was dotted with little night lights, which we carried up to bed and got undressed by. It was like being alive in the olden days! This was our equivalent of Mam and Dad's wartime years, of blackouts and air-raid warnings.

Mrs Pickering gave us books of exercises to work from. We had to find the odd word out in a list, provide the next number in a sequence, fill in missing words and state whether they were verbs, nouns or adjectives. We each had a book of facts we had to learn and were tested on in class the next morning. The list of collective nouns was endless. Some were easy and we knew them already. A pack of wolves. A herd of cows. A flock of birds. Others were downright strange. Mam seemed to derive as much from the exercise as I did. She thought she knew most of them already, but was discovering that this was not the case.

'Well, for heaven's sake, why would a group of crows be called a "murder"? Crows pick at the bones, don't they, like vultures, so a "scavenge" would be more appropriate. Don't you think, Alder?'

Dad grunted. He was trying to write a sermon. We were all in one room, hoping to keep warm. Our own house used oil for its central heating, but the tank was low and we didn't know when it would be filled again.

'And did you know it was a "bench" of bishops?'

Dad didn't reply.

'I wonder what clergymen are,' she continued. 'There must be a word for them, surely. Perhaps it's a "worship" of,' she chuckled. She turned a page. 'Well, fancy that, it's a worship of writers, but not of clergymen. Where's the logic in that?'

It was cold wherever we went – at home, at school, at church. Our house wasn't a particularly warm one anyway, as Aunty Margaret had discovered on her summer visit, and we only had central heating downstairs. If we had kept our fireplaces, I thought, we could have sat round a lovely open fire. Except that there was no coal to burn. One morning Dad apprehended some men pulling down the fence at the end of the churchyard, which they were taking away to use as firewood.

Church was one place that remained open. For the Sunday services it was lit only with candles, but after the first couple of weeks, even these had to be rationed. Dad asked everyone to move forward so that he only needed to light the ones at the front. Most people did, but one or two people remained in their usual seats, including one man who sat behind the pillar he had always sat behind, even though he was now sitting in the dark.

'People don't like being told where to sit,' said Uncle George later. 'It's one of the cardinal rules. And the other one is never change the tunes they're used to singing.'

As we had sung 'Oh Jesus I have promised' to a jazzier tune a couple of weeks before, Dad wondered if he was trying to tell him not to do it again.

Our mothers had to plan more carefully what we ate and when we ate it. When the power was on we boiled kettles and filled thermos flasks with boiling water, and ate meals that could be made quickly, preferably on one ring. We often had Cup a

Soup before bed, and it felt like being on holiday in Aunty Barbie's cottage where we drank it to warm up after our evening walk on the beach. Mam, used to cooking and baking in bulk, fished mysterious packages out of the freezer – she was one of the first people in Ashington to own a stand-alone freezer – and left them to defrost overnight. One dinnertime she stuck her head through the hatch and declared, 'That chicken casserole you were looking forward to has turned out to be an apple dessert. So it's just scrambled egg, I'm afraid.' We were to get used to that happening.

A month after the start of the strike, the government declared a state of emergency and a three-day working week. The power cuts got longer, but when the electricity was on, Mam baked more than ever and Sarah and I were sent round to friends and neighbours with her loaves. We had often had tramps at the door who we fed and watered – one of them, Duncan, was a particular favourite of Mam's, though he terrified the life out of me with his long beard and hair that almost obscured his face, nor did I like the strong smell he gave off – but now one or two miners came knocking for help too. Dad had a discretionary fund he could dip into, but most callers were happy with a meal and a loaf and perhaps a bag of home-made biscuits if they timed it right.

One girl from Sarah's class who came to play occasionally, though she wasn't a particularly close friend, began to turn up every day just before teatime and inevitably ended up staying. One Saturday we were sitting down at twelve-thirty to spaghetti bolognese – one of our favourites, and a dish that there was never enough of – when she and a scruffy-looking companion we had never seen appeared on the doorstep. We weren't happy that our platefuls ended up being even smaller than they usually were.

'Be grateful you have something to eat when some children in the world are starving,' Mam said. 'You can always fill up on bread if you're still hungry.'

It was true that while there might not always be enough for second helpings, we never went hungry. When our grandparents visited, which both sets did every week, Grandma brought gingerbread or treacle tart and a sack of potatoes or other vegetables, while Other Grandma brought fruit, sweets and nuts, and Mr Spedding often left a box of vegetables on the doorstep that he had grown himself.

Mam also sent me and Sarah to check on our elderly neighbours, and to keep them company for a while. Apart from a couple of spinsters, they were mainly widows, many having been on their own for years, as the men in Ashington often died before they were old thanks to their unhealthy occupation. We sat in their kitchens, almost identical and still boasting the old-fashioned ranges that had been installed when the houses were built. Most of them had clippy mats, made from rags, on the floor, big copper kettles on the hob and large items of white underwear drying near the heat.

'What can we talk to them about?' we moaned. 'It's so boring!'

But Mam snapped: 'You weren't born yesterday. Use your initiatives, and hope that someone is kind to you when you're old ladies.'

I didn't think I would ever be that old. It was years before I would even be a teenager, so their sort of old was beyond even my vivid imagination. But we always came away clutching a coin or some sweets to share with our younger brother and sister, for which we then had to return with a thank-you letter from Ruth and Mark, often prompting yet more coins and sweets.

One morning when we girls were at school, Mam took Mark for a walk up the track to see Rip and saw two heads poking out of the ground a few yards in front of her. She couldn't believe what she was seeing. They were two young miners, digging up the path in search of coal, and were already about five feet down. Mam dashed home to get her camera – and a couple of loaves of bread.

The parish parties that Mam and Dad threw early in the new year would become eagerly anticipated annual events during our years in Ashington. This year they took place on two consecutive Sunday nights, just before the power cuts started. The parties were for anyone who helped at either of the two churches – they might be churchwardens, leaders of Brownies, Guides or Cubs, organizers of the Mothers' Union or on the flower-arranging or cleaning rotas. There were about ninety people in all, split into two groups. Mam prepared a hot buffet, as she said it was easier than serving cakes and titbits. There was a chicken casserole and something called chilli con carne, and enough rice to feed the whole of Newbiggin Road.

We were better prepared than we had been for the party in the summer. Sarah and I fished out every ashtray we could find from under the sink – all the fancy glass ones along with all the shells – and dotted them throughout the sitting room and dining room. At a quarter to seven, three-quarters of an hour before the start, we took bets on who would arrive first. Mam said it would be Miss Dobie or Mrs Oliver, another of the old ladies, keen to get a good seat. Dad said old Annie, who cleaned St Andrew's Church. I said the Bennett family and Sarah said the Turners.

Five minutes later, Miss Dobie came down the path, followed closely by Mrs Oliver. They made a beeline for the most comfortable chairs in the sitting room and didn't move all evening, even asking me and Sarah to fetch their food for them. Joyce Turner was next, and went straight to the kitchen to see if she could help, as she always did. The rest followed soon after. For a few hours there was little talk of politics and the strike, and instead, the sound of our parishioners enjoying themselves filled the house. Everyone in both churches loved socialising, and they were still making up for Canon Morton's earlier ban on these events.

They all helped themselves to the hot food, but one or two turned up their noses at the sound of chilli con carne.

'Think of it as fancy mince,' said Mam, and that did the trick.

Later she said she had never seen food disappear so fast. We'd been looking forward to the leftovers the next day, but there weren't any. It was the same story with the puddings, of which she'd made half a dozen. All that remained was a few spoonfuls of fruit salad.

Mrs Pickering asked us to complete a new topic of our choice while we were working at home. Dad suggested the Roman Wall, which he had written his dissertation on at university, but memories of standing among piles of rubble in freezing Northumberland fields whenever we had visitors put me off that idea. Instead I chose our North-East heroine, Grace Darling, who along with her father had rowed out in stormy seas from her home in Longstone Lighthouse on the Farne Islands and rescued several passengers from certain death on the rocks when their ship broke up.

I was wondering if one day I could do something as heroic as she had done, though perhaps not as dangerous, when Mam shouted to us all to come quickly. Her cousin, Beryl Privett, was on television. Mam and Beryl had grown up together, and it was Beryl who had been responsible for introducing my parents to each other at one of her parties. Dad had been interested in the lively young nurse, but when Mam had told him she was leaving for America, he promptly put her out of his mind and they had not met again until her return three years later, soon after he had been dumped by a girlfriend. Today Beryl, who ran night classes teaching men to cook, was appearing on our local news programme, *Look North*, to show people how to make simple, tasty meals with minimal use of electricity. All that sticks in my mind now is her chopping vegetables for soup and reminding us of the usefulness of thermos flasks.

Chapter Twenty-eight

Everyone was looking forward to the arrival of the new curate. Not long after his own arrival, Dad had realized that he and Father Murray were spending all their time burying, marrying and baptising with little time left for anything else. He had been aware before we came to Ashington that Seaton Hirst had a reputation for being one of the busiest parishes in the diocese, but he could hardly have been prepared for what hit him. With an average of 160 baptisms a year, up to 80 weddings and 200 funerals, he was rarely at home, or if he was, would be holed up in his study. And while the job of parish priest inevitably entailed some sort of personal sacrifice, he didn't want to miss out on family life entirely. Now his prayers were being answered. A young curate called Stephen Brown was on his way. A house had been bought for him – a terraced house on the other side of Newbiggin Road, just a few doors from Kathryn's – and Mam and some of the ladies scrubbed it out while the men did odd jobs and gave it a lick of paint.

Stephen Brown bounced into our lives like an enthusiastic puppy. He was good-looking and charming. The older ladies wanted to mother him. The younger ones went weak at the knees. Even some of the hard-faced ones softened when he looked into their eyes so sincerely. Aunty June patted her hair and said she wished she were a few years younger. Even we children knew Mr Brown was young compared to other adults. He had long hair – not as long as some of the lads' in church, but long enough to curl into his collar. Were priests even allowed to have hair that length? It seemed impossibly daring.

Trudy came up to me and Krishna after his first Sunday in church and whispered to us what a shame it was that he had a wife, Margaret, who was as good-looking as he was. 'But don't tell your mam,' she said, tapping her nose as Mam looked over. We laughed, flattered to have been taken into her confidence. Though she still came to church, we had seen less of her in the vicarage since she had started going out with a teacher from the technical college, but rumour had it that this relationship was on the rocks.

Mr Brown – as he was to us children – arrived full of youthful idealism. He spoke about going into the mines and the shops and the factories and spreading the word. But most of all he talked about doing more with 'our young people' and as he let his gaze wander over the younger members of the congregation, I thought perhaps that being young made us special and worth nurturing. He asked us what he could do to make church more fun for us. We didn't dislike church, but we had never before considered that it might be fun. He told us of his plans to bring us all together, the young people from both churches, in a youth and drama club. I felt a flutter of anticipation at the prospect. At last I was going to have the chance to get to know Gary Hunt properly! I supposed Brian, with his cheeky smile, might be there too. Perhaps they would end up fighting over me!

He didn't just court the youth. Over time, Mr Brown brought a group of people into church who Mam called 'Stephen's gang' – people who hadn't gone to church before, or who had lapsed, but were won back thanks to his charisma and personality.

He was a powerful speaker. 'God sees you whatever you're doing!' he boomed from the pulpit one Sunday. 'Yes, he even sees you when you're on the lavatory.'

In the front row we laughed delightedly, and we heard some tittering from behind, but there were gasps as well.

'I'm not happy about that,' Miss Dobie said to Mam when she came to tea the next day. 'I'm not happy at all. We all need some private time, even from the Almighty, and there's some business I'd rather keep to myself.'

Sarah and I exploded and had to leave the table, while Mam twisted her face sympathetically and excused herself to refill the teapot.

We got our snow at last. It fell on a Sunday and had turned the graveyard into a picture like the ones on the cards Uncle Peter sold in his shop by the time we came out of church. We pleaded that Krishna and Nicola be allowed to stay for dinner so that it had a chance to grow thicker. Aunty Beryl said she would go home to do some jobs and come back for them later, but was persuaded to stay as well. Later Kathryn and Sandra both came to play, and so did Sarah's friends Dawn and Linda. We didn't want to come inside that afternoon.

The next morning we walked to school, throwing snowballs all the way, and Mam pulled Ruth and Mark on the sledge when she went to drop Ruth off. We usually did our homework as soon as we had eaten, but Mam let us make the most of the weather. The snowballs we made stuck together better today and we pushed a giant ball around the garden until it was too heavy to push any more. Then Mam insisted I come inside and finish my Grace Darling topic. As darkness fell and the candles flickered around me, the outside world seemed lighter than inside, the brilliance of the ground casting a sheen over the rest of the garden. We were sorry to see the snow melt before the following weekend arrived.

'The country's on its knees,' muttered Ted Nichol when he came to put up a shelf for Mam's cookery books. The strike had been going on for almost six weeks. Workers across the country had been laid off. There were rumours that the lights would be going off and staying off before long. Then, a few days later, it was all over. A deal was reached between the miners and the government, and the miners went back to work. Things returned to normal. We went back to school for full days again, our Brownies meeting resumed on a Monday evening, the electricity stayed on and the candles were put away in a cupboard ready for future emergencies. I was sorry to see them go.

To celebrate, Aunty June and Uncle Andy took me, Kathryn and Sarah on the bus to Blyth one Saturday afternoon to see an Elvis Presley double bill of *GI Blues* and *Blue Hawaii*. We left the cinema carried on a tide of music down the street. We serenaded the man selling hot dogs from a stall: it was mainly Aunty June, the rest of us joining in timidly, responding to her nudges. Uncle Andy bought us a hot dog each, something Mam would never have allowed from a street seller. On the bus we sang 'Rock-a-Hula Baby' all the way home, more confidently now, and the next day Aunty June came round with Carol's *Blue Hawaii* LP. 'She'll not mind, and anyway, she'll never know.' We often played it when she came round. Aunty June could wiggle her hips better than anyone.

Mrs Oliver introduced herself to Mr Brown by taking round one of her chocolate cakes. These were very popular in our house, and a serious rival to the famous Dobie cakes. When Mrs Brown answered the door, Mrs Oliver thrust the cake into her hands, saying, 'I don't suppose Father Brown will have had a home-made cake quite like this before.' Margaret, a trained cordon bleu chef, bit her lip and thanked her.

Mam laughed when Mrs Brown told her, and said that it was best to ignore these sorts of remarks.

'Mrs Oliver was one of the first people to get a colour television, and doesn't everyone know it! I gave her a lift last year when Wimbledon was on, and she suddenly came out with, "Don't the balls show up beautifully on the green grass!" I just agreed with her and changed the subject.'

Sarah and I were perched in the large tree by the front gate. We had filled the Jif lemon with water and were squirting it at passers-by. We got one man right in the middle of his back. He stopped and turned round, failed to see us in the branches then carried on walking, reaching awkwardly for the wet spot as he did so. A few minutes later we saw Mr Brown walk jauntily by on the other side of Newbiggin Road. It was an unusually mild day, and he wore his grey clerical shirt and dog collar and carried his coat. He continued until we could no longer see him, but soon he was coming back, walking faster, and disappearing up Milburn Road. After a few more minutes he appeared back at the junction, crossed the road and began walking past the church and towards the vicarage. Sarah took aim and caught him on his right shoulder. We saw a small dark patch appearing on his shirt. We gave ourselves away by laughing.

'Phew! I thought a bird had got me for just a second,' he said, coming to stand under the tree. 'No, please, please, no more! I'm on my way out! In fact, you can probably help me.'

He explained that he was supposed to be meeting someone in the White Elephant for a drink. He'd been told he couldn't miss it, but he had been up and down Newbiggin Road twice now, and even walked a fair way up Milburn Road in case he had misunderstood his directions.

Sarah and I could hardly contain ourselves. 'It's right there,' we said. 'You're looking at it.'

'But that's the North Seaton Hotel,' he protested. 'I did stop there for a second, but the name couldn't be any more obvious so I carried on.'

'Everyone calls it the White Elephant,' we said, overjoyed to think that grown-ups could make silly mistakes too.

He thanked us for our help and set off once again, calling back over his shoulder, 'I'll get you for that soaking. Just you wait.'

Chapter Twenty-nine

When Krishna and Nicola came to stay one night, we were allowed to stay up late and watch a film, the true story of three shepherd children in Portugal who had seen visions of the Virgin Mary. The Virgin had asked them to make sacrifices, and had made predictions about the future that had come true. One of the girls, Lucia, had become a nun and devoted the rest of her life to God. When the film had finished we took great delight in scaring each other by creeping into each other's rooms draped in sheets and pretending to be the Virgin. But the next night, when I didn't have Krishna in the other bed beside me, there she was in her robes and headdress on my bedroom wall, a dark shadow that moved round the room whenever a car went past outside. Perhaps she was waiting to show herself to me properly and then I too would have to live a holy life, like Lucia.

'If the Virgin Mary appears to you, do you have to be a nun?'

I asked Mam, when she came to say goodnight a few evenings later.

'Who on earth has seen the Virgin Mary appear to them? Don't tell me it's Kathryn.' As Kathryn's dad had seen Santa Claus, perhaps she thought the whole family were starting to have visions. She picked up the book I was reading and turned it over to read the back, as if looking for the answer to her question there.

'Of course not! But remember the film?'

Mam had seen part of it, but had gone off to do something more important, like type Dad's sermon.

She seemed to understand now. She kissed me goodnight. 'Oh, that nonsense! I don't think she appears like that very often, but some people have a calling in other ways. People like Dad and Brother John and Brother Kevin. Now, go to sleep or there'll be more than the Virgin Mary after you.'

'But it wasn't nonsense! It was a true story!'

Mam shrugged and gave one of her tuts that suggested the truth might not be so simple.

'I won't be a nun, even if I do have a vision,' I called after her, hoping that saying it out loud would make it less likely to happen. But I couldn't help adding uncertainly, 'Is that all right?'

Mam laughed as she went back downstairs. 'Don't ask me. That'll be a matter for you and your conscience.'

That wasn't the answer I wanted. How could I marry Gary Hunt if I was shut away in a convent? I wished I had never seen the film.

The announcement came in the notices at the beginning of church. Dad made it, looking across at Mr Brown, who nodded to confirm the details. Anyone aged thirteen or over was invited to see Mr Brown after church about his new youth club. There was a conciliatory glance towards me and Sarah, Krishna and Nicola. 'And any of the younger ones who would like to be confirmed later in the year, can they see me or Mr Brown, please. Classes will start later this spring.'

So that was it. I was too young for the youth club. A dozen of us were going to meet every week in our confirmation class, but that was going to be more like being at school. And to make things worse, as I watched the older children gather round Mr Brown at the end of the service, I noticed that Gary Hunt and Yvonne Dodds were holding hands. How could Gary like Yvonne Dodds? Sarah and I had agreed that Yvonne was a nice girl – she sometimes helped at Brownies – but she had frizzy hair that reminded us of sprouting seeds. It didn't make sense. Later, I consoled myself with the thought that in three years' time I too would be thirteen, and Gary might have grown tired of Yvonne and her hair. Or perhaps, if something happened to me in the meantime – if I recovered from a serious illness, or saved people when Ashington was devastated by an earthquake – I would appear more fascinating in his eyes. I couldn't help hoping that something like that would happen.

Something woke me up in the middle of the night, and it wasn't the Virgin Mary. I opened my eyes, then sank back down into a dream in which a ringing bell took me back to the house when we had first visited it, and Sarah and I had rung the bells that used to summon the housekeeper. What fun it had been! And what a disappointment that we hadn't been allowed to keep them. Krishna was with me in my dream, and I was showing her how they worked. Then I woke up and there really was a bell ringing, but it sounded more like our front door bell. I listened for Mam or Dad on the stairs, for the porch door being opened, words being spoken, but nothing happened. I had no idea what time it was, or if they were still downstairs or in bed themselves. I lay there for a few seconds longer, then, when I heard the bell again, reluctantly got up.

In Mam and Dad's bedroom, the illuminated alarm clock at the side of the bed said three twenty. They were both fast asleep.

'Someone's at the door,' I said, feeling foolish as soon as the words had left my mouth. People didn't ring the doorbell at this sort of hour, even in our house.

Dad stirred, then opened his eyes. 'Eh? What is it?'

'Are you not well?' asked Mam, sitting up suddenly.

I repeated that I thought someone was at the door.

'No,' said Dad. 'You've dreamt it.' But he was getting out of bed and pulling on his dressing gown, slightly annoyed but resigned to going down to see, and Mam was saying that one of them would have heard it if there was.

Then the bell rang again.

'Well I never,' Dad said, and hurried downstairs.

We heard him ushering someone inside, then Mam got up too and told me to go back to bed.

'I'll tell you what it's all about when I come back up,' she promised, but I was alseep before she did.

I found out at breakfast time that the caller had been Ethel Collingwood from over the road, wanting to call an ambulance as her husband, Stan, was doubled up in pain. I only knew Stan vaguely, but I worried about him all day at school. He often walked his dog, Kim, up the track when we were visiting Rip, and passed around a grubby bag of Black Bullets, though Mam said we were taking our life in our hands accepting one.

By the time I got home from school, he was fine. Mam said he had been suffering from nothing but constipation.

'What's that?' I asked.

'It's what you get if you don't eat your fruit and vegetables and my bread,' she said ominously.

On Sunday after church she was telling Aunty Beryl about the episode. As nurses, they always thought of the worst-case scenario when medical matters were being discussed, except when we, their children, were the sick ones, in which case it was 'just a cold' or a 'slight temperature' and 'nothing to make a fuss about'.

'I did think it might have been his appendix,' said Mam as she put the kettle on.

Aunty Beryl got the beakers out of the cupboard. 'An ulcer,' she suggested. 'Gallstones. Kidney stones.'

'Could have been nasty,' said Mam. 'Oh well, all's well that ends well.' She tossed me a bag of crisps to put out for the children and said, almost as an afterthought, 'At least appendicitis is something I don't have to worry about myself.'

'Have you already had it?' asked Aunty Beryl, sounding concerned.

'Yes and no. I'd had the odd rumbling, so when I was doing my training at the General I had it removed. My friend Jimmy was a theatre nurse so I asked him to pickle it for me so that I could see for myself if it was gangrenous. I've still got it somewhere.'

'Gwenda!' laughed Aunty Beryl. 'I've heard everything now.

You're not going to tell me it's sitting on the mantelpiece, are you?'

They both laughed. 'Not quite, but I've got it in a bottle somewhere. I suppose I could put it on display, now you've suggested it.'

A thought struck me. 'Does your appendix look a bit like a snake?'

Mam tried to sound annoyed. 'Have you girls been poking around somewhere you're not supposed to?'

So my mother hadn't killed a snake in the American desert; she had preserved her appendix and kept it for posterity. It was now floating around in a jam jar in the attic. She had done some strange things, but this might be the strangest yet. Even Krishna and Nicola, who were usually more impressed with Mam's tales than Sarah and I were, looked disgusted when I told them.

Chapter Thirty

Though I felt different from my friends in several ways, I still felt as if I belonged in Ashington. Our life in Gosforth – living in a suburban house on a suburban street – no longer felt like my own past, and memories from those days faded when competing with the far more dramatic goings-on that life in a proper vicarage entailed, especially one at the heart of a community of people with such a strong local identity.

Both my parents had North-Eastern forebears going back several generations, so I knew I had as strong a claim to being a proper Geordie as anyone, even if my accent would never be as broad as the Ashington one. Occasionally, when looking at the letters Mam regularly received from America, and the photographs inside them of happy, smiling families gathered round swimming pools, I wished that Mam had stayed there and married one of her admirers and that I too was an American.

Everyone looked far more glamorous than anyone in our country ever looked, their contentment and well-being almost bursting out of the photo. I too could have been the girl with the swimming pool in the yard, or summer camp to look forward to. Mam would remind me that if she had married an American I wouldn't have been me at all, as Dad wouldn't have been my father. However, I was convinced I would still have been myself, just a superior version.

I hoped I might yet become one of the Melendy children from Elizabeth Enright's books set in New York. I had become engrossed in the series, leaving behind Enid Blyton at last, much to Mam's relief. How I would have loved to swap the vicarage sometimes for the delicious freedom of their motherless lives! But if I ever voiced my dreams too enthusiastically, Mam told me that Americans spoke too loudly and were not as polite as British people, that they knew shockingly little about the rest of the world and thought England was a town in Texas or a province of Canada. That I was lucky to be who I was.

She might at least have been pleased, then, when I told her that Sandra and Kathryn and I were going to live in houses next door to each other when we were married and all have children at the same time. But no; she told me I would want to spread my wings a bit and see the rest of the world.

Thankfully, despite being such a dreamer, most of the time I was quite happy to be where I was and just one of the girls. I was nine years old, soon to be ten, and the things my friends and I had in common far outweighed the differences. We went to school, did our lessons, played skippy and chasey and two bally in the playground, fell in and out of friendships, were nice to each other most of the time but occasionally spiteful. We didn't spend much time talking about what our fathers did, or commenting on each other's accents. Sarah and I were never short of friends, and if there was some truth in what Grandma said to us once – 'I wonder if you'd have so many little girls coming to play if you didn't have such a big garden' – we didn't really worry about it.

When one day at school Mrs Pickering sighed when I had finished reading something aloud to her, and said wistfully, 'Oh, and you used to speak so nicely,' I knew this was my home.

One occasion when it was nice to be different was when our friends were different for the same reason. On Ash Wednesday, those of us who went to church had permission to leave school to go to the Ash Wednesday service, which took place at St Andrew's Church. In my class, that included me and Kathryn, Angela, two of the Susans and a couple of other girls. When we got back to school, our classmates surrounded us and looked – some admiringly, some with scorn – at the ash crosses that now adorned our foreheads.

'When are you going to wash them off?' asked one of the Julies.

'I'm keeping mine on,' said Angela.

'Did it hurt?' asked someone else, visibly recoiling.

'No, man! The ash isn't hot.'

'She thinks we've been branded like cattle!' snorted Kathryn.

We were the talk of the class that day.

Mam suggested that Sarah and I were old enough to give something up for Lent this year, and that there was no point unless it was something we would miss. Sweets were the obvious choice. Dad was kind enough to tell us that, strictly speaking,

Lent didn't include Sundays so we could have a day off our fast if we wanted to, but it felt like cheating, especially when nobody else seemed to know this. The sweet tin began to overflow as Other Grandma still brought bars of chocolate and sticks of liquorice every Saturday. She shook her head sadly at Mam and Dad as if she thought it the utmost cruelty that we were being denied them until Easter Day.

That might have been one of the reasons why Easter seemed to take forever to arrive that year, but at last it was Palm Sunday, and just a week to go. Going to church once a week was usually enough for me and Sarah, but we didn't want to miss Mr Brown's youth group's performances at the Holy Week services. The group had their own fancy name, Tableau. We didn't know what it meant, but it made them sound important.

'They all fancy themselves,' we agreed among our pre-teenage crowd. But we were still desperate to see what the older children had been getting up to.

On each day of Holy Week they acted out a different part of the Easter story. They all looked so professional with their bare feet and long robes. The boy playing Jesus was another Brian and had dark shoulder-length hair and spots on his shoulders. Gary played a Roman soldier as well as a disciple and looked more handsome than ever. Yvonne was playing Mary the mother of Jesus and her friend, Fiona, was Mary Magdalene. The actors quickly and quietly arranged themselves into scenes as someone else told the story, then one of them spoke up about what he or she was feeling at that moment before falling silent again.

'Mary Magdalene should have long hair,' I whispered to Sarah. I felt a tiny bit of satisfaction to think that I might have looked the part more than Fiona.

'She's dead good, though,' said Sarah. 'They all are.'

I had to agree. There was something very moving in the simplicity of the production. And it was nice to have an excuse to stare at Gary.

'I'm surprised you're so keen on church this week,' said Mam, looking pleased as we got ready to leave the house on Maundy Thursday, our fifth service in a row. 'People think that Christmas is the most important festival in the Christian year, but in fact it's Easter. Everything is founded on the Resurrection.'

Spring had arrived, and tiny colourful flowers we hadn't seen before sprang up around the trees and bushes in the garden. Bluebells spread thickly through one of the borders, and Papa said that though they looked pretty, they were a weed if they were growing in the wrong place.

Alan told me and Sarah that he was giving up his job as our gravedigger to go down the pit.

'I'll miss this, though,' he added, looking sadly at a half-dug grave. 'I do like being out in the fresh air.'

He and his wife Joan were having a baby any day now. The idea of a little Alan was appealing, but it might mean Alan wouldn't want to spend so much time with us. Sarah and I wondered if the baby was Joan's idea. We thought that Joan was the boss in their house; she was even in charge of the telephone. If we answered the phone to her she would ask for Dad, then say, 'It's Joan here, Father, I'll put Alan on now.'

We were sad to think that we wouldn't see him in the graveyard or at our kitchen table any more. Ruth and Mark were going to miss him too.

*

Mam decided that with all the entertaining she was doing, she really needed a chest freezer. Her present freezer was about the size of an ordinary fridge, and stayed in the garage, but when one day she spent half an hour trying to accommodate a couple of loaves of newly baked bread into the crammed shelves, she decided that something bigger was required.

It arrived, and it was enormous.

'The hospital mortuary will be giving you a call if they run out of space,' said Aunty Beryl when she saw it.

'Everyone has them in the States,' said Mam.

'Are you really sure we need something this size?' asked Dad.

'It'll be worth its weight in gold,' said Mam.

Mam ordered her meat from Arthur Temple, the butcher in Newcastle's Grainger Market. When it arrived she sorted the joints into individual polythene bags, then Sarah and I sat sucking the air out of them using a straw, the method recommended in her instruction booklet to keep things as fresh as possible.

'Perhaps you could start labelling things from now on,' suggested Dad as he came into the kitchen to see if Mam was ready to type up his sermon.

'I already do that, dear,' said Mam.

'So how come that chocolate sauce turned out to be gravy? I was looking forward to that ice-cream before it was ruined.'

Mam started laughing so much she set me and Sarah off. Dad went back to his study, shaking his head in exasperation.

On Easter Day the doorbell went and there stood Jackie, grinning broadly and looking well apart from a cut on her nose. As far as I knew, no one had seen or heard from her since she left us the previous summer, though Sarah and I spoke about her occasionally. I was delighted to see her.

'Your mam said I was invited to high days and feast days, so here I am,' she announced, stepping inside. 'And this is the biggest one of the lot.'

Mam, who must have seen her from the kitchen window, appeared behind me.

'Jackie! How lovely to see you!' Her voice sounded a little clipped. She gave her a kiss, then held her by the shoulders at arm's length, looking into her eyes. 'How are you managing?'

'I'm champion,' said Jackie. 'You know me.' She handed over a carrier bag. 'I brought you all an Easter egg.'

'You shouldn't have,' said Mam. 'You're too generous.' She peeked into the bag. 'And six of them, too – oh, Jackie, it's too much!'

'They're just little,' said Jackie, raising her eyes at me.

'Come and tell me what you're up to these days,' said Mam, shepherding her into the kitchen, 'then I'll introduce you to the old folk.'

Grandma and Papa had already arrived for dinner.

'Who is it?' mouthed Grandma when I went back into the sitting room.

'It's Jackie,' I said, looking at Sarah with a grin.

'Not the one who caused all that trouble before?' said Grandma, though it was more a statement than a question.

'No!' I said adamantly, though I realized I didn't really know.

'She's dead nice!' said Sarah. 'Remember when we went to the Ghost Town and Ruth sat on that old netty?'

Grandma did not look impressed. 'I don't know what your parents are playing at sometimes,' she said. 'Hasn't your mother got enough to do with four children without needing someone else to look after?'

A few minutes later, Mam brought Jackie into the room.

'My parents, Arthur and Gwen Brady,' she announced. 'This is our friend Jackie.'

Jackie nodded briefly at Grandma, then made a beeline for Papa, who had Mark on his lap and couldn't stand up. She crouched down in front of him, put her hand on his knee and said how pleased she was to meet him, and hadn't Mark grown up a lot, all the while keeping her hand on his knee. Papa, who had been complaining about his knee for some time, winced and beamed at the same time. Grandma shook her head at Mam, and left the room. I noticed that Jackie's eyes kept darting from one thing to another and that she had brought that familiar smell with her, not the apple shampoo but the other one.

When Dad got back from that morning's services and was carving the joint, I heard him and Mam talking quietly in the kitchen.

'They said to bring her any time,' Mam was saying.

'But we can't force her,' Dad replied. 'We don't want a repeat of last time.'

'Well, if she agrees . . . ' Mam trailed off.

'Who? Where are you taking her?' I asked.

Mam said to be quiet for now, and they would tell me later.

'Do you still play that bears game?' asked Jackie after dinner.

I nodded. 'Sometimes.' Though I still enjoyed it, we spent more time skipping or playing endless games of two bally against the sitting-room wall. I was getting better at overarms now, but it was harder to throw the ball under your leg and keep control of it. It was only if Ruth and Mark pestered us that we played bears these days.

'Do you know what I thought to myself one day?' she said. 'You know how the mother went and got her kiddy killed by taking a photo? Well, I wonder if she ended up photographing what happened. Can you imagine?' Her eyes gleamed into mine as if she could see my deepest thoughts.

I realized that out of all the questions I had asked Mam, I had never thought of this one, the most intriguing and terrible question of all.

'Now there's a story for you,' she added, giving a self-satisfied nod.

Grandma and Papa left after tea, Grandma mouthing, 'Get rid of her,' to Mam as she left. We had another visitor that evening – Trudy, looking flushed and excited.

'You're not going to believe this,' said Trudy.

Mam's expression suggested that she probably would.

'I met a man at the club a couple of nights ago who's just come back from working in London. It turns out we were living five minutes from each other when I was there. He worked at the Tower of London.'

'Not a Beefeater?' laughed Mam, and Trudy said hardly, they were about a hundred and fifty.

'But we really hit it off. He's a bit shorter than I'd like but you can't have everything. I really think, Gwenda, that he might be the one.'

'Has he got a wooden leg?' I asked.

'Or a glass eye?' continued Sarah, as we both tried hard not to laugh.

Trudy gave us a quizzical look but didn't say anything.

'Well,' said Mam, ignoring us. 'I hope so too. But you've only just met him so don't go building your hopes up too much.'

'I can't decide if he's more like Ryan O'Neal, or Robert Redford.'

Jackie, who had been quiet up until now, snorted. Trudy looked across at her, gave an apologetic shrug that could have meant all sorts of things, then looked back at Mam.

'I'd love a coffee,' she said. 'I'll put the kettle on. Any chance of a ginger biscuit?'

When she and Mam were in the kitchen, Jackie said to me and Sarah, 'She loves herself, she does.' She sounded like a spoilt child who wasn't getting the attention she deserved.

'She's canny,' I said.

'Yeah, she's dead nice when you get to know her,' said Sarah soothingly.

'I'll probably go soon,' said Jackie. Then she brightened up. 'Did I tell you I'm starting a job in Bainbridge's next week?'

This was Grandma's favourite department store, and we always had a drink and cake in the coffee shop there when we went to town with her, which just about made up for spending so long in haberdashery.

'Ooh, we can come and see you when we go to Newcastle,' I said. 'Which department?'

'I don't know yet. I'll tell you when I find out. I might be able to give you stuff cheap.' She almost smiled before her voice took on its sulky tone again. 'Your mam and dad want to send us away, though, so I might have to chuck it in before I've even started.'

'What do you mean?' asked Sarah.

'It wasn't me, you know, who burnt the bedclothes that time. I told your mam, I've no idea how it happened. She said I could have burnt the house down, but I'm not that stupid. I'd have woken up first.'

Sarah and I hadn't a clue what she was talking about. When Mam and Trudy came back into the room she had changed the conversation and was cheerful again, and even managed to be polite to Trudy.

Later, when Trudy had gone, Mam, Dad and Jackie disappeared into Dad's study for a while. Then Mam came out and said that Aunty June was coming to stay the night as she and Dad had to take Jackie somewhere.

It all happened quickly after that. Aunty June was barging into the sitting room, asking if we had seen Christopher Lee on *Stars on Sunday* and telling us there was a good *fillim* on later. 'With Yul Brynner!' she swooned.

'But he's got a bald head!' I protested.

'Ooh, he's gorgeous!'

We forgot about Jackie for a few minutes, and when we went to say goodbye, she was already in the car. Sarah and I looked out of the landing window and saw her small figure in the back seat. When we waved she seemed to move her head in acknowledgement, then turned the other way.

Chapter Thirty-one

Mam and Dad were back at teatime the next day. They both looked exhausted after a six-hundred-mile round trip to Berkshire and back, with very few stops. Mam had done all the driving, as usual. She always felt sick in the car if she wasn't behind the wheel.

I had never learnt much about Jackie. She had never answered many personal questions, or perhaps we had never asked them. When Mam had told me all those months ago that Jackie 'liked a drink', it hadn't occurred to me that this was a real problem, or that she had an illness called alcoholism. Although Mam hadn't wanted to tell us before, now that Jackie had practically spilt the beans she confessed that on the last night of her stay the previous year she had gone upstairs to find singed bedsheets and Jackie nearly unconscious with a cigarette in her hand. She had sat up in the attic with her all night, terrified that she would set fire to the house and to all of us, before insisting to Dad the next day that he find somewhere else for her to go. Mam and Dad were fond of Jackie and wanted to help her, and when they heard about a convent with an excellent reputation for helping addicts of all kinds, they thought of her immediately. Dad had spoken to the Mother Superior, who had agreed to take her any time of day or night, as long as she came of her own free will. Mam and Dad had driven first to Whitley Bay where they had borrowed Grandpa's car, a large, sleek automatic, more suited to the long journey than our Morris Traveller.

The story did have its amusing part, however, and Mam would tell this story for many years to come. When they arrived, a sweet-faced nun had come straight to the car park and gently led Jackie away. Mam had driven all night, and when a second nun appeared and suggested she come inside to wash her face and have a cup of tea or coffee, she went with her willingly. Dad said he wanted some fresh air first, and had a little walk to stretch his legs. When he went into the building, he found his way to the kitchen by following the smell of freshly baked bread. He hadn't eaten since teatime the day before and was famished. There he found Jackie, happily tucking into toast and mar-malade, chatting to a nun who sat beside her at the table, while another stood frying eggs at the stove. The cooking nun asked Dad what he would like to eat, and he gratefully accepted the offer of a fried breakfast – something he had only once a week now, unlike the early days of his marriage when he had eaten one every day.

After about ten minutes, he thought it a bit strange that Mam hadn't made an appearance, and asked what she was doing and if she was eating too. The nun who was cooking said that he was not to worry, the lady was being well looked after. He repeated that it was his wife he was enquiring about, and not Jackie, and that she was taking her time, whatever she was up to. He was aware then that the two nuns were looking at each other strangely.

'You mean, this lady isn't your wife?' asked the one at the table, indicating Jackie, who was now polishing off a plate of bacon and eggs.

'No, it certainly isn't!' said Dad, standing up and feeling a sudden stab of anxiety. 'That's Jackie, the person we rang you about. I thought you knew that.'

Just then, the kitchen door opened and Mam came in grinning, with a sheepish-looking nun behind her.

'I've just been taken upstairs and shown my room,' she said, her laughter containing a hint of hysteria. She saw Jackie and added, 'You're very lucky, Jackie. It's a beautiful place. I could do with a holiday here myself.'

'I'm terribly sorry,' the nun beside her kept saying. 'I didn't realize that Sister Anne had come out before me, and I assumed . . . '

'Well,' said Grandma as the tale came to an end – she and Papa had come to take over from Aunty June that afternoon – 'that might have been the last we saw of you. Mind, that Jackie fell on her feet with you two.'

'It's part of the job, Mum,' said Mam patiently. 'Every parish has their share of Jackies. And there'll be another to take her place, you'll see.' She turned to Dad. 'Remember Gloria, in the last parish?'

'You mean that nice lady who brought me and Sarah the purses we wore round our necks?' I interrupted.

'You see,' said Grandma. 'Your children think it's normal to have all these no-hopers around. I daren't think what it's doing to them.'

'She became a Catholic in the end,' said Dad. 'Saved us a lot of bother.'

I woke one Saturday morning to the sound of music crashing down the road. From my side window that overlooked the street I could see people marching past our house – men holding banners which caught in the wind like the sails of great ships and other men, women and children walking cheerfully behind. I rushed to the large landing window that Sarah and I sometimes sat on at night. The trees in the front garden hid part of the road, but I could see the band striding on ahead and a troop of youngsters twirling their batons expertly behind them. Some of the girls at school were in the jazz band, and I'd watched them throwing and catching their batons in the playground. They looked so clever.

It was the day of the miners' picnic. My schoolfriends had been talking about it for the past couple of weeks, and I had sensed something important. Someone's cousin was the carnival queen. Someone else couldn't wait for the rides, and someone else for the candy floss she'd been promised. But when I told Mam about this day that we would all be celebrating together, she told me that it was a special day for miners and their families, not for us.

'But we can go too,' I pleaded, before adding hopelessly, 'I can get the bus to Bedlington with Sarah!'

But Mam was adamant. 'We've got visitors, and anyway, we go on picnics all the time.' This was true. Picnics were a regular occurrence in our household, whatever the weather or the time of year. A day out usually entailed filling the picnic hamper, a flask of coffee for the adults and making sure we had a couple of rugs in the car.

'Are you going?' asked Sandra, and I just shrugged and said maybe, but we might be doing something else more exciting. Though I wondered if that were possible.

Fortunately, I had the garden party to look forward to. As there hadn't been one for several years, it had been the talk of both churches for ages. I scrambled to the window as soon as I woke up that morning and was pleased to see blue sky, though it also looked breezy. The night before, Mam had burst in on me watching *Crossroads* and said that she'd totally forgotten that she had volunteered to sort out the bran tub, and could Sarah and I quickly wrap one hundred and twenty small items, please. She plonked a couple of cardboard boxes in front of us containing egg cups, plastic combs in little pouches, biros and flip-top mirrors. We pointed out that she had offered to do this, not us, but she said she had enough to do and it wouldn't hurt us to help. The egg cups were Mam's latest discovery from one of her catalogues, and came in two pieces – you sat the egg in one part and put the other part over it, which made it easier to make a clean cut across the top.

We were having breakfast when Mark shouted that there were men in the garden and ran to put on his shoes so that he could join them. There was a group of them with ladders and long strings of bunting, which they used to line the paths and most of the tennis court. Then they erected a large tent on the lawn which would be the tea room, made journeys to and from the church hall to fetch tables and chairs and set up the stalls round the edge of the tennis court.

Later that morning, some of the ladies from the Mothers' Union, which was in charge of the teas, arrived to get things ready. Mam showed them into the kitchen, pointed out the boxes containing the cups and saucers that had been dropped off earlier and some of the cakes and scones that had already been delivered, and told them to make themselves at home. 'Don't mind me, I'll just be popping in and out,' she said.

When she went back ten minutes later, no one had moved.

'Please, treat it as your own kitchen,' she repeated. 'I've cleared the bench for you. There's plenty of sockets for the urn.'

But they still hung back. Then Jean Kirkup arrived and took charge in her forthright manner.

'Right,' she said, looking at each of them in turn. '*You* unpack the cups and saucers, *you* butter the scones, *you* slice the cakes.'

The women sprang into action, happy to be told what to do.

By one o'clock, the tennis court was full of stalls. Vera Bennett and Miss Dobie were on the cakes, sweet Mrs Gascoigne and Joyce Turner presided over a stall selling their knitted goods. 'Tell yer mam I've done a nice two-piece, shorts and a cardigan, just the right size for your Mark,' said Mrs Gascoigne. There was a stall selling little bottles of pop in flavours I'd never tried before – cream soda, Tizer, dandelion and burdock.

Annie, who cleaned St Andrew's Church, had a pound stall, selling items that weighed a pound – a pound of rice, a pound of sugar, a pound of apples. The Kirkups' son, David, was charging ten pence to choose a single of your choice and have it played over the loudspeakers. Sandra Bennett and the Guides had a bathroom stall, and her brother Brian was running something called a buzz wire; you had to guide a metal hoop around an intricate pattern of wire without it touching the sides and buzzing. You won a tiny packet of Refreshers or Parma Violets if you were successful. The Scouts from St Andrew's had organized lots of games – a coconut shy, smash the crockery and roll the penny – and the Brownies were selling ice-creams. One man sold stone garden ornaments that you could paint yourself. There was something for everyone, and I decided that I almost didn't mind having missed the miners' picnic when we had this happening in our own back garden.

Everyone seemed to be in the best of moods. The music put a smile on everyone's face – the Drifters and Lindisfarne were the most popular bands that afternoon, along with Donny Osmond, who had recently declared to the world that his favourite colour was purple, thus ensuring that several of my friends and I decided that it was our favourite colour too.

Trudy was walking around hand in hand with her new boyfriend, the man from the Tower of London.

'Have you met Frank?' she asked me as Krishna and I perused for the twentieth time the list of records on offer on David's stall. I was starting to get interested in the charts now, and just reading the names of the bands and being able to hear them in my own garden felt as thrilling as if they were playing especially for me. I smiled and said hello, and tried not to look surprised when I saw that the resemblance with Robert Redford was far from obvious and that he had what Mam would have described as 'a bit of a tummy' on him.

'She's Gwenda's oldest,' said Trudy to her beau. 'Gwenda's

been so good to me. Well, you all have.' She patted my hand. I smiled shyly.

'Has your mam done any baking for the cake stall?' she called over her shoulder, and went to find out.

Kathryn joined us. We went into the tea tent and bought plastic cups of warm orange squash from the Mothers' Union ladies. Uncle Jim's wife, Doris, was in charge now, helped by Phemie Templey and Sylvia Lewins. Krishna and I had cheese scones with our drinks, and someone must have known Kathryn was coming because there were plates full of meat buns.

Mrs Oliver, sitting with Miss Dobie, who had taken a break from the cake stall, suddenly leant across to a man on the next table and said, 'That's my chocolate cake you've got there, young man!'

The young man, though clearly embarrassed, managed to nod and say, as he wiped the crumbs from his lips, 'It's canny good cake, like, canny good.'

David boomed out over the microphone: 'I'll let someone have a free record if it's not the Drifters or Donny Osmond. Oh, and add David Cassidy to that list, too.' A gang of lads dashed over to have their say.

Joyce Turner said her knitted lady toilet-roll covers (the loo roll went under the lady's skirt) had been selling like hot cakes, and she had saved one of the prettiest ones for Mam. Sarah bought a stone tortoise that she said would look real when it was painted. Every time I looked at Mark, he was being spoilt by somebody. One minute he was on Uncle George's shoulders while Uncle George tried to win him a coconut, then he was with Aunty June being fed ice-cream and clutching a newly bought home-made teddy bear. Ruth, always a favourite with the old ladies, was now walking round hand in hand with Mrs Oliver.

Dad and Mr Brown seemed to be everywhere – welcoming new arrivals, being charming to old ladies, congratulating everyone on their well-run stall. I heard someone tell Dad he expected he was as good as Ilie Năstase now, having the tennis court to play on, and Dad replied that the tennis court was always full of neighbourhood children and that sadly, he rarely had the time. Then one of the tea ladies came to tell him and Mr Brown that Jean Kirkup had put aside some of the nicest cakes for them but that if they didn't come and sit down quickly they were in danger of losing them.

I don't think they were there for long, but I briefly caught sight of Ted Nichol and Simon while Krishna and I sat sucking from our mini-bottles of Tizer at the far end of the tennis court. They were at the music stall, and Simon was standing right below one of the loudspeakers, swaying and stamping his feet.

David announced that he was playing 'Puppy Love' again, adding, 'And if someone will donate fifty pence, I will happily smash this record to smithereens once it's finished.'

The afternoon grew steadily hotter and the morning breeze had dropped to just a murmur. Though some of the casual visitors had been and gone, nobody else seemed inclined to move. Chairs were moved out of the tea tent so that everyone could enjoy the sun on their faces. Miss Dobie and Mrs Oliver, sitting down again now, fanned themselves with their paper plates and said if it was twenty degrees again tomorrow, they wouldn't manage a cooked lunch but would just have cold ham and

tomatoes instead. The stallholders took down and cleared away
their stalls, then joined the people on the lawn. The tea-tent
ladies brought out the food that was left over and sat down
themselves to cups of tea and cake.

Then a big black cloud hid the sun and within a few minutes
most people had disappeared.

'We should have made it a condition that everyone take their
seat back to the hall when they leave,' said Dad, looking at the
chairs scattered all over the garden.

Luckily, the faithful few had stayed behind, and Sarah and I
helped the Bennetts, Wilf Kirkup and brawny David, the Turners
and the Smiths make endless journeys to and from the church
hall, which was over the road behind the White Elephant.

Ted Nichol died that night. He was on foreshift, which meant
starting work at midnight, and when he hadn't come downstairs
for the cup of tea he always drank before leaving the house, his
wife gave him a shout. When he still didn't appear, she went up
to look for him. She found him lying on the bathroom floor. He
had had a heart attack.

Dad said that that was one of the hardest things about
living in Ashington – seeing good men like Ted die before their
time.

'Why did he die?' we asked, and Dad said that there was a
time for everyone, but that working in the pit was a dangerous,
unhealthy job and that might have had something to do with it.
Mam said that though it was a terrible shock for us all, it could
be a blessing when people died suddenly like that, rather than
hanging on for ages with some grim illness. I knew that she was
thinking of some of the people Dad went to visit and whose

names we heard on the prayer list week after week. One lady had been on the list ever since we arrived a year ago. But you could tell by their names that they were old people – Lilians and Godfreys and Ivys – not men of Ted's age.

There was one thing everyone agreed on – that Ted had been the sort of man who made you feel better just by seeing him.

Chapter Thirty-two

After Ted died, the neat order of our world came crashing down for a short time. For a few days it was the first thing anyone mentioned when they came to the house. All the men who dropped in regularly looked solemn when they arrived, though they usually brightened up quickly when Ruth and Mark appeared, making their usual demands to play cars or push them on the swing. Even Mam and Dad, who sometimes seemed inured to death, spoke quietly and sadly between themselves. Dad said that Ted had been a gem, the salt of the earth. Later, I thought how it was funny that he compared him to things that came from the ground when he had spent his working life deep within it, ever since he was a boy of fifteen. I remembered seeing him once, his face black with coal dust, looking as if he was part of the ground he worked in. But how talented he had been in other areas too, how practical and good with his hands! How patient he had been with Simon! Once he had crawled around our sitting-room floor with both Mark and Simon on his back. (Mam told people proudly how, even though Simon had been holding on to Mark too tightly and had hurt him, Mark seemed to understand that Simon couldn't help it and hadn't gone crying to her about it until after they'd left.) And now Ted was gone. He was the first person I had known who had died.

Mam offered to have Simon one Saturday, and we all took turns to entertain him. He seemed the same as ever. He did his war dance to the sound of the vacuum cleaner; we played him records and tried not to protest when the ones he wanted to hear again and again were our least favourite ones. We ran round the garden with him and discouraged him from climbing the trees.

When his mother came to collect him, I realized it was the first time I had seen her. I'd pictured a weedy little woman who could barely stand up without a strong man at her side, but she was younger and more capable-looking than I'd expected.

She was talking to Mam and Dad in the hallway as we tried to entice Simon away from the vacuum-cleaner cupboard.

'We'll miss him, of course we will. But there's folk worse off than me and our Simon. You know what, we're lucky to have had him. Aye, we're very lucky.'

Mam held her hand and said we had all been lucky to have known Ted.

We're lucky. After she'd gone I kept hearing her words and wondering how, with no Ted, they could possibly be true.

I had gone straight into my summer dress as soon as the Easter holidays were over, and didn't take it off again until well into the autumn, but some girls still wore their uniforms of grey tunics and maroon ties, or switched between both depending on the weather. One day, back in the classroom after PE, Kathryn asked Mrs Pickering for help doing up her tie. I don't know why she asked her. I was sure that Kathryn could put on her own tie. Even if her mother put it on for her in the morning, she must have surely put it back on herself countless times after PE lessons. I held my breath as I saw Mrs Pickering's face. She clamped a hand on Kathryn's shoulder and marched her to the front of the class. One of the more spiteful girls we didn't have much to do with if we could help it sniggered and said in a loud whisper, 'This is going to be good.'

'I thought you all knew how to fasten a tie by now, but it seems that Diddums here still needs a hand. You can all watch, and then I don't expect anyone to ask me how to do it again. I shan't be in as good a mood as I am now if they do.'

She didn't look in a good mood at all. I usually laughed when she called someone Diddums, but I could see that today she wasn't trying to be funny, and that laughing would get me into trouble too. She had her grimmest expression on her face. I heard a couple of titters, but most of the girls stood in stunned silence.

Kathryn looked upset when she had finished, but I didn't have time to talk to her as she went home for her dinner straight after.

At the end of the day, as we walked home together with Sandra and Joanna, I asked her what she had been thinking of when she knew how to fasten her tie already.

She shrugged. 'The last time we had PE I saw Michelle ask her for help, and she was really nice to her. I suppose I wanted to see if she'd be nice to me as well.'

We all looked at each other, then burst out laughing.

'She cannot stand me,' said Kathryn when we had stopped. She shook her head like an old woman in disbelief. 'She really cannot!'

'That's not true,' said Sandra.

'Aye, remember last week,' said Joanna. 'She gave you two merits and said we should all start to watch the news, like you. And you got another for knowing who was prime minister in the war.'

'I thought everyone knew that,' replied Kathryn.

'Well I didn't,' said Sandra.

'Nor did I,' I said. 'I never listen when people start talking about the war. It's so boring.'

'And she's like that with everyone, man,' said Sandra.

'Me mam says she blows hot and cold,' said Joanna.

'Remember that we've got her next year, too,' I said.

'I cannot wait,' said Kathryn.

Joanna and I said goodbye to the others. I was going to stay at her house that night. It was the first time I had been invited to stay overnight at a friend's in Ashington, though we often had friends staying at our house. Mam had insisted on ringing Joanna's mam, even though Joanna had told her countless times that it was fine. We stopped at the vicarage first, where I dropped my school things off and picked up the bag I had packed earlier. Mam asked Joanna again if she was sure it was convenient, and shouted after me that she would be round to pick me up at nine the next morning. I was glad to get away.

'Me and Angela were arguing about who taught you to speak Geordie,' said Joanna as we set off, looking at me closely to gauge my reaction.

'None of you taught me,' I said, feeling irritated.

'So how else did you learn, then?'

'Well . . . I just picked it up.'

'Come on, you've got to admit it, you learnt most off me. You're really good now, you know. It's just certain words that give you away.'

'Shall we have a go doing our three-legged race for sports day on the field?' I asked, keen to change the subject. 'Oh, and I want to practise cartwheels, too. Will you show me how you get your legs so straight?'

Joanna laughed delightedly. 'I just practise more, man.'

On the other side of the road a group of miners were waiting for the bus that took them to the pit. I recognized Uncle Andy, and waved. He had a cigarette between his lips, but he took it out to grin and shout hello at us.

I wondered what Joanna's mam would give us for tea.

Sarah and I still liked to climb the mountain ash tree in the back garden – the one that Simon had taken refuge in the previous year – but I had a new favourite place, on the flat garage roof, which I could reach either by shinning up the drainpipe by the back door or climbing out of the little side window in my bedroom. I could sit here and read, enjoying the escapades of Anne of Green Gables, and when I glanced up, though I sometimes longed to stay a little longer in Avonlea with Anne, it was nice to see life on Newbiggin Road carrying on in the satisfying way it did. I might see Aunty June scurrying through the gap between the terraces, waiting to cross the road on her way to our house or to Spedding's, or Kathryn's mam, delivering church magazines.

It was hard to believe that the summer holidays were almost here again, and that we had lived in Ashington for over a year. Such a lot of things had happened. Alan and Joan's baby had been born, a little boy called Alan Alder, looking like a miniature version of Alan. Carol had left the Army and was going to join the RAF. Perhaps she would meet a nice man there and get married and Sarah and I could be her bridesmaids. Everyone had been a bridesmaid apart from us. Paula-from-round-the-corner's baby was walking now, a tiny thing who looked almost comical waddling up the road holding Paula's hand. Jackie had run away from the convent two days after Mam and Dad had driven her all that way, and Mam said she didn't know where she was now, though it wouldn't surprise her if she turned up on the doorstep one of these days.

Other things hadn't changed. Uncle Peter had not got married. Mam said we shouldn't hold our breath. She said the same about Trudy, though she hoped she would settle down with Frank, as she thought he was good for her and Trudy seemed a lot more settled these days.

Kathryn and I still swapped books and looked for adventures in the world around us. Some men had started to build a factory at the end of Newbiggin Road, and we were convinced that the boxes we saw being lowered by crane had dead bodies in them. Krishna and Nicola still spent a lot of time at our house – Aunty Beryl, too – and were considered part of the family.

Aunty Margaret had written to say she was coming to stay again this summer, and Dad had reminded Mam that he wouldn't be putting the heating on for her, she could shiver as much as she liked.

The night before, at Joanna's, we had stood naked in front of her parents' bedroom mirror and looked at our developing bodies to see whose was the most womanly, but there wasn't much sign of anything yet. We wondered if we would be friends when we did eventually grow up, and felt sure we would marry famous men, preferably two who were best friends.

One day I might live in some other town. I knew that Dad's job could take him anywhere, but I hoped that wouldn't be for a very long time. For now, we all belonged in this pit village by the sea. It might not be pretty, it might stink of smoke, but we were proud to call it home.

Acknowledgements

The following people all helped me to relive Ashington memories or contributed in other invaluable ways: Mary Sobey, Mike Kirkup, Chris Spedding, Sandra Davison, Alder Gofton, Gwenda Gofton, Peter Gofton, Elizabeth Fairess, Carol Jarvis, Kathryn Egdell, Krishna De, Nicola De, Mike Fox, Sarah Jordan, Ruth Morris, Mark Gofton, Pat Small, Paul Jarvis, Anne Johnson, Alan Johnson, Helen Forrest, Ann Elliott, Joanne Black, Stephen Brown and Sue Adamson. Thank you, all of you!

Thanks to Helen Surman for the second great cover she has designed for me; to Rhiannon Smith and Jenny Page for their care editing the manuscript; to Kirsteen Astor, publicist extraordinaire. Also to all the staff at literary agencies Watson, Little and Mulcahy Associates.

Thank you to the Society of Authors for a generous grant as well as all the advice they have given me over the years.

A special thank you to Rosie Bailey for allowing me to reproduce her poem 'Druridge Bay' from the collection *Marking Time* (published by Peterloo Poets). Also to Michael Chaplin for the reproduction of 'To a Pit Pony' by his father, Sid Chaplin, taken from *In Blackberry Time* (Bloodaxe Books), an inspirational compilation of Sid's stories and essays.

Last but by no means least, thank you to my agent Sallyanne Sweeney and my editor Hannah Boursnell for being there every step of the way. And to the people of Ashington, Northumberland, for just being.

Some names have been changed. I hope my readers will allow me any liberties I have taken for artistic purposes.

sphere

To buy any of our books and to find out
more about Sphere and Little, Brown Book Group,
our authors and titles, as well as events and
book clubs, visit our website

www.littlebrown.co.uk

and follow us on Twitter

@LittleBrownUK

To order any Sphere titles p & p free in the UK,
please contact our mail order supplier on:

+ 44 (0)1832 737525

Customers not based in the UK should contact
the same number for appropriate postage
and packing costs.